PENSIONS AND LEGAL POLICY

This monograph explores the historical position of pensions law in the UK and the recent influences which have led to the introduction of Auto-Enrolment and subsequent reforms. Alternative models such as the US and Australia are also considered as well as the function of law in bringing about political changes.

The question of saving for retirement is of national and international importance and many governments are wrestling with the issue of how to deal with the pension funding crisis. Consequently political policy has, in many cases, combined with behavioural science to inform new laws which have acted to shift the burden from the state into the private sector. Around the world, responsibility is being moved onto individuals and employers as the state retreats from provision of state support in retirement; this book offers a sophisticated analysis of the role of legal intervention to facilitate this shift.

The book explores the work of behavioural economics, its global influence on understanding financial decision-making and its application to legislation which seeks to influence consumer outcomes. Drawing on qualitative empirical research to explore the experience of implementation of Auto-Enrolment, this timely work considers the interaction with the work of behavioural science to highlight the social costs of the new regulatory regime.

Pensions and Legal Policy

Lessons on the Shift from Public to Private

Amanda Cooke

•HART•

OXFORD • LONDON • NEW YORK • NEW DELHI • SYDNEY

HART PUBLISHING

Bloomsbury Publishing Plc

Kemp House, Chawley Park, Cumnor Hill, Oxford, OX2 9PH, UK

1385 Broadway, New York, NY 10018, USA

29 Earlsfort Terrace, Dublin 2, Ireland

HART PUBLISHING, the Hart/Stag logo, BLOOMSBURY and the Diana logo are trademarks of Bloomsbury Publishing Plc

First published in Great Britain 2021

A catalogue record for this book is available from the British Library.

Library of Congress Cataloging-in-Publication data

Names: Cooke, Amanda, author.

Title: Pensions and legal policy : lessons on the shift from public to private / Amanda Cooke.

Description: Oxford, UK ; New York, NY : Hart Publishing, an imprint of Bloomsbury Publishing, 2021. | Includes bibliographical references and index.

Identifiers: LCCN 2020044047 (print) | LCCN 2020044048 (ebook) | ISBN 9781509929375 (hardback) | ISBN 9781509944729 (paperback) | ISBN 9781509929382 (epdf) | ISBN 9781509929399 (Epub)

Subjects: LCSH: Pensions—Law and legislation—Great Britain. | Pension trusts—Law and legislation—Great Britain.

Classification: LCC KD3131 .C66 2020 (print) | LCC KD3131 (ebook) | DDC 344.4101/252—dc23

LC record available at https://lccn.loc.gov/2020044047

LC ebook record available at https://lccn.loc.gov/2020044048

ISBN: HB: 978-1-50992-937-5
ePDF: 978-1-50992-938-2
ePub: 978-1-50992-939-9

Typeset by Compuscript Ltd, Shannon

In loving memory of my dad, James Cooke, and with love and thanks for the support of all my family and friends; especially Melissa, Callum and Ethan.

CONTENTS

Table of Cases .... *xi*

1. An Introduction to the Work **1**
I. Background 1
II. Pensions 2
A. Public Sector Pensions 2
B. Private Pensions: Occupational Pension Schemes 3
III. Key Policy Considerations 4
IV. The Road to Auto-Enrolment: The Rise and Fall of Voluntary Private Pensions 5
V. The Road to Auto-Enrolment: The Pensions Commission 10
VI. Lessons from Abroad 14
VII. Conclusion 16

2. Introduction of Auto-Enrolment to the UK **17**
I. Auto-Enrolment and Parliamentary Intent 17
A. Increase Saving by Default 17
B. Prevent a Reduction in Existing Pension Benefits or Levelling Down 18
C. Education of the Workforce 19
D. Private Pension Saving Compatible with State Benefits 21
II. Legislative Reality 22
III. Post Implementation Legislative Changes 28
A. Value 29
B. Costs and Charges 30
C. Scheme Governance 33
D. Master Trusts 35
E. Taking Pension Benefits 36
IV. Conclusion 38

3. Legal Paternalism and the Auto-Enrolment Regime **39**
I. Introduction 39
II. Autonomy v Law 40
III. Legal Paternalism 41
A. The Rise of Paternalistic Legislation 45
IV. Soft Paternalism or Nudge 48

V. Paternalism and Contracts 50
VI. Intention of Legal Intervention 55
VII. Proof and Value Measurement 58
VIII. Conclusion 62

4. The Role of Behavioural Economics in Legal Intervention 64
I. Introduction 64
II. Behavioural Economics 65
A. Inertia and Procrastination 66
B. Framing and Presentation 67
C. Social Influences 68
D. Difficulties in Assessing Probability 69
III. The Influence of Behavioural Economics on Law and Policy 70
IV. Regulatory Intervention and Choice Architecture 72
A. Policy of Legal Paternalism 73
B. Choice Architects 74
C. Alternatives to Soft Paternalism/Choice Architecture 77
V. Auto-Enrolment as Choice Architecture 79
A. Auto-Enrolment 79
B. Opting-out 80
C. Defaults 81
D. Auto-Enrolment and Behavioural Bias 84
E. Framing and Disclosure 88
VI. Conclusion 90

5. Empirical Research Findings 92
I. Introduction to the Research 92
II. Research Design and Methodology 94
III. Findings 96
A. Action 98
B. Barriers to Decisions 102
C. Intervention and Implementation 109
D. Engagement and Understanding 115
E. Trust 130
IV. Conclusion 131
A. Choice and Defaults 131
B. Understanding 133
C. Information 134
D. Individual Perception of Auto-Enrolment 135
E. The Employee/Employer Relationship and Auto-Enrolment 136
F. Impact of Gender and Age 137
G. Negative or Unforeseen Consequences of Auto-Enrolment 137

6. Unintended Consequences: Remedies ... 139
I. Introduction ... 139
II. Fiduciary Duties Owed to Employees ... 140
A. When Do Fiduciary Obligations Exist? ... 141
B. The Consequences of Fiduciary Obligations ... 151
III. Duties Owed by the Employer as an Agent ... 153
A. The Agency Relationship ... 155
B. Consequences of Agency ... 157
IV. Duties Arising from the Contract of Employment ... 159
A. Implied Terms ... 161
B. Auto-Enrolment Compliance and the Contract of Employment ... 171
V. Duties Owed to the Employee by the Pension Provider or Advisors ... 173
A. Provision of Advice ... 173
B. Misunderstandings and Mis-statements ... 173
C. Third Party Liability ... 174
D. Reliance on Financial Regulation ... 175
VI. Conclusion ... 176

7. Conclusion ... 179
I. Why Do We Have Auto-Enrolment? ... 179
A. The Ageing Population ... 179
B. Combat Behavioural Traits ... 179
II. Choice Architecture and Justification ... 180
A. Intervention not Persuasion ... 180
B. Behavioural Economics ... 182
III. Has Legislative and Practical Implementation Reflected the Policy Intention? ... 184
A. Defaults ... 185
B. Employer Discretion ... 185
C. Communication and Active Choice ... 186
IV. Are There Unforeseen or Unintended Consequences and How Do These Affect Justification for Legal Intervention? ... 188
A. Barriers and Misunderstandings ... 188
B. Reliance on Defaults ... 188
C. Advice ... 190
D. Detriment and Responsibility ... 191
E. Social Costs and Remedies ... 191

Bibliography ... 193
Index ... 201

TABLE OF CASES

@SIPP Pension Trustees v Insight Travel Services Ltd [2016] SLT 131 (2015) [2015] CSIH 91, [2016] S.L.T. 131 166
Attorney General of Belize v Belize Telecom Ltd (PC) (2009) 1 Weekly Law Reports, 1988–1998 161
Anderson Smyth and Kelly Customs Brokers v World Wide Customs Brokers (1996) 7 WWR 736 147
Autoclenz Ltd v Belcher and Others [2011] UKSC 41 (2011) [2011] 4 ALL ER 745 160
Bathurst Regional Council v Local Government Financial Services Pty Ltd (No5) [2012] FCA 1200 [2324] (2012) FCA 146
Batt Cables Plc v Spencer Business Parks Ltd (2010) SLT 860 156
Beach Petroleum v Kennedy (1999) 48 NSWLR 1, 188 .... 145, 148
Braganza v BP Shipping Ltd and another (2015) 2015 1 WLR 166
Bristol and West Building Society v Mothew (1988) CH 1 150
British Groundschool Ltd v Intelligent Data Capture Limited (2014) 2014 EWHC 2145 (Ch) 166
Clark v Nomura International [2000] IRLR. 76 (QB) 166
Clyde & Co LLP and another v Bates van Winkelhof [2014] UKSC 32 22
Collidge v Freeport [2007] EWHC 1216 (QB) 147
Commonwealth Bank of Australia v Smith [1991] FCA 375; (1991) 42 FCR 390,391 146
Credit Lyonnais Bank Nederland NV v Burch [1996] EWCA Civ 1292 148
Crossley v Faithful & Gould Holdings Ltd [2004] EWCA Civ 293 (2004) ICR, 1615 170
D & G Cars Ltd v Essex Police Authority [2015] EWHC 226 (QB) 166
Emirates Trading Agency LLC v Prime Mineral Exports Private Limited [2014] EWHC 2104 (Comm) 166
F & C (No 2) [2011] EWHC 1731 (Ch); *F & C Alternative Investments (Holdings) Ltd v Barthelemy and another (No 2)* [2011] EWHC 1731 (Ch) 144, 149, 152, 165
Grant Estates Limited v RBS plc [2012] CSOH (2012); *Grant Estates Limited (in liquidation) v Royal Bank of Scotland Plc* [2012] CSOH 133 .... 169, 176
Greenclose Ltd v National Westminster Bank Plc [2014] EWHC 1156 (Ch) 166
Grove Investments Ltd v Cape Building Products Ltd [2014] CSIH 43 166
Hagen v ICI Chemicals and Polymers Ltd [2002] IRLR 31 165

Hedley Byrne & Co Ltd v Heller & Partners Ltd [1964] AC 145; (1963) 3 WLR 101 174
Hilton v Barker Booth & Eastwood [2005] UKHL 8; (2005) 1 WLR 567 149–50
Hines v Sturge LLP [2010] CSIH 86; (2011) SLT 2 174
Hodgkinson v Simms [1994] 3 SCR 377; (1994) SCC 146
Hospital Products Ltd v United States Surgical Corporation [1984] 156 CLR 41 ....147, 150, 152, 158
Hunter v Hanley [1955] SC 200 174
Imperial Group Pension Trust v Imperial Tobacco [1991] 1 WLR 589 ....160, 162
JM & JH Robertson v Beatson, McLeod & Company Ltd (1908) SC 921 157
Johnson v Unisys [2003] 1 AC 518. *Johnston v Unisys Ltd* [2001] ICR 480 (HL) (2001) Industrial Case Reports (HL) 165–66
Kelly v Cooper [1993] AC 205 150
Lakshmi v Mid Cheshire Hospitals NHS Trust [2008] EWHC 878 (QB) 53–54
Loosemore v Financial Concepts (2001) Lloyd's reports PN 235 174
Mahmud (Malik) v Bank of Credit and Commerce International S.A [1997] ICR 606 163–64
Marks and Spencer plc v BNP Paribas Securities Services (SC(E)) [2015] 2 WLR 1843 161
McWilliam v Norton Finance [2015] EWCA Civ 186 156
Mettoy Pension Trustees Ltd v Evans [1990] 1 WLR 1587 160
Myers v Kestrel Acquisitions Ltd [2015] EWHC 916 (Ch) 166
Outram v Academy Plastics Ltd [2001] ICR 367 168
PDPF GP Ltd v Santander UK Plc (2015) WL 1839062 161
Pearce v Foster (No 2) (1886) 17 QBD 536 (CA) 160
Pension Ombudsman (Major R Farrimond) (April 2013); Pensions Ombudsman cases (PO-680) 161
Pensions Ombudsman complaint (Mrs Oona Perret) (November 2014); Pensions Ombudsman, PO-3750 168
Jo Reading v Attorney General [1951] UKHL 1; (1951) AC 507 147
Rodewald v Taylor [2010] CSOH 5 154
Rosetti Marketing Ltd v Diamond Sofa Company Ltd [2012] EWCA Civ 1021 150
Samsung Semiconductor Europe Ltd v Docherty [2011] CSOH 32, [2011] SLT 806 ....147, 160
Sao Paolo Alpargatas SA v Standard Chartered Bank [1985] SLT 433 158
Scally v Southern Health and Social Services Board [1991] ICR 771 ....160–61, 163–65, 168–69
SEC v Chenery Corporation (1943) 318 U.S. 80, 85–86 141
Smith v Bank of Scotland (1997) SC (HL) 111 166

Spring v Guardian Assurance [1995] 2 AC 296 170
Stoelwinder v Southern Health [2001] FCA 115, [39] 147
The Commissioner of Police of the Metropolis v Lennon [2004] EWCA Civ 130; (2004) WL 170
The Pensions Regulator, April 2014. Report under s 89 of the Pensions Act 2004 in relation to Dunelm Soft Furnishings Ltd. s.l 3, 10, 25, 27–28, 33–36, 58, 83, 103, 110–11, 113, 125, 127, 131, 133, 165, 168, 171–72, 178
University of Nottingham v Eyett [1999] ICR 721 163
University of Nottingham v Fishel, [2000] EWHC 221 (QB); (2000) IRLR 471 .... 147–48, 160
Visa International Service Association v Paul [2004] IRLR 42 164
WRN Ltd V Ayris [2008] EWHC 1080 (QB) 51
Yam Seng Pte Ltd v International Trade Corporation Ltd [2013] EWHC 111 165–66
White v Jones [1995] 2 AC 207 174
Wingecarribee Shire Council v Lehman Bros Australia Ltd (in liq) [2012] FCA 1028 [733] (Rares J) 146

1

An Introduction to the Work

I. Background

This book considers the regulatory intervention of the Auto-Enrolment (AE) pensions' regime and whether the social costs of the regime are recognised within United Kingdom (UK) legislation. It also considers whether there are unintended consequences of this change in UK pensions' policy, examining and evaluating the AE regime which was introduced in 2012. In considering the history of private pensions and regulation in the UK it is possible to track the journey from regulation designed to protect rights, voluntarily given by employers to employees, to a new approach where pension regulation actually creates rights and obligations in relation to private pension provision. If the Pensions Act 1995 was a response to fears over trust then the Pensions Acts of 2007 and 2008 represent a response to lack of saving and poor public finances. This book considers the costs and benefits of this legal intervention. For example, whilst the law results in more people saving privately this could be at the expense of a higher level of savings for some who would pay more if they made personal choices rather than relying on default positions. Further costs are the administration and compliance costs to employers and in amending existing benefits to fit into the new regime.

The book considers the effects of the state and public sector pensions on occupational pension legislation in the UK but also reflects on different balances and policies in other countries. Pension schemes come in many different forms and are provided in the UK by the state and privately. The introduction of AE into workplace pensions in 2012 marked a significant legislative change to UK pensions law.[1] This is part of a public policy change but also reflects a change in the social balance and the significance of private pensions in the UK. Since 2012 all employers must automatically enrol eligible employees into a qualifying pension scheme, pay contributions on behalf of the employee and deduct employee contributions to the scheme from the employee's pay. Each employer had its own date for compliance based on its PAYE (Pay As You Earn) number in 2012 which was known as 'staging'. This is the date when most obligations came into force for that employer, although the legislation is fully implemented now. Employers must assess workers

[1] Pensions Act 2007, Pensions Act 2008, Pensions Act 2008 (Commencement No 13) Order 2012 (SI 2012/1682).

to identify who is already in a qualifying pension and who must be enrolled into one. It is possible to modify an existing pension arrangement to become a qualifying arrangement under AE or the employer can set up a new pension arrangement, including by joining a multi-employer master trust.[2] There is also the government-established National Employment Savings Trust (NEST) which is an occupational defined contribution pension scheme set up under trust.[3] This might be chosen as a low-cost option. Employers can choose to use a three-month postponement period before enrolling employees into the AE pension. Minimum contribution requirements were phased over the period up to 2018. Now all employers must pay in minimum contributions of three per cent of employee qualifying earnings and employees must pay the balance, to ensure a minimum of eight per cent total contributions are paid in (including tax relief). The employer may pay more but the employee is responsible for meeting any shortfall between the employer contribution and the eight per cent minimum.

II. Pensions

A. Public Sector Pensions

i. State Pension

The state pension in the UK is essentially a promise by the state to pay a certain amount of pension to those who have paid adequate contributions on reaching a certain age. This is not funded by a centralised fund but through taxation and, where the proportion of those working to those retiring decreases, this can result in a strain on public funds. Historically the state pension was comprised of a basic and top up part but this was recently replaced by a flat rate system.[4] Changes were also introduced to equalise state pension age for men and women.[5] This means that if an employee also has a workplace pension with an earlier retirement age they will need to make up the gap if they retire as they will not get the state pension until later. For this reason, compulsory retirement age has been abolished unless it can be objectively justified because of the nature of their work.[6]

[2] Pension Schemes Act 2017.

[3] NEST Pensions website www.nestpensions.org.uk/schemeweb/NestWeb/public/home/contents/homepage.html.

[4] Pensions Act 2014, s 19.

[5] Pensions Act 2007 provided for a gradual increase in women's retirement age but this was accelerated by the Pensions Act 2011. This has been heavily criticised as failing to give women adequate opportunity to prepare for this loss of benefit.

[6] Equality Act 2010, Equality Act (Age Exceptions for Pension Schemes) Order 2010/2133.

ii. Public Sector Pensions: Public Sector Schemes

In addition to public liability for state pensions, there is also a liability in respect of public service pensions. Most workers in the public sector are entitled to join public-sector pension schemes such as the Local Government Pension Scheme (LGPS) or the Principal Civil Service Pension Scheme, depending on their employer. These schemes historically provided defined or salary related benefits, but affordability has led to a reduction of these benefits. The Independent Public Service Pensions Commission, headed by Lord Hutton of Furness, led to the Public Service Pensions Act 2013 which changed the benefit calculation from final salary to an average salary figure. Whilst this is still a good pension benefit, it is much less valuable than the previous benefit promise and caused widespread industrial action in the public sector. The change effectively varies the benefits originally promised in respect of future service accrual and the unhappiness underlines the value that workers place in pensions as deferred pay. This is another example of state pension costs requiring amendment because of affordability concerns.

B. Private Pensions: Occupational Pension Schemes

The majority of this book is concerned with private pensions but there is a clear relationship between private and public schemes. Within this private pension sphere the focus of this work is on workplace pensions. Workplace pensions are further divided into occupational trust-based and contract-based schemes:

- Occupational pension schemes established under trust will be governed by a trust deed and rules, supplementary documentation and overriding pensions, tax, employment and other applicable legislation. In a trust-based scheme, the assets of the scheme are held in trust and the scheme is run by trustees who manage the fund for the purpose and benefit of the beneficiaries. The trust deed and rules will provide for the appointment and retirement of trustees, scheme administration, funding and investment of assets, termination and winding up of the scheme, insolvency provisions and method of calculating benefits. Whilst the trust deed and rules are generally applied, these may be overridden by statute, case law and varied contractually.
- Pension arrangements which form a collection of personal pension schemes. In contrast to the trust-based scheme, a personal pension policy is written in the name of the individual member and payments are directly made to the policy which is administered by the product provider on behalf of the individual member. These can be grouped together into a grouped personal pension (GPP) to make administrative savings but it is still a collection of entirely portable individual pension policies. The Pensions Regulator has a supervisory role in relation to work-based personal pensions but the Financial Conduct Authority also has authority in relation to aspects of sales and the policies.

In contrast to the public sector, benefits provided in the private sector often do not make any benefit guarantees. Pensions, which make a promise of a certain level of benefits related to salary, are described as salary related or defined benefit (DB) schemes. In such arrangements, the employer undertakes the risks involved in ensuring that the pension fund has sufficient assets to meet the pension promises and employees are only obliged to pay a fixed contribution. The other type of arrangement, which is more popular now, is defined contribution (DC) or money purchase benefits. In this type of arrangement, both the employer and employee will pay a fixed contribution and the employee bears the risk of how much their share of the fund will be worth when they come to retirement. This will depend on the amount of contributions paid, charges and fund performance. The introduction of the pensions drawdown allows individuals with defined contribution funds much more flexibility in taking benefits at retirement and is discussed further in Chapter 2.[7] This is significant as the flexibility to use this saving as a lump sum may both encourage more people to save and then encourage members to view pensions as deferred cash rather than a sum to create income until death.

III. Key Policy Considerations

Pensions' policy and regulation in the UK has been evolving over the past 70 years and has most recently been influenced by the demographics of an ageing population and the difficulties of state funding of benefits in retirement. This is a serious social problem and involves the consideration of interests of varied and sometimes conflicting stakeholder groups. The retired population has an interest in maintaining income, the state seeks to minimise its obligations to fund benefits and today's workers who choose not to save to support themselves conflict with the interests of future generations required to support them if private savings are inadequate. The introduction of AE marks a significant change in direction for pensions policy in the UK and will result in an extra £19.7 billion pension savings every year by 2020.[8] The policy focus was to increase the numbers of individuals saving for a pension privately and much of the evaluation to date has also focussed on this.[9] It was estimated that AE will have resulted in ten million new pension savers

[7] Pension Schemes Act 2015, s 55, Taxation of Pensions Act 2014.

[8] Department for Work and Pensions, *Automatic Enrolment Review: Analytical Report*, December 2017, 5: https://assets.publishing.service.gov.uk/government/uploads/system/uploads/attachment_data/file/668657/automatic-enrolment-review-2017-analytical-report.pdf.

[9] Department for Work and Pensions, *Automatic Enrolment Review 2017: Maintaining the Momentum CM 9546* (December 2017): https://assets.publishing.service.gov.uk/government/uploads/system/uploads/attachment_data/file/668971/automatic-enrolment-review-2017-maintaining-the-momentum.PDF.

by 2018.[10] The success of the regime has been measured by low rates of members leaving the schemes they are enrolled into, known as opt-outs. However, there is a gap in research which considers the intended effects and justifications for the AE legislation and then compares it to the reality of implementation to test for actual benefits and unintended or negative consequences and effects. The increased volume of business is a benefit for the financial services sector which will benefit both in terms of increased demand for pension products and investment in financial instruments and products by the increasing volume of pension fund assets. Previous scandals in the sector have proved that market forces do not always work to the advantage of the ultimate consumer and so it is important to identify any issues at this stage rather than wait until problems arise for individual pensioners in 20 or 30 years' time. This policy places that extra £19.7 billion of pension savings into the hands of private pension providers from the pockets of many workers who might otherwise choose to do something else with their money. That fact alone makes this topic worthy of further consideration.

AE operates to enrol employees into a pension which they have not chosen and payments are deducted from their salary automatically without the employee having to consent. Employees may choose to leave the regime after enrolment but this relies on engagement and understanding of the information given to the employee. The legislation makes employers responsible for implementing the regime and the government has a more limited role, although it may benefit if reliance on state benefits in retirement is reduced. There is potential for conflict of interests to exist between these parties and this book considers the role of each of the stakeholders and whether there are adequate protections for the freedom of choice and interests of the individual workers affected by AE.

IV. The Road to Auto-Enrolment: The Rise and Fall of Voluntary Private Pensions

UK pensions have changed significantly since being introduced as means tested payments to those aged over 70.[11] Private pensions were also developing around the same time and the introduction of tax relief on employer contributions and investment income within the fund led to increased use of pensions as an efficient way of remunerating staff.[12] Beveridge first introduced the universal benefit system in 1946.[13] Beveridge himself saw pensions as a form of insurance for times when

[10] Department for Work and Pensions Workplace Pensions: Update of analysis on AE 2016: https://assets.publishing.service.gov.uk/government/uploads/system/uploads/attachment_data/file/560356/workplace-pensions-update-analysis-auto-enrolment-2016.pdf.

[11] Old Age Pensions Act 1908.

[12] Finance Act 1921, s 32.

[13] National Insurance Act 1946.

individuals were unable to work rather than creating a right to retire at a particular age. Whilst the practicalities and costs of provision meant that he accepted that there could be accumulation of benefits for those who could contribute he anticipated that this would be a short-term measure with most workers using private savings to retire without the means tested top up.[14] He was also very concerned about the declining birth rate and saw age as a 'moving frontier' arguing that it would be unjustifiable to give a full income just for reaching a certain age.[15] These very concepts are still debated today and are the roots of the pensions' crisis leading to the AE legislation.

The public and private pension systems complement each other. There are varying pension models in Europe and the US placing greater or less emphasis on the state pension component. Even within Europe there are large differences in approach, but most European countries use the three pillars approach to pension policy. The first pillar is formed by the state funded pension, dependent on workers contributions during their working life. In the UK this is funded by NICs.[16] The second pillar is represented by the occupational pensions funded by contributions from employers and workers. The third pillar represents any additional savings for retirement planned by the individual. In the UK the state pension represents a fairly small portion of income compared to working income for many and so the second and third pillars should complement this. The state pension is not linked to actual income and, where individuals have failed to appreciate the value of the state pension, this may result in a poorer retirement than expected or further reliance on complementary state benefits. Mediterranean countries such as Spain and Italy follow a different emphasis with higher guaranteed compulsory state pensions and less complimentary pension provision from the private sector. The costs of this burden on the public finances have led to reforms and the need for development of a private sector pension industry in recent years.[17] Sweden has recently overhauled its pension system with each worker contributing a higher level of compulsory pension contributions and receiving attributable pension credit for this.[18] Effectively it is an unfunded defined contribution plan relying on government benefit promises.[19] The introduction of this system known as 'notional defined contribution' has the benefit of being linked to longevity and employment through contribution calculations and may instil a sense of

[14] Inter-departmental Committee on Social Insurance and Allied Services, *Social and Allied Services* (Cmd 6404-6405, 1942) 90–101.

[15] H Pemberton, P Thane, and N Whiteside, *Britain's Pensions Crisis: History and Policy* (The British Academy: Oxford University Press, 2006) 34.

[16] UK Government, 'The New State Pension', www.gov.uk/new-state-pension.

[17] LF Agudo and AM Garcia, 'The Reform of Some European public pension systems: Spain, Italy and Sweden: A Breakthrough?' (2010) 15 *Pensions: An International Journal* 297, 300.

[18] D Andrews, 'Why Sweden's Notional DC Pension System Needs a Correction Calculation' (2012) 5(2) *Rotman International Journal of Pension Management* 40.

[19] A Borsch-Supan, 'From Traditional DB to Notional DC Systems: The Pension Reform Process in Sweden, Italy and Germany' (2005) 3 *Journal of the European Economic Association* 458, 461.

responsibility in workers to save and which may actually increase private saving as well.[20] Whilst the state pension in the UK has a defined benefit, this is not linked to salary or lifetime contributions meaning that it is poor value and does not replace income for many. The Australian Superannuation system has also developed with the three pillars and introduced mandatory saving in the second pillar to reduce reliance on the first.[21]

In the UK, the private pension provided by employers has a long tradition of supplementing the state pension benefit but the balance is changing and the introduction of AE is evidence of this. The concept of AE in the UK was borrowed, at least in part, from the Australian system. In 1986, Australia introduced a compulsory three per cent contribution by employees into a private pension and this was extended in 1992 to require employers to make contributions as well.[22] This is essentially a legislated, compulsory private pension contribution and is subjected to complicated taxation arrangements.[23] This is an alternative to the reform of the first pillar seen in Europe and came about after agreement with labour groups, employers and government.[24] However, it has been heavily criticised because of the inherent gender inequalities of the system which relies on payment of contributions when women often work fewer years because they undertake caring roles without receiving a credit in the system for this.[25] The Australian Superannuation Scheme is referred to throughout the book.

Since Beveridge introduced the state pension as a support for private saving, pensions in the UK have gone through highs and lows. Increased wealth brought more occupational pension schemes in the private sector and workers were encouraged to save in their employer's schemes to supplement state pensions. Between 1971 and 1975 the number of those in final salary schemes rose from eight to ten million workers.[26] Unionised workforces increased the numbers of members of salary related pension schemes which were seen as a form of deferred pay and pensions were an integral part of the benefit package.[27] Saving in advance for retirement benefits was a major contributor to the development of large institutional investment in the UK and created conditions for growth in the financial sector. Increasing funding obligations further influenced the type of investments favoured by such schemes.

[20] ibid, 464.

[21] Crawford School of Public Policy, Heng et al 'Retirement Policy: a review of the role, characteristics, and contribution of the Australian superannuation system' (2015) *Asian Pacific Economic Literature*.

[22] K Sadiq, 'Prescriptions for Reform of Australia's Superannuation Tax Concessions' (2012) 27 *Australian Tax Forum* 371, 373.

[23] T Jefferson, 'Private Retirement Savings in Australia: Current Policy Initiatives and Gender Equality Implications' (2012) 38 *Australian Bulletin of Labour* 234, 234.

[24] Also see part VI below.

[25] ibid, 237.

[26] Government Actuary's Department, 'Occupational Pension Schemes: Fifth Survey' (HMSO,1975).

[27] Pemberton et al, *Britain's Pension Crisis*, (n 15) 148.

Not everyone benefitted from membership of final salary schemes and it was often a divisive issue amongst the workforce where the 'generous promise to some workers was effectively cross-subsidised by the poor treatment of others'.[28] Women were often excluded and, until 1975, there was no obligation to provide a preserved pension for those leaving the company so anyone leaving could lose all pension benefits. Funding was less of a problem in these circumstances. Although pension funds also suffered losses in stock market crashes, there were disproportionately higher numbers of workers to those reaching retirement and so the funding difficulties could be evened out over time. As the membership demographic changed and more employees reached retirement, the costs increased and there were less contributions to smooth over funding. This is one reason why the recent global financial crisis had such a large impact on pension funds as the fund value crashed but liabilities increased with the increasing age profiles of schemes closed to new members.

A number of factors played a part in the decline of occupational pension savings, particularly in defined benefit or final salary schemes. Economics and finance always play a part in the funding of such arrangements but the confidence of those saving into such schemes is not always influenced by the economy. A number of high-profile scandals knocked consumer confidence and subsequent increased legislation has made final salary schemes more expensive to run. It was estimated that there was a 60 per cent drop in access to salary related schemes between 1995 and 2002.[29] Closure of a salary related scheme generally results in employees being offered membership of a defined contribution scheme instead. This allows the employer to reduce and fix contributions and costs. Changing business structures and ways of doing business have meant that inflexible and highly regulated defined benefit occupational pension schemes have fallen out of favour as employers look for other ways to incentivise the workforce and maintain skilled workers.[30] The balance between business needs and those of the workers need careful consideration and the two may not always be aligned. Employers may have competing obligations to account to shareholders for value; or are competing in a global market where employee costs are lower. This has quickened the speed of decline of final salary pension schemes. The legacy of dealing with historic schemes now in deficit also weighs in the consideration of many businesses and in their balance sheets with the introduction of stricter accounting standards and reporting of pension scheme deficits.[31]

Another factor which has heavily influenced pension membership is lack of trust. A number of scandals dented confidence in pensions, schemes and

[28] Pensions Commission, *Pensions: Challenges and Choices, The First Report of the Pensions Commission* (HMSO, 2004), 120.

[29] ibid, 84.

[30] ibid, 157.

[31] Pensions Act 1995, s 75 creates a debt on the employer to pay such deficits.

providers over the years. In the 1990s it became clear that retirement policies sold by Equitable Life as guaranteed were far from that.[32] The pensions mis-selling scandal further tarnished the image of the pensions industry when it became clear that millions of employees were convinced to transfer benefits from valuable final salary schemes into personal pension policies with no benefit guarantees. A report at the time by the Financial Services Authority and Personal Investment Authority identified more than two million mis-sold personal pension cases and estimated losses greater than £10 billion.[33] All of these individuals had been advised to leave good quality employer pension schemes in order to set up a personal pension with no guaranteed benefits. The consequences were a loss in membership of workplace pensions and personal detriment to those involved. The scale of the problem required industry wide redress and led to the review of all such sales with affected individuals receiving compensation from the relevant pension provider. The reputational damage to the financial services industry was huge as it became apparent that advisors were motivated by large commissions which conflicted with the best interests of the clients. It seems that even after this scandal, some employees are still poorly advised about pensions and cases continue to arise where employees are advised to leave good quality pension schemes in favour of riskier private pension policies.[34] As well as damaging the reputation of the industry and individuals, this had a negative effect on many employer-sponsored schemes as the funds were transferred from these schemes into private pension policies on a large scale. The reputational damage to pension products and providers remains today.

Perhaps the most famous was the Maxwell pensions' scandal where it was discovered that millions of pounds of investments had been misappropriated by Robert Maxwell from the Mirror Group Newspaper Pension Fund.[35] Corporate insolvency also challenges trust in the concept of saving for retirement. In the aftermath of the Lehman Brothers collapse the Pensions Advisory Service (TPAS) reported a 10 per cent increase in calls to its helpline.[36] In response to the Maxwell and other scandals, the Pension Law Review Committee was established in June 1992 (the Goode Report) to 'review the framework of law and regulation within which occupational pension schemes operate'.[37] Recommendations were made to create a legal framework and guarantee the funding of pension promises as this

[32] BBC News *Equitable Life: Timeline of key events* 20 October 2010: www.bbc.co.uk/news/business-10725923.

[33] Financial Services Authority & Personal Investment Authority, 'Pension Transfers and Opt Outs Review, Phase 2' (March 1998), 13.

[34] E Simon, 'A £20bn Pension Mis-selling Scandal?' *The Telegraph* (London, 4 March 2012) www.telegraph.co.uk/finance/personalfinance/pensions/9120476/A-20bn-pension-mis-selling-scandal.html.

[35] RJ Laugharne Thomas and RT Turner, 'Mirror Group Newspapers plc: Investigations under Sections 432(2) and 442 of the Companies Act 1985' (Department for Trade and Industry, 2001) https://webarchive.nationalarchives.gov.uk/+/http://www.dti.gov.uk/cld/mirrorgroup/summary.htm.

[36] www.pensionsadvisoryservice.org.uk/.

[37] Pension Law Review Committee, *The Report of the Pension Law Review Committee* (Cm 2342-1, 1993), iii.

was seen as being key to restoring employee trust lost after the Maxwell scandal. Imposing minimum scheme solvency would also reduce risk from fraud or underfunding.[38] Where these regulations fail a further safety net was established to assume responsibility for defined benefit schemes where the employer becomes insolvent, now embodied in the Pension Protection Fund.[39] The Goode Report also recommended regulatory oversight to ensure that new regulation was properly enforced and this role is currently performed by the Pensions Regulator.

As a result of the Goode Report, the Pensions Act 1995 was introduced, which imposed a number of funding and other restrictions on salary related pensions. Restrictions on employer-related investments were introduced and regulation requiring employees to be given more information on schemes, benefits and investments were introduced. Regulation of occupational pensions has increased ever since and some have questioned the value of this regulation compared to the resulting decline of salary related pension schemes.[40] The increased regulation has contributed to the decline of DB schemes which means in a way that current employees are paying for the scandals of the past with poorer benefit promises in the future. Lack of trust by employees and increasing costs of administration for employers as a result of increasing legislation played a part in the reduction of numbers of workers contributing to private pensions generally.

V. The Road to Auto-Enrolment: The Pensions Commission

AE was brought in as a result of cross-party support, having been instigated by the Labour Government (1997–2010) and completed by the Coalition Government (2010–2015). This research explores the legislative intention of AE and compares this to the actual legislative requirements enacted and the effects of implementation. Whilst the first AE legislation was issued in 2007, the idea for AE came much earlier. In 2002 the Pensions Commission (The Commission) was established to review pension provision in the UK in light of increased life expectancy and a reduction in savings. The Commission produced three reports recommending wide ranging reforms to the state and private pension system in the UK.

The first report found that many people were not saving enough, if at all for retirement, and that the population was ageing, meaning that there were fewer workers to support the growing number of pensioners.[41] The number of people

[38] ibid, 195.

[39] Pensions Act 2004, pt 2.

[40] J Jones, 'Maxwell Pension Scandal "Could Happen Again" Despite Regulations' (*Professional Adviser*, 4 November 2011) www.professionaladviser.com/ifaonline/news/2122739/maxwell-pension-scandal-could-happen-again-despite-regulations.

[41] Pensions Commission, *Pensions: Challenges and Choices*, (n 28).

over state pension age is expected to increase by 32 per cent over the next 25 years but the working age population is only expected to increase by 14 per cent.[42] The state pension system needed reform and the fact that the pensions system was so complicated meant that many were put off making decisions about pensions as they did not understand what they might get from the state or other pensions. The first report noted that the UK's state pension was among the least generous in the developed world[43] and significantly worse than Europe where earnings related formulas in excess of between 70 and 80 per cent of earnings were targeted as retirement income.[44] Even the US system of social security provided a gross average replacement of 45 per cent of earnings in retirement compared to 37 per cent in the UK.[45] It was noted that the UK was in a group with New Zealand and Canada where state pension is designed to prevent poverty rather than replace income. New Zealand pays a universal flat rate irrespective of assets or income, in a similar way to the UK. This might cushion mistakes in savings decisions of the individual but is of a very low level in proportion to weekly pre-retirement wages.[46] Australia had been in the same category until the introduction of mandatory saving in the 1990s and it has now moved to the intermediate group on a similar footing to the US.[47] The UK's smaller percentage of salary as a retirement pension can be traced back to the roots of the state pension, discussed previously, which was designed to 'insure' against poverty rather than replace income. Changes to the state pension were one aspect of the proposed solution along with reforms to the private sector.

The Commission noted a number of barriers to the voluntary pension saving system.[48] An end to means testing for state pensions was one difficult issue which needed to be addressed if people were to be encouraged to commit to private pension saving. Individuals required advice and encouragement to make rational decisions about long-term saving and the cost of providing advice would significantly affect the benefit of savings. The Commission examined the difficulties of unavoidable choices and made suggestions based on the least unfavourable options. As the UK state pension system is funded from taxation of current workers, the fact that the population is ageing has a significant effect. Fewer and fewer workers are supporting more and more pensioners. The choices posed were to accept poorer pensioners, increase taxation to pay for pensions, save more privately to support the state pension or increase retirement ages. The increase in retirement age has a double benefit in that it both increases the size of the workforce contributing

[42] NAPF, *Fit for the Future: NAPF's Vision for Pensions* (March 2010) www.plsa.co.uk/portals/0/Documents/0123_Fit_for_the_future_NAPFs_Vision_for_Pension_0310.pdf, 4.

[43] ibid, 58.

[44] Ibid, 58.

[45] Ibid, 59.

[46] Crossan et al 'Financial Literacy and Retirement Planning in New Zealand' (2011) 10 (4) *Journal of Pension Economics & Finance* 619, 620.

[47] ibid, 60.

[48] ibid, xii.

through taxation and reduces the number of years to be funded for retirement for the individual. This takes account of the increasing longevity. The Commission found that a 'conscious and well-formed' choice had to be made.[49] Age discrimination legislation has now removed compulsory retirement ages.[50] Pension schemes, employers, trustees or managers of occupational pension schemes may not directly or indirectly discriminate against members or prospective pension scheme members on grounds of age.[51] It might be possible to objectively justify such discrimination on the basis that it is to support a social good but this can be difficult to identify. As a consequence, employers which previously matched higher pension contributions on an age-related basis may have withdrawn these enhancements to prevent a breach of the age discrimination legislation. This would have been a valuable benefit lost if employers reduced the level of contributions for some and also a useful prompt for those automatically enrolled at a low level who might have been motivated to benefit from higher matching contributions as their career (and age) progressed. This demonstrates how one legislative intention can impact on another. The powerful effect of employer matching contributions is discussed throughout the book and is illustrated by the empirical findings reported in Chapter 5.

A decision having been made to reform the state pension, the Commission turned its attention to improving private pension saving in the UK. Private saving on a voluntary basis had not been successful. The previous attempt to encourage more saving in the workplace by the introduction of stakeholder pensions had been a failure with few employers contributing and the schemes becoming 'empty shells'.[52] In order to make these successful, a change was needed both in the level of contributions and the voluntary nature of joining. Behavioural economics and the failure of assumed rational behaviour of investors was used as justification for introducing some compulsion in private saving for retirement. The report describes how 'very few individuals actually operate in this rational and well-informed fashion'.[53] There was discussion about the fact that 'inertia and a tendency for people to accept the situation regarding saving that requires the least decision making means people do not save for retirement'.[54] 'Harnessing the power of inertia to bring individuals into pension saving and keep them there' was justification for the AE aspect of the regime.[55] The perception was that some workers, particularly on lower earnings or those working for smaller employers, have difficulty accessing pensions. The relevant findings for the pensions market are that people will be put off making complex, long-term financial decisions unless

[49] ibid, 20.
[50] Employment Equality (Age) Regulations 2006, SI 2006/1031, Equality Act 2010.
[51] Equality Act, s 61.
[52] Pensions Commission, *Pensions: Challenges and Choices*, (n 28) 92.
[53] ibid, 206.
[54] ibid.
[55] P Johnson, D Yeandle and A Boulding, *Making Automatic Enrolment Work: A Review for the Department for Work and Pensions* (TSO, October 2010), 13.

they are pushed by some external agent and that the individual is heavily influenced by the way questions are framed and inertia. The Commission relied on evidence that people procrastinate unless they are forced to make a choice and that trading off means that people will always value the ability to consume today more than the ability to consume in future retirement.[56] On this basis it was decided that, where the default position is pension membership, this will result in much higher rates of participation.

The Commission consulted on its findings and then issued a second report in 2005 which restated objectives to address gaps in the current pension system, prevent the spread of means testing and overcome the barriers of inertia and high cost which deter voluntary private pension provision. The Commission identified 45 per cent of earnings as a suitable target for retirement income (considering reforms to take the state pension to meet around 30 per cent and the remainder to be met privately).[57] It suggested that this would require eight per cent of earnings for 40 years to achieve this figure.[58] As a result, it was recommended that employees be auto-enrolled into a personal account with a minimum eight per cent contribution paid in by employers and employees. It was anticipated that the private pensions market would not be able to meet demand for this volume of individual accounts, at the low cost required and so it recommended that the government establish a national pension savings scheme for this purpose. After considering a number of options it was agreed that a national scheme would be established, known as the National Employment Savings Trust (NEST). Other complimentary and supporting measures included the simplification of the tax and benefits system, major reductions in selling and administration costs and a major increase in the level of customer understanding of pension related issues. Throughout all of these changes to state and private pensions, it was noted that specific consideration should be given to the fact that female pensioners are poorer than male pensioners and that this should be redressed.[59] My work considers the effectiveness of AE in dealing with these concerns. The recommendations of the Commission received broad political support in principle although the mode of delivery was more difficult to agree.

The main recommendations were in two parts:

(1) The creation of a low cost, national funded pension savings scheme into which individuals will be automatically enrolled, but with the right to opt-out, with a modest level of compulsory matching employer contributions, and delivering the opportunity to save for a pension at a low annual management charge.

[56] Pensions Commission, *Pensions: Challenges and Choices*, (n 28) 206.

[57] Pensions Commission, *A New Pension Settlement for the Twenty-First Century: The Second Report of the Pensions Commission 2005*, 7.

[58] ibid, 356.

[59] Pensions Commission, *Pensions: Challenges and Choices*, (n 28) 259.

(2) Reforms to make the state system less means tested and closer to universal. In order to achieve this while maintaining the standard of living of the poorest pensioners it will need to be more generous which implies a mix of tax increases, devoted to pensions' expenditure, and an increase in state pension ages.[60]

Two White Papers were subsequently issued in 2006. The Pensions White Paper, *Security in Retirement: Towards a New Pensions System*, resulted in the reform of state pensions implemented by the Pensions Acts of 2007 and 2014.[61] The second paper, *Personal Accounts: A New Way to Save*, set out the framework for AE and introduced the National Pension Savings Scheme (NPSS) which was the forerunner to NEST.[62] The scheme was introduced to ensure that even if the pensions industry failed to supply sufficient private pensions meeting the AE quality criteria, employers could still fulfil their obligations to employees under AE legislation. The policy of AE was implemented by the Pensions Act of 2008 as amended by the Pensions Act 2011.

VI. Lessons from Abroad

In reviewing the UK system, the Pensions Commission referenced international experiences of auto enrolment in pensions.[63] It identified Australia as a good comparison to the UK as a developed country seeking to add a compulsory savings element to cover a savings gap. I will also refer to the example of New Zealand which introduced AE in 2007 and also to the US which does not have a mandatory savings system but which has a large body of research into the effects of AE where it is introduced on a voluntary basis.

The Australian Age Pension is funded through general taxation and is means tested rather than the earnings-based system of the UK and the US.[64] This works to support those with the lowest earnings and so provides a subsidy to those who do not have additional savings. The UK system in comparison is based on National Insurance contributions and is of a standard amount irrespective of wealth.

[60] Pensions Commission, *The second Report*, (n 57) 18.

[61] Department for Work and Pensions, *Security in Retirement: Towards a New Pensions System* (White Paper, Cm 6841, 2006).

[62] Department for Work and Pensions, *Personal Accounts: A New Way to Save* (White Paper, Cm 6975, 2006). The Pensions Act 2007 established the framework for AE and created the Personal Accounts Delivery Authority (PADA), which advised the government on establishing NPSS which is now NEST. It also reduced the number of years of qualifying service needed to get the full basic state pension and increased state pension age.

[63] Pensions Commission, *Pensions: Challenges and Choices*, (n 28) 252.

[64] D Muir 'Building Value in the Australian Defined Contribution system: A Values Perspective' (2011) 33 *Comparative Labor Law and Policy Journal* 93, 104.

The Australian Superannuation Guarantee is a mandatory employer contribution to a private pension plan which was introduced initially in 1992.[65] Employers are not required to contribute to the plan where employees earn below a minimum threshold, are under 18 or over 70 and for some employment less than 30 hours per week.[66] The details of the Australian regime are considered further in the next chapter which looks at the legislation and main principles of the UK regime.

The KiwiSaver is a dramatic policy change for New Zealand which had previously offered a non-contributory flat rate pension which people could chose to supplement or not.[67] Withdrawal of tax benefits for pension schemes had seen a decline in private saving and so there was a heavy reliance on the state to fund retirement.[68] KiwiSaver was introduced 'to assist members smooth their pre-and-post retirement living standards and to reduce the likelihood that individuals would experience a significant decline in living standards once retired'.[69] Effectively a cushion between existing and expected standards of living.[70] It operates as a voluntary savings scheme but on an AE basis. All new employees are automatically enrolled but they can choose to opt out.[71] KiwiSaver schemes are a distinct form of saving product unlike the workplace pensions used in AE in the UK, which only need to meet certain criteria. It also offers significant tax incentives and a tax free contribution on first joining.[72]

The US calculates mandatory pensions based on only part of total career earnings and has high levels of relative income poverty amongst the retired population.[73] In a similar way to other countries, the employer pension plans have changed over the years from defined benefit to defined contribution and are also entirely voluntary.[74] The most used defined contribution plan in the US is the 401k plan which is portable and available even to temporary workers.[75] The experience of the US has been similar to the UK in this regard in that DC plans were offered by employers, often with little incentive, and employees did not join for a variety of reasons.

[65] Department for Work and Pensions, Collard & Moore, Research Report No 663 (2010) 'Review of International Pension Reform' 16.

[66] ibid, 17.

[67] Gibson et al 'The Distributional Impact of KiwiSaver Incentives' (2009) 36 *Social Policy Journal of New Zealand*, 111.

[68] Department for Work and Pensions, Collard & Moore, Research Report No 663, (n 65) 23.

[69] New Zealand Treasury Working Paper 11/04, Law et al 'KiwiSaver: An initial Evaluation of the Impact on Retirement Saving' 13.

[70] ibid.

[71] ibid, 1.

[72] Gibson et al 'The Distributional Impact of KiwiSaver Incentives', (n 67) 112.

[73] OECD Pensions at a glance 2019 www.oecd.org/unitedstates/PAG2019-USA.pdf.

[74] Secunda 'The Behavioural Economic Case for Paternalistic Workplace Retirement Plans' (2016) 91 *Indiana Law Journal* 505, 509.

[75] ibid, 514.

VII. Conclusion

Several themes emerge from the discussion of AE before enactment which allows conclusions to be drawn about parliamentary intention and concerns about the introduction of AE. The interaction between the state and private sector was integral to the introduction of AE. The system required simplification and change to ensure that people understand the system and believe there is a benefit in saving privately in addition to the state pension. Changes to a flat rate state pension and increasing the retirement age are part of this process but individuals may still perceive the state pension system as changeable and unpredictable. My empirical study demonstrates this and how these doubts affect thinking about private workplace pensions.

It is also clear that individuals need to save more for their own good. Even with a simplified state pension system, individuals would need a higher proportion of income in retirement than they could achieve and so it would be in their interests to save more for retirement. It was found that individuals do not always behave rationally when making financial decisions. Behavioural economics provided evidence which supported legal intervention to make choices easier and harness inertia to work in favour of additional pension saving rather than against it. Some have described this as a paternalistic motivation for legislation and this will be discussed in detail in Chapters 3 and 4 which will consider paternalism and behavioural economics in this context as well as the more general policy considerations for legal intervention in this way. Linked to this is the question of affordability. The policy intention from the Pensions Commission is considered throughout this book as the implementing legislation is considered from a practical and policy perspective. Reference is made to other jurisdictions such as the US, Australia and New Zealand to compare and consider the particular approach to implementation of the UK and the consequences for the individual.

2

Introduction of Auto-Enrolment to the UK

I. Auto-Enrolment and Parliamentary Intent

As a result of the Commission's recommendations, a number of changes to pensions were announced. The new pension system was intended to promote personal responsibility and be fair, simple, affordable and sustainable.[1] The 2008 Act is the main legislative mechanism for introducing the rights and obligations under AE. Discussion of the Bill, which became the 2008 Act, demonstrates that whilst there was broad consensus that something had to be done to encourage more private retirement saving, there was disagreement about the exact method of achieving this. Parliamentary debate[2] raised many issues about the practical effects of implementation of AE and this book explores these and provides commentary on whether concerns were adequately addressed in subsequent legislative developments. The Secretary of State for Work and Pensions, Mr Peter Hain, introduced the second reading of the Bill with a statement about renewing the contract between the state and the individual. The state pension had been overhauled but it needed support from private saving.

A. Increase Saving by Default

The main intention of the legislation was to increase saving for retirement [and respond to]

> [A] serious problem of under-saving, with perhaps as many as 7 million people not saving enough to fulfil their aspirations in retirement … a chasm will grow between the income that they want and that which they receive in retirement.[3]

This reference to individual aspiration identifies the intention for the legislation to help people do what is good for them. When law intervenes with personal choice

[1] House of Commons Library, 'Research Paper 07/94: Pensions Bill' (19 December 2007) http://researchbriefings.files.parliament.uk/documents/RP07-94/RP07-94.pdf.
[2] HC Deb 7 January 2008, vol 470, col 6.
[3] ibid, 60.

(self-enrolment) for the good of the individual this constitutes a form of legal paternalism (discussed in the following chapter). The form of AE rather than self-enrolment was deliberately chosen as a way to combat 'people's tendency not to act when faced with difficult financial decisions [and AE is] the most effective way of combating inertia and myopia'.[4] However, there could be reasons, other than inertia and myopia, for not joining pension schemes, such as financial constraints or lack of trust in providers. It was acknowledged in the parliamentary debate that scheme failures and frauds had caused a loss in confidence in pensions. The establishment of the Pension Protection Fund may have provided comfort for those in salary related pension schemes but the investment risk in defined contribution schemes remains with the individual and so doubts remain. Perhaps individuals had good reasons not to join under self-enrolment.

A key feature of AE is to put employees into a default investment fund and this book considers the effect this has on future decisions about investing in the fund and responsibility for decision making by the individual. The regime does not acknowledge the problems of the ability to pay and how this interacts with the identified inertia that is now operating to keep people auto-enrolled. A real test of the justification for legislative intervention is the effect of implementation. The difficulties of enrolling individuals into default savings positions is explored in detail in Chapters 4 and 5. It is important to note that the default envisaged is intended to fulfil individual aspiration and was not intended to be at all costs. This clearly requires assessment of the individual experience and consideration of the question of how to assess whether individual aspirations are met and to what extent negative consequences are acceptable.

B. Prevent a Reduction in Existing Pension Benefits or Levelling Down

One concern for Parliament was whether employers might use AE as an excuse to reduce existing pension benefits known as 'levelling down'.[5] An employer might discontinue an existing pension arrangement in order to pay the minimum three per cent contribution required under the AE obligations. There was emphasis in the debate that the three per cent is a floor and should not become a ceiling. It was suggested that by creating a simple qualifying scheme test for the purposes of AE, many employers would choose to use existing schemes to enrol workers and that the phasing in of contributions would allow employers to adjust to the increased numbers of employees receiving contributions.[6] My empirical research suggests that employers have found it difficult to use pre-existing schemes with

[4] ibid, 63.
[5] ibid, 57.
[6] ibid.

providers unwilling to amend existing schemes to qualify as AE compliant. This is particularly the case for pre-existing personal pension plans. When these cannot be changed, employers must re-negotiate contractual terms with employees as employers do not wish to continue with these other arrangements in addition to the new AE obligations. Reliance on the private sector allows it to dictate whether it will agree to amend existing products and it may not be cost efficient to do so. Parliament was certain that 'Employers will not suddenly go down-market'[7] but difficulties of implementation and continuing regulatory compliance may increase costs and require changes to be made to existing benefit packages during the implementation of AE.

The parliamentary emphasis was on increased numbers of workers saving but would AE still be considered successful if the numbers of people contributing to pensions increased but overall contributions do not? Whilst not strictly levelling down of pensions, there were also fears that the overall benefits package would be reduced to take account of increased pension costs. Employers may deduct the extra costs from future salary increases but this may be an acceptable foreseen consequence of the legislation. Chapters 4 and 5 demonstrate the anchoring effect of defaults where the minimum contribution levels are often not reconsidered. This could effectively reduce the value of pensions for some which contravenes the policy intention.

C. Education of the Workforce

Parliament acknowledged that:

> For the new personal accounts to be successful, those on lower than average earnings will need to be persuaded that it is in their interests to invest in the new pensions. If they are not so persuaded, there is a danger that they will opt-out, and that the whole system, and the benefits that it is supposed to bring, will collapse.[8]

It was acknowledged during the parliamentary debate that the Bill represented a 'consensus solution' and that there would be no certainty that the three per cent employer contribution and five per cent employee contribution would provide a good return to everyone.[9] The investment and performance risks are borne by the individual in DC plans often used for AE. Personal responsibility for retirement saving was also discussed but some questioned how realistic it was to expect people to save when they have no idea what they will get in return for saving. The intention was that it would be difficult not to auto-enrol and difficult to opt-out without a good reason.[10] It seems that this is not so much about persuasion of the

[7] ibid.
[8] HC Deb 7 January 2008, vol 470, col 6.
[9] ibid, 58–59.
[10] ibid, 61.

workforce as it is about making legislative default decisions. My work considers whether people now have sufficient understanding of workplace pensions to make decisions and whether active choices are made, including whether to stay in or opt-out and how much to contribute.

Financial literacy is also a key concern if AE is to do more than enrol people at a minimum level without employee engagement. Parliament also considered the level of understanding and advice individuals need as AE relies on generic advice being sufficient.[11] The pensions industry is involved in creating new pension products which comply with AE and past experience shows the industry does not always put member interests to the forefront.[12] Also, the government sponsored NEST scheme is unsuitable for some employees but there is little scope for advice to be given to employees within the cost margins of private AE compliant pensions. My research looks at issues facing employers when dealing with advisors and in providing information to employees about AE. The question of advice and responsibility for communications is also considered in Chapters 5 and 6. It is also interesting that the most basic concept of personal financial advice has been set aside in favour of the policy objective of increasing pension saving. Basic financial planning dictates that a client should deal with protection (life cover for debts), income protection (for death or inability to earn income), pension, savings, investment in that order. Financial planners would generally advise the payment of all expensive debts before making savings and, whilst pension saving is very tax efficient, the poorest of households with debt attracting high interest may be better paying off these debts before saving for a pension or otherwise. The lack of financial advice in AE should therefore not be written off as trivial and it is important to remember that, irrespective of whether the personal account used by employers to comply with AE is in NEST, a private or occupational pension, they are all financial products of some sort with varying risks and potential benefits. In most instances where a payment is made for an investment, the individual will have made a positive choice in that investment and will have made decisions about the provider and product but not with AE.

Default positions influence the decision making of individuals and AE may actually promote disengagement from pension planning or seeking financial advice. If the pension provider chosen by the employer performs badly it will be the individual member who suffers the consequences. Chapter 6 considers whether there is any responsibility by the employer for the choice of provider for the employee. Even if the employer satisfies the basic obligations under AE is there any legal obligation to take care when selecting products of providers? Does the provider owe any duty to the employer or employees to ensure that the employees understand the pension and options or is the employee considered to be self-advised?

[11] ibid, 64.

[12] For example, the mis-selling of personal pensions discussed in ch 1.

Having decided that generic advice would be sufficient for AE, the government had to ensure that generic advice would be available[13] and a study to research and design a national approach to generic financial advice was commissioned.[14] The aim was to ensure greater access to high quality affordable financial advice for those most vulnerable to the consequences of poor financial decision making. The review found varying levels of access to advice across the UK and that there was no existing provider of advice which could comprehensively provide Generic Financial Advice (GFA).[15] Perhaps unsurprisingly, those not-for-profit organisations providing GFA were concentrated in large urban areas.

The Financial Services Authority (FSA) also considered generic advice as part of its Retail Distribution Review (RDR) in 2007.[16] In light of the impending introduction of AE, the FSA looked at the possibility of creating a scale for the depth of advice required in given situations.[17] The FSA anticipated that GFA might lead to demand for regulated advice services.[18] As a result of the review, the Money Advice Service (originally established under the Financial Services Act 2010 as the Consumer Financial Education Body) was set up as an independent body with responsibility for improving people's money management. The Financial Services Act 2010 sets out statutory objectives to enhance the understanding and knowledge of members of the public of financial matters and enhance the ability of members of the public to manage their own financial affairs. Statutory functions include promoting awareness of the benefits of financial planning and providing information and advice to members of the public and also provides debt advice. This book considers whether and how individuals engage with information and advice and how the giving of information as part of the AE requirements is regulated. It is clear from the empirical data that individuals react in different ways to information on workplace pensions and many reported disengagement with pensions and decisions at the most basic level. My research finds that there is more work to be done in relation to educating the workforce about workplace pensions and making active choices to preserve the intended benefits of the AE regime.

D. Private Pension Saving Compatible with State Benefits

If people are to be persuaded to save, it must be clear that there will be a benefit to this. If there is a fear that means testing of the state pension will lead to individuals being entitled to lower state benefits because of pension saving then this

[13] HM Treasury, *Financial Capability: The Government's Long-term Approach* (HMSO, January 2007).
[14] O Thoresen, *Thoresen Review of Generic Financial Advice: Final Report* (HMSO, March 2008).
[15] Experian, 'Thoresen Review, Generic Financial Advice: Target Market and Infrastructure Mapping' (January 2008) http://files.datapress.io/london/dataset/financial-capability-and-child-poverty/financial-capability-technical-model.pdf.
[16] Financial Services Authority, 'A Review of Retail Distribution' (DP07/1, June 2007).
[17] ibid, 21.
[18] ibid, 31.

will operate as a disincentive to saving more in personal accounts. There has to be a tangible benefit for saving and, whilst the state pension has been reformed to remove means testing, there is always a concern that 'the rules of the game will be changed by a future Government'.[19] The Pensions Act 2014 introduced a single tier state pension system to replace the previous basic and second state pension system.[20] The increased state pension retirement age will also increase to 67 by 2028 and may be subject to further increases.[21] The increased age reflects increased longevity and an ageing population. It will no longer be possible for any occupational pension schemes to contract out of the state pension which demonstrates the commitment to the first pillar: a state pension.[22] The supporting second and third pillars are then bolstered by the AE legislation which compels an element of private saving as the default position.

II. Legislative Reality

The parliamentary intention outlined above,[23] highlighted a number of aims for the AE legislation. The main provisions of AE were brought into force on 30 June 2012[24] with employers subject to the requirements in a phased period from 2012 to 2018. The employer is responsible for checking all employee information to ensure that each employee is informed of their status and automatically enrolled into a suitable pension, where appropriate. This requires consideration of the age, salary and contractual status of each employee.[25] The legislation defines eligible workers as jobholders. To be defined as a jobholder the employee needs to be a worker in the UK under a contract, be aged over 16 and under 75 and earning qualifying earnings. The creation of this new term of jobholder means that employers cannot always rely on existing employment law definitions to consider eligibility but the term 'worker'[26] may cause confusion with the definition of 'worker' used in other employment legislation.[27] Agency workers are specifically included as workers under the AE legislation with an assumption that whoever pays the agency worker will be responsible for effecting AE.[28] The specific contractual arrangements of the contract of employment may need to be examined to assess whether individuals require to be included as workers for the purposes of AE.[29]

[19] HC Deb 7 January 2008, vol 470, col 65.
[20] Pensions Act 2014, s 2.
[21] ibid, ss 26–27.
[22] ibid, s 24 and sch 13.
[23] Part I, above.
[24] Pensions Act 2008 (Commencement No 13) Order 2012, SI 2012/1682.
[25] Occupational and Personal Pension Schemes (Automatic Enrolment) Regulations 2010, SI 2010/772.
[26] Pensions Act 2008, s 88.
[27] Employment Rights Act 1996, s 230.
[28] Pensions Act 2008, s 89.
[29] *Clyde & Co LLP v Bates van Winkelhof* [2014] UKSC 32; [2014] 1 WLR 2047.

AE legislation includes a wide scope of potentially eligible jobholders. It is for the employer to determine the status of each person and then consider whether employees are to be automatically enrolled, can opt-in to the pension or fail to meet the AE criteria. Only eligible jobholders, who are aged between 22 and the state pension age, have qualifying earnings (currently between £6,240 and £50,000), exceed the earnings trigger (currently £10,000)[30] and who are not already members of a qualifying pension scheme with the employer must be automatically enrolled into a qualifying pension.[31] The qualifying earnings criteria is defined as gross earnings, which includes bonus, overtime and maternity pay, falling within a specific band of earnings.[32] The definition of earnings used for AE is quite wide and may differ from the definition of earnings used in contracts of employment and in pre-existing pension schemes. This often required contractual changes and scheme changes with the costs being met by employers. This complication can be criticised as a negative aspect of this regime and another potential barrier to saving. It makes it more difficult and costly for employers to ensure compliance and also means that some employees with higher earnings will only be eligible for contributions on a portion of their earnings. This is an important policy difference from the KiwiSaver Scheme in New Zealand which requires both employers and employees to pay contributions as a percentage of gross earnings.[33] However the process of automatic enrolment only applies to new employees in New Zealand,[34] as opposed to all eligible jobholders in the UK. In the US, pensions are entirely voluntary but some employers have introduced a policy of auto enrolment since this was permitted in 2006.[35] This allows employers to enrol all employees into a 401k plan with the option to opt out and has produced a volume of research on the benefits and consequences of the policy in the US.[36]

To ascertain whether a worker has qualifying earnings in the UK, an employer needs to consider the actual pay in the period, whether that is a week, month or other period. If a worker has variable pay, because of overtime or bonus payments for example, this will need to be considered. This means that even if contractual pay is below the earnings trigger of £10,000, if the trigger is met in any period such as monthly or fortnightly then the worker must be enrolled. So, for example, if a part time student working on a Saturday throughout the year and earning less than £10,000 earns more than £192 per week because they do overtime in the holidays then this would trigger the AE requirements. Employees who do not trigger the

[30] Automatic Enrolment (Earnings Trigger and Qualifying Earnings Band) Order 2020 (SI 2020/372) Art 3.

[31] Pensions Act 2008, ss 3(1), 5(1) & 87A.

[32] Pensions Act 2008, s 14; Pensions Act 2011, s 8.

[33] Department for Work and Pensions, Collard & Moore, Research Report No 663 (2010) 'Review of International Pension Reform' 24.

[34] KiwiSaver Act 2006, ss 10–15.

[35] Pension Protection Act 2006.

[36] P Secunda, 'The Behavioural Economic Case for Paternalistic Workplace Retirement Plans' (2016) 91 *Indiana Law Journal* 505, 526.

£10,000 earnings will not be eligible for automatic enrolment but may be entitled to opt into AE if they earn more than the minimum band of earnings figure.

There has been some criticism of the complexity for employers in assessing workers. The legislation also fails to ensure the poorest workers are included within the regime which was identified as an issue at the outset.[37] A worker with several jobs with different employers may still have no access to a pension and no entitlement to an employer contribution. There is particular concern about the position for women who may not be entitled to a full state pension, because of a broken national insurance record when undertaking caring responsibilities. Women are also more likely to fall into the category of undertaking several part-time jobs making them more likely to be excluded from AE. As part of my research into the experience of workers, I consider employees' understanding of state benefits and also whether women have any experience of this broken career path impacting on pensions.[38] Entire sectors may gain little benefit from AE because of the pay thresholds. This can be contrasted to the Australian Superannuation Guarantee which applies to all employees and which requires employers to pay contributions for those earning above a statutory minimum.[39] In the UK, the limitations mean some workers still miss out and the policy misses part of the target group. The tourist and food and drink industries often have work patterns that mean that individuals do not meet the threshold conditions. For example, a worker who has multiple part-time contracts may find that they are not eligible to receive contributions from any of their employers because they do not reach the threshold of earnings for any of the contracts. It may be the case that a worker holding multiple contracts with the same employer can be considered to have an umbrella contract which would require the employer to consider all the contracts together for the purposes of AE but this will depend on the nature and terms of the contract of employment.

The obligation to contribute to the AE plan for money purchase/DC schemes equates to a minimum three per cent employer and minimum eight per cent total contribution from October 2018. DB schemes provide guaranteed pensions and operate on a minimum criterion but the same concerns about value and quality in return for member contributions do not arise for DB because the employer underwrites the guarantee to the member. The focus of this work is on DC arrangements used in AE compliance as the risks are all borne by the member. Some employers may only contribute the statutory minimum three per cent employer contribution whilst others may pay a higher contribution reducing the compulsory employee contribution. There has been criticism that the contribution levels are very low, particularly if this anchors contribution levels as a norm rather than a minimum threshold. In Australia only the employer is required to contribute. The superannuation guarantee was introduced in 1992 with an initial mandatory

[37] HC Deb 7 January 2008, vol 470, cols 6, 55.
[38] See empirical findings in ch 5.
[39] Department for Work and Pensions, Research Report No 663, 16.

contribution rate of 9 per cent of employee ordinary earnings from 1 July 2002 until 30 June 2013. On 1 July 2013, the rate increased to 9.25 per cent, before increasing again on 1 July 2014 to 9.5 per cent. The government has legislated that the superannuation guarantee rate will remain at 9.5 per cent until 30 June 2021. After this, the rate will increase by 0.5 percentage points each year until it reaches 12 per cent on 1 July 2025.[40] There is no requirement for employees to contribute.[41] There is currently no progressive model of contributions for AE in the UK. In New Zealand, the employee could choose either four or eight per cent contributions with the default initially set at four but reduced to two per cent the year after introduction. There are now a range of employee contribution options.[42] Employer contributions have been phased in from one per cent in 2008 and reaching three per cent in 2011.[43] Whilst this appears similar to the UK, it should be noted that the contribution is based on gross earnings rather than a band of salary like the UK so the net effect is a much larger monetary contribution. Employees can also take a contribution holiday from the KiwiSaver and may also be able to access funds for a house deposit in New Zealand.[44] These flexibilities might encourage saving as it seems like a more tangible, accessible and flexible plan than the AE pensions in the UK. Accessibility concerns are reported in the empirical research as a barrier to motivation for saving and so might be considered in future development of the policy in the UK. The low value of contributions raises the question of justification for the legal intervention of AE and whether it can achieve its purpose of helping individuals to make better savings decisions. It may be that the low contribution rate was designed to ensure that the policy appears successful with a low opt-out rate, discussed further in Chapter 4. It should also be noted that the obligation to contribute is in respect of the qualifying earnings band only and so this adds a further complication when assessing what contributions are to be made.

This assessment process is continual and the employer is responsible for monitoring employees who satisfy the AE criteria, for example because they reach age or salary triggers. Even for those employees who have been auto-enrolled but choose to opt-out, the employer must re-assess them every three years and re-enrol them as necessary.[45] Some employers find this administrative burden too great and this has led to the practice of contractual enrolment.[46] In contractual enrolment, all

[40] OECD Pensions at a glance 2019 Profiles Australia: www.oecd.org/els/public-pensions/PAG2019-country-profile-Australia.pdf.

[41] Ibid, 18.

[42] KiwiSaver Act 2006, s 64.

[43] Department for Work and Pensions, Research Report No 663, 25; Inland Revenue KiwiSaver Employer Guide, 14: www.ird.govt.nz/-/media/project/ir/documents/forms-and-guides/ir1---ir99/ks4/ks4-2020.pdf.

[44] ibid, 25.

[45] Pensions Act 2008, s 5(2).

[46] The Pensions Regulator Detailed guidance 'Opting in, joining and contractual enrolment: How to process pension scheme membership outside of the automatic enrolment process' April 2017, 22: www.thepensionsregulator.gov.uk/-/media/thepensionsregulator/files/import/pdf/detailed-guidance-6.ashx.

employees join the qualifying pension scheme at the point of joining the employer and are contractually obliged to contribute to the scheme at a level which meets the minimum criteria for AE. The employee must consent to contractual enrolment and the payment of contributions and it runs parallel to the AE obligations which still need to be met. Contractual enrolment allows all employees to join, irrespective of satisfying AE criteria and negates the need to continually assess the workforce as employees who are already members of a qualifying scheme do not need to be automatically enrolled. However, if employees cease payment of contributions then they would need to be assessed for AE purposes and if the AE qualifying scheme criteria changes in the future then the scheme used for contractual enrolment would have to be changed and consent obtained again from members. Employees may feel pressured to stay in the pension with contractual enrolment and this is another example of an unintended consequence of AE leading to changing employment practices.

The scheme used for AE must meet certain minimum criteria and pre-existing schemes or arrangements were not always suitable. This required the employer to change or add to existing pensions. A qualifying scheme can be an occupational or personal pension which meets the quality requirements, such as access and minimum contributions and it must be capable of accepting all employees who are to be auto-enrolled without them having to make any choices of fund or otherwise.[47] An existing scheme might be used for this purpose although it may require amendment as pension schemes often contain minimum service, age or salary restrictions which are inconsistent with the AE regime. Many pension providers were unwilling to make requisite changes to existing plans, for example, to meet the charging criteria of AE compliant schemes and this has increased the volume of new pension schemes being created. The pensions industry may also choose to exclude lower earning employees if this is more profitable. This is a further difficulty of relying on a competitive free market to provide AE compliant products. An employer can instead use the NEST scheme rather than a private pension scheme for some or all of the workforce. The scheme is run by the NEST Corporation but because of its unique status, having been established under the AE legislation to meet AE requirements, it is not governed in entirely the same way as an ordinary occupational pension scheme.[48] Contributions and transfers to NEST were restricted until 2017. This led to a two-tier system for higher and lower paid employees from the introduction in 2012 until this was amended in 2017.[49] Again this highlights the difficulties of meeting AE requirements and the variety of different products that employees can be enrolled into.

This approach to saving model contrasts to the KiwiSaver which is a particular type of scheme with limits on fees, funds and with a specific design to meet the

[47] Pensions Act 2008, ss 20–27.

[48] NEST Website: www.nestpensions.org.uk/schemeweb/NestWeb/public/home/contents/homepage.html.

[49] The National Employment Savings Trust (Amendment) Order 2015, SI 2015/178.

legislative criteria.[50] Defaults are used in a similar way to the UK to ensure that no fund selection is needed before activation of membership but a member can also choose a different scheme to which their contributions are made which is a key difference to the UK policy.[51] Kiwisaver has been described as a model of a simple and unified national scheme whereas the UK is a model for those wishing to add a further option into an existing market.[52] In Australia, there is recognition of the importance of default funds in a system of compulsory membership.[53] The overhaul of the system and introduction of MySuper defaults in 2014 confirmed this.[54] In reviewing the original design, the Cooper review found that: 'Member interests are not always paramount: Superannuation is compulsory and fully outsourced to the private sector. System design and regulatory settings have perhaps not taken this into account.'[55] In addition, the regulatory model was found to be too focused on prudential regulation and the system was too complex. Disclosure to members failed to achieve its objectives and the improvements were designed to address these concerns.[56] In introducing a new cost effective product known as 'MySuper' the reforms sought to address worries about fund performance, disclosure, high fees and complex products in a default environment.[57] All of these issues appear to exist in the UK system of AE and are explored further in Chapters 4 and 5. Part of the new Australian measures include a choice-based system focussed on four sectors: retail, industry, public sector and corporate funds. Individuals can also add self-select investments.[58] In addition to the default restrictions, providers or trustees have to apply for a licence to provide a MySuper product and can only nominate one product in keeping with the member base they have.[59] Products must be offered on a diversified, balanced or lifestyle option; including a diversified, balanced option with standard fees.[60] When you contrast the UK with NEST, personal and occupational schemes all used for AE, it is clear that the UK could have chosen a more simple form of implementation and scheme design and the implications of this are explored further in Chapters 5 and 6.

A key duty under AE requires employers to provide workers with information and the Pensions Regulator has issued guidance which requires employers to

[50] Department for Work and Pensions, Research Report No 663, 24.

[51] KiwiSaver Act 2006, ss 44–52.

[52] O'Connell, Institute of Policy Studies, 'KiwiSaver: A Model Scheme' (2009) 36 *Social Policy Journal of New Zealand* 130, 140.

[53] Butt et al, 'Design of MySuper default funds: influences and outcomes' (2017) 57 *Accounting and Finance* 47, 48.

[54] Superannuation Legislation Amendment (MySuper Core Provisions) Act 2012 No 162, 2012.

[55] Australian Government '*Super system review: final report*' 2010, 6.

[56] ibid.

[57] Crawford School of Public Policy, Heng et al 'Retirement Policy: a review of the role, characteristics, and contribution of the Australian superannuation system' (2015) *Asian Pacific Economic Literature*, 9.

[58] Butt et al, 'Design of MySuper default funds: influences and outcomes', (n 53) 50.

[59] ibid.

[60] Heng et al 'Retirement Policy' (n 57), 10.

fully inform the workforce without inducing opt-outs.[61] Employers must notify employees in advance if they are to be automatically enrolled and provide information on the scheme and the date of enrolment. Employees who are not to be enrolled, either because they are already members of an eligible scheme or do not qualify for AE must also be informed of this. Employees must also be advised of their right to opt-out of the AE scheme and told where to find further information on this. Employers must be very careful when providing this information as the legislation specifically prohibits conduct which might induce employees to opt-out of AE.[62] Employers should not provide the opt-out notice directly to employees unless the employer is also the administrator of the scheme. Usually this means that the information notice contains details of the pension provider or administrator and the employee must be automatically enrolled into the scheme before they can elect to opt-out of it. For those with a right to opt-in or join another scheme, this information must also be provided. Employment contracts must also contain a statement of particulars about pension provisions and AE.[63] To avoid creating specific contractual obligations to provide a particular pension benefit or access to a particular scheme employers often draft a generic statement of compliance with AE within the contract of employment and do not specify benefits or pension schemes.

The Pension Regulator is responsible for enforcing compliance with the AE legislation, although there is some limited right to bring a claim in relation to detriment or dismissal connected to AE in the Employment Tribunal.[64] This is discussed in more detail in Chapter 6 which consider remedies and enforcement in more detail. The Pensions Act 2014 also gave the Department for Work and Pensions (DWP) regulation-making powers to make a range of technical changes to the legislation governing AE in workplace pension schemes.[65] As a result, employers are no longer required to enrol workers who are working in a notice period at any point within six weeks of AE or who the employer believes are covered by the lifetime allowance protection.

III. Post Implementation Legislative Changes

Since the introduction of AE in 2012 there has been a huge volume of pensions' legislation and those hoping for simplification will be disappointed. Some of this legislation is a direct result of the introduction of AE and might also be an illustration of the 'slippery slope' described in Chapter 4. For example, the increased

[61] The Pensions Regulator, 'Automatic Enrolment Detailed Guidance' (April 2017) www.thepensionsregulator.gov.uk/en/document-library/automatic-enrolment-detailed-guidance#s11556.

[62] Pensions Act 2008, s 54.

[63] Employment Rights Act 1996, s 1(4)(d)(iii).

[64] Pensions Act 2008, ch 2; Pensions Act 2004, s 5.

[65] Pensions Act 2014, s 38.

volume of private pension saving has led to an increase in membership of defined contribution schemes (DC). Key concerns related to the increase in DC saving as a method of AE compliance have produced more regulation on a number of issues including: value, costs, charges, scheme governance and flexibility in taking pension benefits.

A. Value

A review of workplace pensions found that a free market and competition in the financial industry cannot be relied on to deliver value for money for DC pension savers. The review identified weaknesses on the buyer side of the market with members relying on employers to make key decisions whilst lacking capability or incentive to ensure that good value schemes are chosen.[66] The findings of my study support this. In AE the employer chooses the pension plan but may have conflicting interests, insufficient time or resources to ensure that the best product is chosen. The pension products themselves are complex with opaque charging structures which make the employer's job more difficult. The OFT found that employees did not understand or engage with pensions, but members retain all the risk of the pension plan with DC schemes.[67] As the employer chooses the scheme without the employees' consent an added protection is required to ensure that all DC schemes meet minimum quality standards.

A major review of the value of workplace pensions produced the report, *Better Workplace Pensions: Further Measures for Savers*.[68] This report considers standards in pension schemes, charges/commissions and active member discounts. The introduction of AE has seen the volume of pension funds increase significantly but whilst AE provides for minimum contributions and access to pensions it does not create a governance framework to ensure that the schemes provide good value to employees. In relation to employers who use pre-existing workplace pension schemes for AE, the charges could be 'around 26 per cent higher than schemes sold after 2001'.[69] In this paper the government 'recognises that the process of defaulting millions of individuals into savings plans brings with it a new responsibility to set minimum quality standards'.[70] It is interesting that quality was only considered two years' after the introduction of AE. This may indicate that some of the consequences of AE were unforeseen and this quality standard is reactionary.

[66] Office of Fair Trading, 'Defined Contribution Workplace Pension Market Study' (OFT1505, September 2013 (revised February 2014) https://webarchive.nationalarchives.gov.uk/20140402194810/http:/www.oft.gov.uk/shared_oft/market-studies/oft1505.

[67] ibid.

[68] Department for Work and Pensions, *Better Workplace Pensions: Further Measures for Savers* (Cm 8840, March 2014).

[69] ibid, 9.

[70] ibid, 5.

B. Costs and Charges

As the employer makes all the decisions relating to the provider and fund under AE this leads to varying employee experiences because some funds will perform better than others and some will suffer as a result of high costs and charges. There is no obligation to ensure that the best value scheme is chosen for employees and a small difference in charges can create a large difference in the accumulation of assets in the fund. In light of the effect the default has on employee choice there was a real risk that some employees would suffer as a result of being enrolled into more expensive and inefficient pension plans than others. This is another potential cost of the policy. The Pensions Act 2014 allowed regulation of charges and the imposition of governance and administration requirements on AE pensions.[71] A charge cap of 0.75 per cent was introduced from April 2015 which applies to all default pension funds in AE qualifying pension schemes.[72] The reforms aim to control charges and make it easier for employers and employees to compare schemes. This is particularly important as many employees will be auto-enrolled into a default scheme and fund and will not make active decisions to change this. The charge cap will only apply to those members who remain in the AE default fund. Those workers who have elected to switch funds from the default will not be covered by the charge caps which may operate as a further barrier to active choices being made. This is the legislative equivalent of an acknowledgement of the vulnerability of employees subject to defaults under AE. In having to legislate further to protect those in the default fund, it seems to have been accepted that most individuals will stay in the default position created by AE. It may also make the default fund choice more appealing as it appears that it is the cheaper and best option where members perceive the cap to be a benefit.

The introduction of the cap may provide better value or it may act as a price anchor to pension providers, as discussed in Chapter 4. That is to say that in setting the 0.75 per cent charge cap, this could be viewed as the normal or standard amount even for providers who previously charged less than this. There is also a danger that schemes will become very basic to allow providers to operate the scheme within the charge cap or the market may not be willing to offer pensions for all employees if it is not profitable. Some believe that the new cap will prevent active investment management but it can also be argued that any benefits gained by such active investment are negated by managers' fees. The charge cap has not been changed since it was introduced which could also have the effect of

[71] Pensions Act 2014, s 43.

[72] The Occupational Pensions Scheme (Charges and Governance) Regulations 2015, SI 2015/879; Department for Work and Pensions, 'The Charge Cap: Guidance for Trustees and Managers of Occupational Schemes' (March 2015, updated October 2016) www.gov.uk/government/uploads/system/uploads/attachment_data/file/420215/charge-cap-guidance-apr-2015.pdf; Financial Conduct Authority, 'FCA Instrument: Personal Pension Schemes (Restrictions on Charges) Instrument' (FCA 2015/15, 2015) www.handbook.fca.org.uk/instrument/2015/FCA_2015_5.pdf.

stifling competition to provide products. Another concern has been that the lack of understanding of the pension products and complex charging structures could make the cap ineffective. Providers may add charges elsewhere to keep within the charge cap – the so called 'waterbed' effect.[73] Transaction costs are excluded from the charge cap and if this is not monitored it may lead to additional charges being added under this heading. Genuine transaction costs cannot be included in the charge cap as this could prevent advantageous trades of underlying fund assets but it will be difficult to monitor and enforce.

As the cap applied to all old and new schemes, employers who established schemes in 2012 had to review compliance again within a short timescale. With so much demand for new compliant schemes, this could put pressure on providers and may result in demand outstripping supply of AE compliant pension schemes. It has been argued that this could lead to a lack of competition and may result in providers declining to offer plans for the lowest paid workers. This leads to a concentration of employers with too few providers, and a higher risk of failure or non-compliance with auto-enrolment duties.[74] There has also been speculation that the charge caps will result in the 'levelling down' or reduction of scheme quality with features such as financial education and advice being removed. My empirical study suggests that more education or advice needs to be built in but this is less likely now as the policy seems to expect that defaults are the norm and that protections should assume defaults will continue.[75]

In the past, it was possible to apply a discount to active scheme members to encourage continued payments into the scheme. However, this may be unfair to those who leave (deferred pensioners) because their costs will increase even though it does not cost more to administer their funds. This practice was banned from 6 April 2016[76] as it was argued that it was unreasonable to expect people to be proactive when 'the policy has been built on harnessing inertia'.[77]

Commission and consultation charges were, in the past, recouped from employees' contributions as a method of paying for advice after the pension is taken out. The OFT found that commission acted as a barrier to switching because advisors were unlikely to advise employers to establish a new scheme, which could not have the charges built in, when they could recommend continued use of an existing arrangement, with built in charging, for new members. From April 2016, commission was removed from all qualifying schemes and members can only be charged for advice or services explicitly requested by the member.[78] Some employers argued that the removal of these commission and consultancy charges

[73] Department for Work and Pensions, *Better Workplace Pensions*, (n 68) 52.
[74] ibid, 55.
[75] ibid, 47.
[76] ibid, 67.
[77] ibid, 69.
[78] The Occupational and Personal Pension Schemes (Automatic Enrolment) (Amendment) Regulations 2013, SI 2013/23/28.

would mean that they could not access the same quality of scheme with services such as advice sessions, educational seminars and electronic marketing no longer included. For example, EasyJet was critical of the change and reported that it had a 100 per cent take up with over 60 per cent making additional contributions and attributed this in part to the '1-2-1 advice and electronic marketing provided by our advisers'.[79]

Employers may see the new position as a barrier because they will have to either pay for advice or choose an AE compliant scheme without any advice. This could mean that poorer value schemes are selected without professional advice or that employer contributions are reduced to compensate for upfront fees. Punter Southall suggested that 'Employers are not expecting to pay for advice and have not budgeted for it. Any additional costs may cause employers to make savings elsewhere.'[80] However, these arguments were rejected on the basis that employers do not need advice as the 'process has been designed to be as simple as possible and that employers can always use NEST'.[81] This so-called simplicity is questioned by many employers and it is clear from my empirical research that there are complications with the practical implementation of AE and integrating the duties within existing benefit packages. The employer must now incur all costs of establishing the scheme.[82] These findings appear to accept that members will not engage so there is little benefit in building advice into the pension product. This new legislation appears to be motivated by an acceptance that members are disengaged from their AE pension and it is an attempt to improve the consequences of default positions for those members.

Some costs are excluded from the charge cap and this has raised concerns that charges, such as transaction costs, will simply move to the excluded areas. Generally transaction costs are those charges and costs associated with the buying, selling, lending or borrowing of investments.[83] The response has been to increase the disclosure of transaction costs to ensure that costs are not simply moved around beyond the charge cap.[84] Some transaction costs are direct and visible but others are more difficult to identify.[85] Additionally, pension funds operate in a way that produces many layers of investment and potential for costs. Whilst disclosure of transaction costs is an understandable goal, it will be difficult to achieve in a meaningful and comparable way. It might be possible to estimate the costs, but this would not allow a real comparison between competitors in the financial services

[79] Department for Work and Pensions, *Better Workplace Pensions*, (n 68) 78.
[80] ibid, 83.
[81] ibid.
[82] ibid, 85.
[83] The Occupational Pensions Scheme (Charges and Governance) Regulations 2015, SI 2015/879.
[84] Department for Work and Pension and Financial Conduct Authority, 'Transaction Costs Disclosure: Improving Transparency in Workplace Pensions, Call for Evidence' (Discussion Paper 15/2, March 2015) https://assets.publishing.service.gov.uk/government/uploads/system/uploads/attachment_data/file/407942/workplace-pensions-transactions-costs-consultation.pdf.
[85] ibid, 26.

industry and transaction costs published out of context could provide a misleading picture. Consequently, employees are only to be given information that is not 'difficult to understand or may drive perverse behaviour'.[86] This refers to the suggestion that alarming levels of transaction costs may produce a negative reaction and cause members to opt-out.[87] My empirical study found that people were unaware of the costs and charges associated with their pension and also wanted information to be given in a less complicated way and so any efforts to disclose information in a straightforward manner which allows comparison should be welcomed. However, it is a very difficult line to tread. Oversimplification may skew the appearance of performance because there are many types of costs that may be incurred depending on the fund. If information can be presented in a manner which resembles a bank statement, with a clear and understandable indication of the costs and performance of funds, then this might be a way to re-engage workers with their pensions. Costs and charges are also addressed by The Markets in Financial Instruments Directive (MiFID II),[88] requiring overall costs to be disclosed to clients in a way that allows them to understand the effects on the investment and may lead to more standardised presentation of information across the market.[89]

C. Scheme Governance

The trend has seen a decline in salary related pension schemes in favour of defined contribution arrangements.[90] This allows the employer to fix pension costs but means that investment risk is borne completely by the member who must ensure that he pays adequate contributions into an appropriate fund to accumulate a sufficiently large capital sum to fund his retirement. With the introduction of AE, employers must nominate qualifying schemes, often defined contribution, and scheme quality may not always be the top priority. Convenience of administration and working relationships are also important to employers who want to comply with the regime with the minimum inconvenience. Consequently, not all the workplace pensions used for AE represent the same standards of value or quality for members. In trust-based schemes, the scheme trustees will have considered governance as part of their overall obligations which are enforced by the Pensions Regulator. Regulator guidance to trustees suggests that they may want to facilitate

[86] ibid, 48.

[87] ibid.

[88] European Parliament and Council Directive 2014/65/EU of 12 May 2014 on markets in financial instruments and amending Directive 2002/92/EC and Directive 2011/61/EU Text with EEA relevance [2014] OJ L173/349.

[89] Financial Conduct Authority, 'Developing our Approach to Implementing MiFID II Conduct of Business and Organisational Requirements' (Discussion Paper 15/3, March 2015) www.fca.org.uk/publication/discussion/dp15-03.pdf, 40.

[90] Pensions Commission, *Pensions: Challenges and Choices, The First Report of the Pensions Commission* (HMSO, 2004), 114.

access to financial advice for members and that it should be clear who is paying for this.[91] As part of the trustees' governance role they must consider investment performance, design of the default strategy, financial advice for members, support at retirement, scheme administration and the quality of advice provided to trustees.

The OFT was concerned about 'governance gaps' that 'increase the risk that members of less well-resourced schemes will not get value for money'.[92] Improved governance is also seen as a key element for ensuring the longevity of suitability of DC schemes as they continue to replace defined benefit pensions. Employers bore the risks of defined benefit schemes which increased incentive to ensure that schemes were well governed and performed well, as employers would have to fund gaps between the pension fund and cost of benefit promises. With the decline of defined benefit schemes, employers have fixed contribution and administration costs, but employees may suffer reductions in fund value from costs, performance and poor governance which can lead to reduced benefits.

The governance of trust-based and contract-based schemes is now more tightly regulated.[93] All schemes should be governed by a body acting in the members' interests with the majority of individuals on the governing body being independent of the pension provider. Default investment strategies must have clear aims and be designed in the interests of members and reviewed regularly.[94] It is acknowledged in the government report that the majority of individuals automatically enrolled into a scheme will remain in the default fund. So, whilst AE was justified at the outset as policy intervention which preserved free choice, the reality is that people do not make choices under AE. Defaults act as a strong anchor and this report acknowledges the need for extra care when considering default positions. Whilst trustees of occupational trust-based schemes have always had a fiduciary duty to act in the best interests of the members and been subject to strict governance standards, the increase in the number of employers using contract-based group personal pension schemes has led to these new standards of governance being applied to all pension schemes.

For contract-based schemes, such as personal pensions or group personal pensions, the introduction of these governance standards was a new response to the reality of AE. The existing FCA rules continue to apply minimum standards for the conduct of business but the FCA implemented changes as part of its rules (COBS 19) and no legislative reforms were needed.[95] Independent Governance Committees (IGCs) were introduced to supervise the value for money and compliance with quality standards for each scheme. In practice this means that pension providers must arrange for the setting up of IGCs but providers have to operate at arm's length. The IGC must act solely in the interests of members (which includes

[91] The Pensions Regulator, 'Regulatory Guidance for Defined Contribution Schemes' (April 2015) 6.

[92] Office of Fair Trading, 'Defined Contribution Workplace Pension Market Study', (n 66) 21.

[93] Financial Conduct Authority, 'Personal Pension Schemes (Independent Governance Committees) Instrument' (FCA 2015/2, 2015) www.handbook.fca.org.uk/instrument/2015/FCA_2015_2.pdf.

[94] Department for Work and Pensions, *Better Workplace Pensions*, (n 68) 12.

[95] Financial Conduct Authority, *Conduct of Business Sourcebook* (2015).

active and deferred members), assess value for money of the personal pension and raise concerns if it finds problems. This marks a significant change as, whilst the FCA rules require firms to act fairly, honestly and professionally, this is not the same as acting solely in the members interests. The NAPF was critical of this plan in its response to the OFT report.[96] It suggested instead that it should be for employers to set up governance arrangements to support employees rather than product providers which have conflicting interests between shareholders and members. The IGCs must resolve any conflicts of interest which arise in this regard and it may cause some issues in practice, particularly when the existing obligations owed by providers to shareholders and under contractual obligations are considered. The IGCs assess value by considering the default investment strategies, level of charges and costs relevant to policyholders.[97] IGCs also play an important role in assessing the value of older workplace pension schemes which continue to be used. All of these issues with governance and costs should not have been surprising given the way the policy was implemented relying on free market products and reflects international experience. In Australia a number of reforms were made to the Superannuation scheme in 2012 with legislation providing for default superannuation products called 'MySuper'.[98] Since 1 January 2014, only funds offering a MySuper product have been eligible to receive default superannuation contributions relating to new employees and since July 2017, all member accounts in default investment options are required to be invested in MySuper products. The changes were intended to improve value 'for the vast majority of Australian workers who are invested in the default option'.[99]

The NAPF also criticised the lack of longevity in pension planning in the UK. In making its case for an Independent Retirement Savings Commission,[100] the NAPF talks of agreeing a 'collective vision for what a good retirement savings system looks like for the long term'.[101] The key benefit of a commission would be its political neutrality and long-term approach which is lacking in pensions regulation and policy; changed with every general election.

D. Master Trusts

As part of the efforts to improve governance there has been a development in large multi-employer trusts known as master trusts. These trust-based DC schemes developed as a direct result of the AE policy.[102] These have been developed as an alternative to small trust-based arrangements which have been criticised for value

[96] NAPF, 'OFT: Defined Contribution Workplace Pensions Market Study'.
[97] Financial Conduct Authority, *Conduct of Business Sourcebook*, para 19.5.5.
[98] Superannuation Legislation Amendment (MySuper Core Provisions) Act 2012, No 162, 2012.
[99] Australian Government MySuper https://treasury.gov.au/programs-and-initiatives-superannuation/mysuper.
[100] NAPF, 'OFT: Defined Contribution Workplace Pensions Market Study'.
[101] ibid, 7.
[102] The Pensions Regulator Automatic enrolment Commentary and analysis: April 2016–March 2017, 3.

and governance. Master trusts are now tightly regulated[103] and consolidate assets of smaller schemes into larger more efficient ones. There is always a danger with consolidation that this creates over dependence and consolidated risk of failure, hence the additional regulatory requirements to be met by master trusts. Master trusts provide money purchase or defined contribution benefits and are used by multiple unconnected employers. They are established and governed in the same way as ordinary trust-based schemes but must be authorised and supervised by the Pensions Regulator.[104] There is concern that existing small scheme pension scheme trustees can exhibit inertia in the same way as pension scheme members and 'may persist in running a scheme because the barriers to exiting – whether those stem from a lack of knowledge, time or awareness – appear to be high'.[105] It therefore seems likely that there will be a push to further consolidate existing DC schemes into master trusts[106] and this will have to be carefully supervised to ensure that the master trusts are secure, well governed and genuinely provide a better outcome for individuals.

E. Taking Pension Benefits

New pension freedoms to allow individuals to access their entire DC fund after the age of 55 were announced in the budget of 2014.[107] This means that individuals no longer have to buy an annuity for any part of their pension. It is also possible for individuals with final salary pensions to convert these to a defined contribution arrangement in order to access these freedoms. This policy seems to clash with the policy intention of AE of ensuring individuals have accumulated sufficient pension assets to ensure a better standard of living in retirement but is in keeping with some international approaches to annuities and pension flexibilities.[108] Australia and New Zealand both have a policy of being able to take savings as a lump sum with no compulsory annuitisation. In New Zealand it is also possible to access cash early for a first home deposit in prescribed circumstances[109]

[103] Pension Schemes Act 2017, s 1.

[104] The Pensions Regulator (2018) Master trust authorisation Supervision and enforcement policy www.thepensionsregulator.gov.uk/-/media/thepensionsregulator/files/import/pdf/master-trust-supervision-and-enforcement-policy.ashx.

[105] Department for Work and Pensions, (2019) Investment Innovation and Future Consolidation: A Consultation on the Consideration of Illiquid Assets and the Development of Scale in Occupational Defined Contribution schemes, 24 https://assets.publishing.service.gov.uk/government/uploads/system/uploads/attachment_data/file/776181/consultation-investment-innovation-and-future-consolidation.pdf.

[106] ibid.

[107] HM Treasury, 'Budget 2014: Greater Choice in Pensions Explained' (2014) www.gov.uk/government/uploads/system/uploads/attachment_data/file/301563/Pensions_fact_sheet_v8.pdf.

[108] OECD Pensions at a Glance Country Profiles 2019 Profiles Australia: www.oecd.org/els/public-pensions/PAG2019-country-profile-Australia.pdf.

OECD Pensions at a Glance Country Profiles 2019 New Zealand: www.oecd.org/els/public-pensions/PAG2019-country-profile-New-Zealand.pdf.

[109] ibid.

and there is limited use of annuities.[110] On the one hand AE requires individuals to save for retirement, but on the other the whole fund is available to spend on whatever the individual wants at the age of 55. The emphasis is on compulsory saving but there is no requirement for advice during the accumulation phase as discussed previously. At the point of accessing the savings, active choices need to be made and the government has recognised the need for some form of advice at that point. For the wealthy, the freedoms will be welcomed, but the freedom may also result in some poorer members spending too much of their pension early and then relying on the state during retirement. This is a universal concern with lump sum benefits.[111] Research has found that individuals consistently make poor choices when given decisions about what to do with lump sums.[112] There are also concerns that members of defined benefit pensions might be tempted to transfer their valuable benefits to a DC scheme in order to access the freedoms. The reforms include a requirement for such individuals to take independent financial advice before making any transfer from defined benefit schemes. The need for advice at this stage has been accepted to ensure that people are advised of their options and the government has introduced the 'guidance guarantee' which entitles members of defined contribution schemes to access impartial guidance for free. It is hoped that the new guidance delivered at the point of retirement can help redress some of the issues identified with the annuity market,[113] and concerns about whether competition in the retirement market is working for consumers.[114] Parliamentary discussion of the guidance guarantee describes the limits of this advisory service cautioning about what 'this relatively limited conversation can cover or achieve'.[115] These changes have been effective since April 2015. Whilst there was concern about consumer use of the annuity market,[116] this policy seems to contradict the paternalistic intentions of AE and must raise some concern about future mistakes, particularly as the volume of private pension savers has increased so significantly under AE. In the US, it has been argued that annuities should be part of the solution to poor retirement planning, providing certainty and security despite the initial high costs.[117] The contradictory nature of the UK policy also strengthens calls for an independent pensions' commission which has long-term aims and is beyond political influences.

[110] MacDonald et al 'KiwiSaver and Retirement Adequacy' 2012 6(4) *Australasian Accounting, Business and Finance Journal* 61, 65.

[111] P Secunda, 'The Behavioural Economic Case', (n 36) 537.

[112] ibid, 538.

[113] Financial Conduct Authority, 'Thematic Review of Annuities' (TR14/2, February 2014) www.fca.org.uk/static/documents/thematic-reviews/tr14-02.pdf.

[114] Financial Conduct Authority, 'Retirement Income Market Study: Final Report – Confirmed Findings and Remedies' (MS14/3.3, March 2014) www.fca.org.uk/static/documents/market-studies/ms14-03-3.pdf.

[115] HC Deb 25 November 2014, vol 588, col 834.

[116] FCA Thematic Review October 2016 Review of annuity sales practices, 11 www.fca.org.uk/publication/thematic-reviews/tr16-7.pdf.

[117] P Secunda, 'The Behavioural Economic Case', (n 36) 546.

IV. Conclusion

There is great reliance on market forces and competition to ensure quality in private pension schemes but it must be recognised that products will only be offered if they are profitable. Past scandals such as personal pension mis-selling also caution against over-reliance on competition as a market regulator. The super-trust schemes, in particular, the NEST scheme created to comply with AE, could be used by employers as an alternative to personal pension arrangements but questions of performance and suitability remain with those as well. Such arrangements may not be suitable for higher earners which could lead to employers using different pensions for different workers or reducing the level of benefits for those who previously had better pensions. The policy has also seen the development of other master trust/multi-employer schemes. Again these are in the private sector without government guarantees and only as good as the companies which run them. It should also be recognised that there are different and competing interests between workers and employers and it may be difficult to meet all of the intended objectives for all workers.

Some in the industry still believe that it would have been better to establish a system built on competitive industry super trusts rather than with individual providers offering personal pension plans. It is noted in one parliamentary report that the KiwiSaver scheme in New Zealand (which was influential on the decision to implement AE) has a higher level of protection for savers increasing value for money.[118] My research also indicates that employers rely heavily on product providers for guidance and advice when dealing with AE but that the relationship and responsibilities are sometimes unclear and lead to misunderstandings.

The legislation which introduced AE places a heavy administrative burden on employers which requires time and incurs costs for advice to ensure compliant implementation. Not all employers will have the same resources available to allocate to implementation and administration of AE which might result in varying experiences and benefits for employees. The earnings limits operate to exclude part-time workers with multiple contracts which appears to contradict the stated intention of increasing the pension saving for poorer workers. The minimum contributions and other defaults need careful consideration as they impact on the consequences of the policy intervention. The minimum scheme standards also mean that many existing schemes will need to be changed or new schemes established to effect compliance. It is clear that the regime was intended to increase saving in a manageable way whilst preserving choice. The next two chapters consider in detail the justification for legal intervention for the good of the individual and the consequences of the policy intervention on the operation of choice.

[118] Work and Pensions Committee, *Automatic Enrolment in workplace pensions and the National Employment Savings Trust* (HL 2010–2012, 8-I), 19.

3

Legal Paternalism and the Auto-Enrolment Regime

I. Introduction

Auto Enrolment (AE) was introduced as a result of the lack of pension saving by individuals and fears of an underclass of poor pensioners needing support from the state. It was assumed that this failure to save was the result of faulty decision making on the part of those individuals which needed correction. This chapter considers whether the introduction of AE is paternalistic or justified by other motivations. Conflicts of interest, experience of affected individuals and parliamentary intention will all be considered to question both the legal validity and effects of AE.

The individual right to freedom to contract and otherwise conduct themselves may be fettered for the protection of harm to others, but is it as easily justified to protect the individual from self-harm? This chapter identifies paternalistic traits in the AE regime and considers how to value the restrictions of the regime against individual autonomy. Using these traits, it will be possible to classify the AE regime as paternalistic and then consider the effect and justification of implementation. This work may be defined as a discussion of narrow paternalism in that it considers state coercion of the individual.[1] Legal paternalism is a concept defined to some extent by the user, depending on whether the user is in favour of the intervention or not.[2] The starting point is the full autonomy of the individual and then restrictions are imposed to ensure that other individuals are not harmed or adversely affected by the actions of the fully autonomous individual. The extent that restrictions to freedom should be imposed to prevent self-harm is a different question and from this comes the concept of legal paternalism. This has developed into a new form of paternalism designed to nudge individuals into doing that which is in their best interests.

Justification of this intervention is complicated further by the question of identifying the will of the individual and considering how far this could be usurped

[1] G Dworkin, 'Paternalism' in J Feinberg and H Gross (eds), *Philosophy of Law* (Dickenson Publishing Company, 1975), 174.

[2] AL Ogus and WL Van Boom, *Juxtaposing Autonomy and Paternalism in Private Law* (Hart Publishing, 2011) 2.

by the well intentioned will of the state. The work of behavioural economists has considered the effects of human behaviour on decision making and seeks to justify those laws which nudge individuals to act in a particular way.

II. Autonomy v Law

If there was a line of autonomy with one end representing full autonomy, where individuals are completely at will to do as they please, and the other end representing prohibition, where the state restricts all individual freedom other than specified exceptions, neither point is likely to represent the ideal legal model. The question with all law is where to fix intervention by law on this line of autonomy. To what extent can you justify the compromise or restriction of individual autonomy (and to some extent the will of the individual where they are consciously aware of it) for some greater good? This line may not be permanently drawn and will move with the attitudes of society. The least controversial limitations are those laws designed to prevent the individual harming others. Much of the criminal law is based on this principle. However, even criminal laws are based on value judgements of what is right and what should be protected and will evolve as society changes and values change. As such, laws may still be subject to challenge as an imposition of one moral position over another.

In this respect the key concern is the balance of ensuring that the individual has the maximum amount of freedom to act to the perimeter of where the action impacts negatively on others. This boundary, where it occurs, and which individual's freedom is protected is the crux of legitimacy of legislation. In restricting choice, the state acts in the interests of the individual will and also imposes its own morality. However, the question of identifying the will of an individual will always be fraught with difficulty, involve an element of subjectivity and will rarely form a collective societal acceptance of a moral position.

Laws designed to protect an individual from self-harm are referred to as legal paternalism and encompass a vast spectrum of compromise on personal autonomy. It is important to recognise that the debate in relation to paternalism has been more prolific in the US than in the UK which, perhaps, reflects the attitudes of the two legislatures in relation to rights of autonomy. The debate has historically focussed on the right to autonomy versus the right of the state to intervene to prevent harm (to others or self). However, there are many situations where the state intervenes and this chapter seeks to explore the justification of the intervention of AE. If the AE regime is paternalistic, is it prima facie justified? The empirical findings in Chapter 5 consider the individual experience of implementation of the AE regime which allows greater evaluation of the justifications established by the policy. Are all stakeholders affected in the same way and how does that influence the classification of this regime as paternalistic?[3]

[3] DN Husak, 'Paternalism and Autonomy' (1981) 10 *Philosophy and Public Affairs* 27.

III. Legal Paternalism

Legal paternalism is a term used to describe a law which behaves in a way a parent might behave towards their children: protecting them from harm even against their will. It is used to describe the situation where the state takes on the paternal role looking after its population. Such a state might legislate to create laws which sometimes require the individual to act against their own will, for their own good, to protect them from the consequences of their own actions. It might be argued that restriction on personal autonomy cannot be justified on these grounds alone. Indeed, those against paternalism argue that not only does it affect autonomy in that matter legislated for but that it also 'leads to serfdom' destroying the ability to make decisions in other areas and in the future.[4]

A difficulty with paternalism is that it always represents the reduction of freedom of the individual in their exercise of choice in preference for the view of the law maker, which enforces its own perception of what the will of the individual must be. It may be difficult to determine if the reason given as justification for the restriction of freedom is the only reason for the action or limitation. In the case of AE, paternalistic or economic motives may seek to justify the regime. This is contrary to the libertarian view that the individual should retain responsibility without state intervention where there is no harm to others. Mill argued that 'The only purpose for which power can be rightfully exercised over any member of a civilized community, against his will, is to prevent harm to others. His own good, either physical or moral, is not sufficient warrant.'[5]

This raises the difficult question of how do you define harm to others? At first glance it may appear that the only potential harm by not saving for retirement is to the individual who sees out old age in poverty. However, it can be argued that the state would be obliged to support this individual and accordingly society as a whole may be damaged if the ageing population does not save and future generations of workers have to support them through increased taxation. This raises the debate about the collective will of society and how to identify harm. This is described as the utilitarian argument of competence that nobody is a better judge than oneself with respect to whether your interests are harmed.[6] Private choices should only be valued by the individual's satisfaction at having made the choice, the individual creates better outcomes for themselves by making unfettered choices and the outcome will be at least as valuable as any alternative suggested. Critics would argue that this statement is not correct and the individual may operate under misunderstanding, irrationality or are unable for a number of other external factors to carry out that which we know they really want to in the long term. In paternalistic legislation it is implied that the 'State can know the interests

[4] EG Valdes, 'On Justifying Legal Paternalism' (1990) 3 *Ratio Juris* 173, 176.
[5] JS Mill, *On Liberty* (Currin Shields, 1969) 13.
[6] Valdes, 'On Justifying Legal Paternalism', (n 4) 174.

of individual citizens better than the citizens know themselves … a permanent guardian of those interests *in loco parentis.*'[7]

Those who argue for autonomy in all but essential decision making point to the difficulty in establishing an acceptable line if legislators are permitted to prevent individual will other than to prevent harm to others. Strict paternalism will intervene and require the individual to behave in a particular way rather than try to persuade them that they should choose to act differently themselves. An illustration might be the prohibition of alcohol (strict paternalism) versus an obligation on those selling alcohol to display clear warnings of the dangers of over consumption. If instead another method is used to influence choice this is a softer form of paternalism.[8]

The study of paternalism is concerned with identifying in which risks the state may intervene on behalf of individuals and which it cannot. There must be a balance somewhere as a key function of law is to be predictable and fair.[9] The question may come down to degrees of harm, foreseeability, probability, and necessity but this is also a subjective test. Is there an implied consent by the individual that the state may intervene both to prevent a certain level of harm to others and to themself? If an individual acts in a way which is completely irrational is the law justified in intervening to establish whether the will of the individual is really to harm themselves? Cigarettes and alcohol are known to be harmful if abused but are permitted where recreational drugs are not. The question here is where the legislative line should be drawn between the points of individual will/consent and public interest.

Rationality can play no part here. The example of smoking shows us that, despite constant advertising showing the health effects of smoking and links to disease, people still choose to smoke and in doing so behave irrationally. It may be that individuals discount factors, inflate their own powers to buck the evidence or simply give too much weight to immediate pleasure and the perceived pain of giving up that the decision to keep smoking seems rational. These behavioural traits operate in all individual decision making and will be discussed further in the next chapter which considers the work of behavioural economics and its influence on the introduction of AE. If it is unsafe to assume that individuals want to behave rationally, then it becomes more difficult to justify intervention by the state on behalf of the individual. It may be argued that past failures in thinking which prevented voluntary contributions to private pension scheme savings were irrational and that AE corrects this faulty decision making. However, there may be other rational and justifiable reasons for choosing not to save in a pension which might weaken the justification for intervention.

[7] J Feinberg, 'Legal Paternalism' (1971) 1 *Canadian Journal of Philosophy* 105, 105.

[8] For example, minimum alcohol pricing: www.gov.scot/policies/alcohol-and-drugs/minimum-unit-pricing/.

[9] Mill, *On Liberty*, (n 5) 260; J Rawls, 'Justice as Fairness' in J Feinberg and H Gross (eds), *Philosophy of Law* (Dickenson Publishing Company, 1975), 276.

Feinberg discusses this difficulty with reference to self-harm and consent to harm done by another.[10] In legal paternalism it might be argued that where an individual consents to the harm then there is no harm done, by analogy with the principle of *volenti non fit injuria.*[11] However, the analogy seems more successful by saying that the consent simply removes any remedy or right to recourse arising from the harm rather than artificially saying that no harm occurred. Whether this consent can ever be inferred by an individual is another matter. When a state imposes law for the protection of oneself then the question of coercion will go to the heart of any consent given and destroy any notion of tacit agreement and consent to wrongs.

Increasingly, paternalism has been inferred into contracts and other areas of private law to protect abuse or asymmetries of power or information. Even those who support full autonomy would support some paternalistic intervention where the individual purports to restrict their future freedom to act for example to prevent a contract of enslavement.[12] Voluntariness of individual decision making is another key consideration when deciding whether the state should intervene to prevent or require action or to enforce contractual terms. Hospers gives the example of a patient in hospital being force fed as they refuse food: is it right to assume that the long-term goals of the individual are to live?[13] The justification for intervention in this instance is to preserve the right of the individual to make the decision another day but can the law ever really know what the long-term will of the individual is or whether a particular action is really voluntary? This might be described as soft paternalism or intervention only when it is unclear whether the individual acts voluntarily and with adequate knowledge.

Any paternalistic legislation inevitably makes assumptions about the long-term wants and needs of an individual and in so doing imposes the state's view of the will of the individual which may not be what the individual wants. For pension saving, the assumption is that the individual really wants to save for retirement but just lacks the willpower to do so and so justifies the state requiring the individual to pay NICs for a state pension. This does not consider that the individual might be willing to spend everything now as he is expecting an inheritance to see him through old age. This also exposes the difficulties of assessing harm externally, as the individual may feel it is more harmful to have less money now in order to be able to afford a good pension on retirement later. The AE regime differs from this model of strict paternalism seen in state pension saving. It makes the same assumption about the individual's desire for long-term savings but allows the individual to opt-out of this if they strongly disagree. However, as will be discussed further in the next chapter, behavioural traits favour the status quo and individuals

[10] Feinberg, 'Legal Paternalism', (n 7) 106.
[11] Interpreted conventionally as no harm can be done to one who has consented.
[12] JS Mill, *On Liberty* (White Crane Publishing, 2011) 100.
[13] J Hospers, 'Libertarianism and Legal Paternalism' (1980) 4 *The Journal of Libertarian Studies* 255.

are less likely to opt-out of the arrangement once it is in place unless it provokes a strong negative reaction. This cannot be said to be an entirely voluntary state either.

The more an action appears to be the will of the individual, the less the law might be justified in intervening to correct it, but the will of the individual is difficult to assess externally. The work of the behavioural economists has added much to this debate but individuals should be free to choose and make decisions free from coercion. If coercion occurs from external economic factors, or overt threats this affects the degree to which any decision can be said to be made voluntarily.

The state may also evaluate the knowledge of different individuals as having different levels of credibility. Feinberg describes a doctor having an opinion about the dangers of a prescription drug which disagrees with a non-medically qualified individual's opinion of the drug and its potential for harm.[14] In this example the state prefers the view of the medically qualified doctor and agrees that the law should intervene to protect individuals from potential harm caused by the drug. If full autonomy was allowed then individuals may decide for themselves whether the drug is harmful but in the paternalistic state, the risk is assumed to be too great and individuals are prohibited from making this choice. If the financial industry is of the opinion that individuals must be compelled to put more money into pension savings, is this the same as the perceived expertise of the doctor and should the state intervene even if the individual has an opposing view? A further difficulty with consent and knowledge is whether a lack of understanding by parties frustrates consent and voluntariness. If full information and knowledge is required to provide consent to medical treatment can this ever be achieved by the non-medically qualified patient? Following this to its conclusion, uninformed consent cannot ever be said to be voluntary. So, if people are uninformed about their pension, can this consent in AE really justify the intervention? Chapter 5 explores the understanding of those with workplace pensions and Chapter 6 considers whether the law adequately deals with negative consequences, including those arising from misunderstandings.

It is also possible that the AE regime was not created with paternalistic intent but is in fact an example of one part (the state) of the stakeholder group asserting its own interests over the others (employers and employees). If the true motivation was actually to protect the state from rising state benefit costs then AE could be viewed as coercive and to the disadvantage of the other parties who are required to implement the regime for the benefit of the state, even if the rhetoric surrounding the introduction of the regime to Parliament sounded paternalistic. However, the freedoms in drawdown, discussed in Chapter 2, would tend to rebut this. If pension freedoms permit individuals to spend accrued pensions and then continue to rely on the state, costs are not managed as effectively as the position where the accrued pension must be invested to produce retirement income.

[14] Feinberg, 'Legal Paternalism', (n 7) 114.

Alternatively, in paternalism the law intervenes to assist the individual to do what they really should. There is clear potential for conflict if the state simply assumes that the financial services industry is better placed to assess the need for saving than the individual. The self-interest of the financial services industry is a clear conflict. In setting up the NEST scheme the government might also be seen as a player in the industry, competing with the private sector and not neutral when considering employees' needs.

A. The Rise of Paternalistic Legislation

There has been considerable work by behavioural economists in recent years into the questions of the assumed norms used for regulation of many areas, including financial services. The body of work known as Behavioural Decision Theory has made a strong case for changing the way regulations are drafted to ensure they are effective on individuals who are shown to respond to previously unrecognised factors.[15] The influence of this work has created increasing legal intervention for the benefit of individuals, which is essentially paternalistic in nature, but which has options so that the individual may choose to go back to their pre-intervention position. This is considered in detail in the next chapter and the following is a summary of the key issues which have resulted in increased use of paternalistic legislation.

The first challenge by this work is to the concept of a rational person which is assumed in many aspects of law but particularly financial services regulation. It can be difficult to live up to the standard of a rational person with 'a consistent set of preferences, and behaving in a purposive, goal-oriented, and self-commanding manner'.[16] The entirely rational person would be unaffected by the way a choice is presented or framed and would never make impulsive purchases. Whilst the decision is still the free choice of the individual, the influence of these other factors may indicate that the choice does not properly reflect the deeper values or long-term aims of the individual – so justifying intervention to help the individual stay on the path. Further doubt about the certainty of the will comes from the fact that people change their mind for a variety of reasons. The cooling off period for financial products may allow the individual to realise that they do not really need the product or value the company. Alternatively, it may provide an opportunity to thwart what was a good decision made in keeping with the long-term goals of the individual but which now seems to be taking up too much disposable income. If the individual cannot tell what will influence his decisions and whether this is

[15] E Avgouleas, 'Cognitive Biases and Investor Protection Regulation: An Evolutionary Approach' (*SSRN* 15 May 2008).

[16] P Burrows, 'Analyzing Legal Paternalism' (1995) 15 *International Review of Law and Economics* 489, 492.

for his long-term good, then how could legislation hope to intervene and do any better?

The model which assumes that a rational investor will always invest to create maximum gain without reference to irrelevant factors has also been significantly challenged. The classical economic assumption is that people know what they prefer and act consistently with this preference. The introduction of rationality will consider whether the behaviour is successful in pursuit of the good of the individual. However, it is difficult to define the good of the individual externally and not all investors are focussed entirely on making the most money they can. Other factors play a part in the decision making which might seem irrational to the outsider but which are the will of the individual at the time. If the state intervenes to try and correct these wobbles from the straight path then this is paternalism as it is intended to nudge the individual into making more rational decisions. Essentially, the state intervenes to mitigate irrational bias. Legal intervention which intends to 'persuade, induce or compel any individual to do something that he would not otherwise have chosen to do, in order to bring benefits to that individual' is paternalistic in nature.[17] The question of rationality, as explored previously, is difficult to identify and so any intervention must be measured to some extent on the response by the individuals to the intervention. In AE, it might be justified if it is shown that employees are happy to contribute to the pension scheme and choose not to opt-out. It might be argued that the inherent irrationality used previously not to save for a pension is used in the same way not to make a decision about whether to opt-out or how much to contribute to the scheme.

Even if the individual can identify what they would choose under differing circumstances, they might find it difficult to evaluate what is best for them, not asking all the necessary questions and screening out relevant information for some irrational reason. Individuals might underestimate risks or discount benefits as it allows them to opt-out of making a decision for longer.

A number of key influences on decision makers have been identified and regulation then attempts to counter these biases or influences to produce a better result for the individual. For example, the endowment effect whereby people are willing to pay less for something they do not own than if they were selling the item. This might explain why individuals are unwilling to pay sufficient amounts into a pension to secure sufficient retirement income or this might be explained by procrastination.[18] Narrow framing, whereby investors do not look at the whole of their circumstances when considering a potential investment/risk but only the one in contemplation in isolation, and loss aversion theory which explains that individuals are much more affected by a potential loss than a potential gain are other examples. This might be assimilated to pension saving where an individual

[17] ibid, 495.

[18] RH Thaler and S Benartzi, 'Save More Tomorrow: Using Behavioural Economics to Increase Employee Saving' (2004) 112 *Journal of Political Economy* 164, 168.

has to accept a reduction in income now to save in a pension, even though the money will still (probably) be there in the future and will have a higher value at retirement. If people think in the short term then the result may be an inability to see through the long-term ideal of saving so regulation which produces saving as a default may be the best thing. Behavioural traits of the individual and their particular bias may explain the lack of pension saving in the UK or there may be perfectly rational alternative reasons for not saving in pensions. For example, genuine concern about capital return of the pension, preferred alternative pension saving, financial hardship etc. These behavioural traits are in evidence in the qualitative research in Chapter 5.

A policy is paternalistic if it 'is selected with the goal of influencing the choices of affected parties in a way that will make the parties better off'.[19] There are many issues to consider when analysing AE. Is the goal of the legislation to influence choice? Has this been done in a way to make the parties better off? Does it make the parties better off? How do you decide who is better off? It can be argued that the softness or element of choice of such policy intervention does not justify the legal interference with individual decision making and will produce effects which are not the will of the individual and may cause harm to some. It may be unclear who the targeted parties are and how the policy affects parties who were not in the target group. Thaler and Sunstein argue that there is no real alternative to paternalism as someone will always have to make decisions influencing the behaviour of others.[20] It is argued that this does not represent coercion as the individual can choose but the policy 'is selected with the goal of influencing choices … in a way that will make the parties better off'.[21]

This is described as libertarian paternalism. In relation to pensions, if there is no AE, then employers still have to make choices about whether pensions should be offered to employees. In the US, 401(k) plans are similar to money purchase pension schemes in the UK and most use the self-enrolment model. However, some use the AE model and this increases plan participation significantly. The fact that there is a default fund choice and contribution amount may mean that employees are steered into selecting or staying with that option as inertia may operate to pull individuals toward the status quo. This raises issues about the discretion to set the status quo of fund default and minimum contributions as this may be followed closely by employees.

As a policy, AE is described as 'New Paternalism' relying on the consent and element of choice by the individual being maintained. 'Surely the virtue of "new" paternalism's automatic enrolment process is the opt-out option.'[22] New paternalism is described as an example of law showing greater understanding for the real

[19] RH Thaler and CR Sunstein, 'Libertarian Paternalism' (2003) *American Economic Review* 175, 175.
[20] ibid.
[21] ibid.
[22] GL Clark and J Knox-Hayes, 'The New Paternalism' in GL Clark, K Strauss and J Knox-Hayes (eds), *Saving for Retirement* (Oxford University Press, 2012), 143.

biases and anomalies used in financial decision making. However, if behavioural economics teaches us that inertia causes people not to join pension plans does the same inertia prevent individuals exercising choices after AE and if so, is this really a free choice and the will of the individual? If the legislation limits individual freedom, is it justified? To consider this it is necessary to somehow value the good results against any negative effects and this is discussed further below.[23]

IV. Soft Paternalism or Nudge

Libertarian, new or soft paternalism is distinguished from classic legal paternalism on the basis that there is no coercion and the individual may still choose to do something other than the default position. This softness may lie in the fact that the individual welcomes the nudge in a particular direction but retains choice or in the fact that it is not clear that all will benefit so the law is imposed with exceptions. Where hard paternalism is prohibitive or requires action, an element of free choice is retained in the alternative soft paternalism or nudge.[24] Soft paternalism, recently often described as nudge, may take the form of regulation or could be less intrusive, for example by requiring disclosure of information. This is sometimes discussed using means and ends where ends paternalists prohibit an activity, even though people want to undertake the activity.[25] Behavioural economists focus on means rather than ends and use choice architecture to allow people to 'promote their own ends, as they themselves understand them'.[26] The justification for the nudge lies in the imperfect decision making described in detail by behavioural economics and it is argued that 'so long as people are not choosing perfectly, it is at least possible that some policy could make them better off by improving their decisions'.[27]

Choice architecture is used to describe the range and form of options available to the individual in a given situation, discussed in Chapter 4. With AE the underlying assumption is that the poor record of self-enrolment was caused by imperfect or faulty decisions and that the intervention of AE will make individuals better off by improving their decisions. Evaluation of the legislation requires testing whether individuals are better off and whether they make better decisions as a result of the intervention. There may be a number of perfectly good reasons why individuals have chosen not to self-enrol into a workplace pension, such as pension scandals, poor fund performance and competing financial interests, and it is important to consider how the implementation of AE affects individuals, their exercise of

[23] Part VII below.
[24] CR Sunstein, *Why Nudge?* (Yale University Press, 2014), 17.
[25] ibid, 19.
[26] ibid.
[27] CR Sunstein and RH Thaler, 'Libertarian Paternalism Is Not An Oxymoron' (2003) 70 *The University of Chicago Law Review* 1159, 1163.

choices and whether there are any negative consequences. This influence of behavioural economics or nudge on regulation is increasing and the starting point is that 'nudges are usually the best response, at least where there is not harm to others'.[28]

In interfering with the employer/employee relationship, the policy needs to demonstrate a higher level of justification than, for example, an employer placing fruit in the cafeteria before other sweet snacks.[29] If justification is based on choice then the legislation must ensure that individuals are aware of and can exercise such choice. AE represents an intervention in the agreed contract of employment between the employer and employees and so it could be countered that this is an agreed bargain.[30] If choice justifies the intervention then it must be easily exercisable by those affected to avoid the risks of going down a 'slippery slope' to 'unacceptably intrusive forms of paternalism'.[31] Some would argue that in intervening at all the slippery slope to more extensive or hard paternalism is inevitable.[32] Many factors are at play and it can be difficult to predict the result of one action.[33]

It seems that the choices available to those exercising choice (choice architecture), within the paternalistic intervention, is key to the legitimacy of the policy. If the employer is put in the position of having to make choices which affect the employees, which they might not have made pre-intervention, the standards and requirements of implementing AE are key as they will provide the limits of free choice within which the employer can choose the form of implementation. This choice architecture demonstrates that the method and form of implementing the paternalistic legislation is just as important as the intervention itself. This could be in the form of legislation or in the mode of implementation by employers and product providers. For AE there are many conflicts of interest between the parties which complicates the justification. This difficulty with employer discretion, which impacts on employee choice, is discussed in Chapters 5 and 6.

It is also important to recognise that where behavioural economics demonstrates that individuals make choices based on irrational bias, this may also be the case for planners attempting to intervene in a paternalistic way. This is discussed in detail in the next chapter which looks at the interplay between behaviour and pension plan design. Whilst policy makers may react to a particular market failure when creating policy, they might also be affected by other non-relevant factors which can affect the consequences of the policy. Who will monitor those creating paternalistic policies? Whilst hard paternalism is prohibitive it is clear and highly visible. A key concern with soft paternalism or nudge is that it is more difficult

[28] Sunstein, *Why Nudge?* (n 24) 17.
[29] Sunstein and Thaler, 'Libertarian Paternalism Is Not An Oxymoron', (n 27) 1166.
[30] ibid, 1164.
[31] ibid, 1199.
[32] MJ Rizzo and DG Whitman, 'Little Brother is Watching You: New Paternalism on the Slippery Slopes' (2009) 51 *Arizona Law Review* 685, 687.
[33] ibid, 685.

to see and is perhaps more subject to abuse than hard paternalism.[34] If there are concerns that the government will make errors with hard paternalism then the same potential for error exists with soft paternalism and it relies on correction by those affected by it. This requires affected individuals to have an awareness of the effects and be motivated to take action. The data in Chapter 5, demonstrates that individuals often lack this awareness and proactive thinking and so this results in an unchecked policy. In AE, the nudge is not always visible and does not promote active choosing. In using a number of default positions for fund and contribution amount, AE enlists inertia and is seen to operate 'behind the back' of the employee.[35] My empirical study finds clear evidence of this and so it is difficult to see how individuals, who are unaware of the consequences, will be motivated to take action.

V. Paternalism and Contracts

From the fully autonomous libertarian perspective, all contracts free of fraud and fear, which do not harm third parties, should be enforced. However, contractual limitations are often imposed as it has been argued that the economic consequences of freedom to contract have resulted in inequality, exploitation and wasting resources under capitalism. When terms are implied into contracts or contracts are set aside on grounds of unconscionability these are examples of intervention in individual freedom. Where the intervention purports to be for the benefit of the individual this may be a paternalistic intervention. Many financial contracts have a compulsory cooling off period which may recognise the differing bargaining positions of the parties or the fact that consumers make impulsive decisions which, for financial products, can relate to long-term complex products. An employment contract will have certain terms implied to have an ongoing effect – such as keeping trade secrets and an ongoing duty of good faith. What of restrictions to working hours or minimum levels of pay which may result in the employee earning less than they want or being given less hours of work? This may be motivated by paternalism, seeking to protect workers from exploitation but what about the will of those who are prepared to work longer for less pay to have greater economic wealth in the long term? In fact, a large number of terms and conditions are implied by law into a great many contracts.

All of these restrictions operate to protect people from contracting themselves into binding agreements with a view to protecting them and so may be considered to be paternalistic in motivation to some extent. There may also be

[34] EL Glaeser, 'Paternalism and Psychology' (2006) 73 *University of Chicago Law Review* 133.
[35] Sunstein, *Why Nudge?* (n 24) 149.

concern for the interests of third parties which are not paternalistic motivations. The extent to which individuals may contract away freedom seems to be based on the reasonableness of the bargain in many instances rather than on paternalistic principles. The way that the decision maker intervenes on behalf of either party in interpretation can completely change the nature of the contract. A current example might be the ability to agree to non-compete clauses in partnership agreements and other commercial contracts. Restrictive covenants may be set aside on the basis that the individuals cannot have intended to contract such a matter and this is separate from duties of good faith that may be implied into partnership agreements.[36] Feinberg argues that states set aside such clauses or contracts for sound commercial reasons rather than paternalism.[37] He explains that:

> Reasonable contracts in restraint of trade are a limited class of exceptions to a general policy designed to protect the economic interests of third parties (consumers) rather than the expression of an independent paternalistic policy of protecting free bargainers from their own mistakes.[38]

The fact that industry utilises standard contract terms might give weight to this. An example is the LOGIC standard set of contracts used by the UK offshore oil and gas industry.[39] Efficiency of business and saving time and money negotiating terms are reasons given for industry wide agreements such as this – there is no paternalistic intent.

Freedom to contract may also be restricted because of the effects on third parties, described by economists as transaction costs. For example, the contract between two parties for the cultivation of crops may seem to be entirely self-contained but if the farmer uses fertiliser which impairs water quality this could be an external effect of the contract. In theory all the parties affected by this could be compensated by the parties to the contract but this may not be possible as the numbers of affected others increases. This external cost becomes too high and legal remedies must be invoked to deal with this.[40] If the external effect is positive rather than negative then this is an external benefit. For AE it might be argued that the state or future generations benefit from the creation of private pension contracts by those workers auto-enrolled under AE. This would be an external benefit. Conversely the past under-saving by workers could be described as an external cost on future generations of workers who will be required to fund retirements through increased taxation. All of these reasons may be employed depending on the nature of the contract and parties. It is important to recognise that a variety of paternalistic and non-paternalistic reasons may be deployed to nudge the parties'

[36] *WRN Ltd v Ayris* [2008] EWHC 1080 (QB); [2008] IRLR 889.
[37] Feinberg, 'Legal Paternalism', (n7) 123.
[38] ibid, 123.
[39] LOGIC, 'Standard Contracts' (LOGIC 2019) www.logic-oil.com/standard-contracts.
[40] AI Ogus, *Regulation: Legal Form and Economic Theory* (Hart Publishing, 2004), 20.

intentions. Kronman describes three categories of paternalistic intervention in contracts, namely:

(1) Economic Efficiency and Distributive Justice;
(2) Personal Integrity; and
(3) Judgement and Moral Imagination.[41]

An example of economic efficiency is the oil industry standard contracts discussed above but with the difference that the state intervenes to imply terms, warranties etc.[42] Another example is the implied term of habitability in leases of residential property.[43] This implied warranty cannot be negotiated out of the contract as the tenant is protected from being tricked by the landlord who controls the property, but who may also be dishonest. The tenant might still have a remedy for fraud if the term was not implied but this leads to litigation, uncertainty and costs. It is more efficient to have a number of standard terms which cannot be varied and give rise to lengthy negotiations and considerations of risks and disclosures. The warranty might also be viewed as a form of insurance against undisclosed risk – if the landlord does not know of a problem which will render the property uninhabitable no fraud is involved but who will bear the risk of this happening? If the term is not implied into the contract then its inclusion will depend on the respective bargaining positions of the parties and their knowledge. As the landlord has greater knowledge of the property than the tenant this could be unfair to prospective tenants. This would involve additional legal costs and perhaps insurance against fraud or error. Examples of enforced contracts where the property is not habitable and the tenant bears the risk would cause future negotiations to become more complicated and expensive and would not be economically efficient. Even if the contract might be void if fraud is proved then there is still the question of proving fraud/fault. Again, this is inefficient and the most straightforward answer is to imply habitability and then the additional potential costs are avoided.

Similar principles are employed in consumer protection legislation which imply terms that cannot be negotiated away. As with the landlord, it is assumed that the seller has greater knowledge and resources and it would be more difficult to prove a fraud or dishonesty where these informational asymmetries exist. As well as the economies of efficiency, it might also be argued that the imposition of implied terms allows redistribution of power between the bargaining positions of the parties. Only by making the term non-variable can this be achieved as a variable term might be bargained away by the weaker party. This implied term is not about transfers of wealth which is key in its status as a paternalistic intervention. If the costs of applying the implied term are passed to the consumer or tenant in our examples, the party who had the stronger bargaining position is not disadvantaged

[41] AT Kronman, 'Paternalism and the Law of Contracts' (1983) 92 *The Yale Law Journal* 763, 766.
[42] ibid.
[43] ibid.

and the weaker party will bear the costs of the added protection in the contract – such as insurance. Whilst many will see the benefit of the implied term, some might have preferred a cheaper lease or product and have paid the price for the intervention which purports to be for their benefit.

Intervention on grounds of personal integrity is difficult and may include legal intervention to preserve the future will of the individual. For example, this would prevent parties binding themselves to stay married. Kronman illustrates the point explaining the difference between disappointment and regret.[44] You can be disappointed in the results of a contract but may not necessarily regret it. All contracts are premised on certain assumptions and where an assumption by one party is wrong he may be disappointed. For example, a seller of strawberries may be disappointed with his bargain to sell at £2 per box (at a point when he assumed the rain would make customers leave the market), when he discovers he could have sold at £2.50 per box if he had stayed until later in the afternoon when the sun came out again. He still makes money on the £2 box so he does not regret his contract to the point of feeling it was an irrational deal as he might not have been able to sell any if he waited. Regret is a different thing entirely and will cause the bargainer to wonder why they ever thought such a contract was a good idea as they have changed their objectives entirely. To some extent this reintroduces the question of rationality. Where the will of the individual has changed, previously rational bargains may look irrational. Certainty and predictability of contract requires consideration of the rationality of the bargain considering the will of the individual at the time the bargain was made rather than with hindsight. It may be that the individual regretting the bargain can void his obligations under the contract in return for compensation paid to the other party.

A difficulty arises where specific performance of the contract is required by the party now regretting the bargain. The law may consider that this is not possible, as in the case of a contract for service where the implied duty of trust and good faith is found to have broken down. For example, the courts will not force an employer to re-employ an employee even where the relationship has been terminated in breach of the contract. This is because the employment relationship is one of mutual trust and confidence and if this has broken down the law cannot intervene to reinstate it and may only deal with the breach by way of financial remedies.[45] The intervention here by the law is not explained on economic grounds, as appropriate compensation must be paid and the process of determining this through litigation is costly but in the fact that delivery of personal service requires the will of the individual to be co-operative. The implied duty of good faith works both ways and an employee cannot be compelled to perform work nor an employer compelled to give work where the relationship has broken down to this degree. This implied term may not have been what the parties would have wanted, for example the doctor in the

[44] ibid, 780.
[45] *Lakshmi v Mid Cheshire Hospitals NHS Trust* [2008] EWHC 878 (QB).

Lakshmi case above did not want the relationship to be terminated, but it was deemed to be in the parties' best interests.[46]

The third of Kronman's paternalistic categories is judgement and moral imagination: intervention where there are concerns about errors in the reasoning of the bargainer. This is the justification for setting aside decisions made by children and those with mental disabilities and acknowledges that there is a much wider category of individuals who may make rash decisions based on faulty logic, irrelevant external factors or error. As a method of looking after these individuals many contracts have a cooling off or reflection period built in to allow the individual an opportunity to change their mind in the cold light of day. In the same way as a child might not foresee all the issues with a bargain, an individual may not behave rationally and realise the error during the cooling off period. Consumer or financial contracts operate in this way to acknowledge lack of understanding or asymmetries of power or knowledge. Some would argue that in requiring these terms to be implied and limiting consumer choice, the policies are examples of stronger paternalism.[47] As such it is important to consider the potential benefits and losses of the intervention.

Considering the value of intervention on economic grounds may prove useful in evaluating the AE regime:

> When we say that a child (or anyone else) lacks good judgement, we often mean that he lacks the capacity to evaluate critically his own interests and desires … Judgement … involves a critical reflection on one's interests and desires and hence presupposes some distance from them; indeed, we associate judgement with sobriety and dispassion … requiring disengagement from the immediacy of desire.[48]

Many individuals find it difficult to value a distant benefit such as a pension in retirement compared to spending money now. That does not mean that individuals have judgement like children but may indicate a propensity to irrationality in making choices. If the ultimate goal is happiness of the individual a choice between happiness now or later will require a process of valuation or deliberation by the individual. Kronman argues that judgement is not related to irrationality in this way but is formed by the individual having a greater imagination of the options being considered and how they may impact on their life and their ultimate goals.[49] The work of the behavioural economists supports intervention to correct the faulty decision making where individuals discount risks or the value of future gains against something smaller held now. This has been described as 'moral imagination' or the art of valuing the moral effects of an action in context.[50] How successful the individual is in this judgement making will therefore depend

[46] ibid.
[47] Rizzo and Whitman, 'Little Brother is Watching You', (n 32) 698.
[48] Kronman, 'Paternalism and the Law of Contracts', (n 41) 789.
[49] ibid.
[50] ibid, 791.

on how good they are at objectively considering the options whilst suspending the immediate desire for action. It is suggested that those who cannot do this objective consideration will live to regret the decision made as they will reflect back on it as an irrational decision rather than merely a mistaken one. In the cold light of day, the individual sees that the decision was never one that would further their aims in life. All of this may explain in part why people make bad decisions but not why the law intervenes in some, but not all, instances of poor decision making.

VI. Intention of Legal Intervention

Not all interventions are primarily motivated by paternalism and may be for other economic or social reasons. If the consequences of intervention can be valued and compared to the situation that existed before then this allows evaluation of the success of the intervention. If it is a paternalistic intervention, for example, then an evaluation would test whether individuals are better off as a result. If the reason for intervention was to prevent harm to others then an evaluation would test whether this had been the result of the intervention. For AE this involves valuing benefits of AE, as perceived by the recipients of the intervention, compared to the pre-AE self-enrolment position. If there is no genuine intention to make the subject better off as a result then a number of other justifications might be used to support legal intervention. There are at least six non-paternalistic reasons for interference with free choice namely:

(1) Distributional concerns;
(2) Egalitarian rights – prevention of discrimination/harm to others;
(3) Positional theories – personal choice limitations of freedom such as religious restrictions, temporary limitations whilst serving in the armed forces;
(4) Collective choice concerns – where some may be harmed by allowing others full freedom to contract, for example permitting voluntary euthanasia which is argued might put pressure on some to make decisions they would not otherwise;
(5) Externalities; and
(6) Perfectionism – where the state determines the morality of the day and imposes it.[51]

Distributional motivations relate to mandatory transfers of wealth such as taxation of workers to provide for benefits for those not working. Buckley argues that most people agree that there should be some state redistribution of wealth which justifies taxation which 'is not regarded as a fetter on free choice – but try to tell that to the people who pay their taxes and can't buy what they would in a world without taxes'.[52]

[51] Buckley, *Fair Governance, Paternalism and Perfectionism*, (Oxford University Press Inc, 2009) 7.
[52] ibid, 8.

Clearly it does represent a limitation of choice as the individual would otherwise have all of his salary to spend or save as he pleased, whether it is perceived as such or not, but the motivation for limitation is not strictly for the benefit of the individual. Taxation may provide benefits for the individual such as the free NHS and state benefits but the weaker the link to individual usage the less likely the intervention will be perceived as paternalistic in its intentions. Paternalism is based on intervention for the good of the individual and potentially some social good to others. However, with compulsory NICs there is a stronger link to individual benefit as all who have paid will be entitled to state pension on reaching the requisite age.

It might be difficult to distinguish between state intervention which is motivated by distributive aims, for example, intending the improved welfare of one group at the expense of another, and that which is paternalistic and aimed at improving the individual's welfare. Where there is little chance of the individual accessing the benefit, such as unemployment or income support benefits where the individual has great personal wealth, then the argument that the taxation is paternalistic seems quite weak unless it is argued that he benefits from the knowledge that he is helping the poor. This strong justification means even libertarians are unlikely to protest unless the balance is pushed too far one way.

In the case of AE, critics have argued that it would have been better if the government had either increased NICs or created a separate tier state pension which required contributions by employers and employees and resulted in a guaranteed state benefit at retirement to link the 'goods' to the individual.[53] This was deemed politically unacceptable and the government desired to shift responsibility away from the state into the private sector as described in Chapter 2. The fact that this was deemed politically unacceptable might indicate that the public are not willing to accept the distributional concerns justification even where there is a direct link to a benefit by the individual suffering taxation. This degree of acceptability by the public would therefore affect the nature of the intervention itself. This is described:

> As in the distributive case, the decision-maker changes a rule because he believes that under the new regime the objects of his benevolence will end up with a set of experiences that will be better for them … what makes this change paternalist rather than distributive is, first, that those who have supposedly benefitted do not agree that they are better off, and would return to the previous regime if given a choice in the matter.[54]

Any external effects are side effects rather than the design of the paternalistic policy. This is key to the justification of AE. If some affected individuals do not agree that they benefit from the policy then they perceive the regime as

[53] P Burrows, 'Patronising Paternalism' [1993] *Oxford Economic Papers* 542, 567.

[54] D Kennedy, 'Distributive and Paternalistic Motives in Contract and Tort Law, with Special Reference to Compulsory Terms and Unequal Bargaining Power' [1982] *Maryland Law Review* 563, 572.

paternalistic rather than distributive and feel they are harmed as a side effect of the policy. The extent to which the decision maker tips the scales for redistribution or personal interest in the decision will determine how acceptable this intervention is. This might be a key issue in determining whether AE is paternalistic or not. Is it perceived as something which is not beneficial in which case will workers opt-out as they have the choice to return to the previous position? It could take many years for the true consequences of AE to be clear but the current evidence suggests that the majority of those affected do not opt-out of AE.[55] However, there may be a number of reasons why workers do not opt-out, including inertia.

Externalities as a reason for intervention are those instances where the personal choices have an impact on others. It may be that what looks like a paternalistic piece of legislation is motivated by other competing interests. For example, it is possible that the potential harm to the state and future generations of citizens paying increased taxation and NICs to support an ageing population was the real motivation for introducing AE. Ogus describes externalities using the example of the wearing of cycle helmets.[56] If the individual is injured then there is clearly harm to the individual but there may also be harm to the state or employers who deal with hospital care, sickness cover and pay etc. This may enhance the justification for paternalistic reasons for intervention, as well as harm to self, there is also potential harm to others. In AE, there are a number of competing objectives: state affordability of pension benefits in future; employer's commercial interests in running a business and complying with the laws; and the individual who themselves have competing interests both for money to live now and to avoid poverty in retirement. If an individual does not save anything then they may become reliant on the state in future for benefits and pension payments. This will have to be funded by the state through increased taxation and National Insurance Contributions.

It is useful, however, to consider why the legislature chose the form of legislation enacted. In the AE regime the external effects (cost to the state of impoverished ageing population) might alternatively be dealt with by limiting state benefits to top up the income of those who have inadequate pensions. This would leave individuals to ponder their future poverty but would leave the state and current taxpayers free from the economic consequences of their reckless decision making. However, the fact that the legislation nudges employees into saving privately for their retirement must indicate to some extent that parliamentary intention was paternalistic rather than simply motivated by externalities.

[55] RS Consulting on behalf of Department for Work and Pensions, *Automatic Enrolment: Experiences of those who have Opted Out, A Qualitative Study* (Research Report No 862, February 2014) www.gov.uk/government/uploads/system/uploads/attachment_data/file/288530/rrep862.pdf.

[56] AI Ogus, 'The Paradoxes of Legal Paternalism and How to Resolve Them' (201) 30 *Legal Studies* 31, 64.

VII. Proof and Value Measurement

Dworkin asks whether there is a burden of proof attached to paternalism in terms of establishing and justifying its use.[57] As it represents a reduction of autonomy is it for the state to justify on the grounds that it is for the good of the party governed by the legislation or does it depend on the category of individual? Should we start at one end of the imaginary autonomy line we started with – all paternalism is wrong and must be justified? If so then how do we measure justification and success? Empirical research into the experience of those compelled to join a workplace pension allows an assessment of the impact of intervention to consider the effects and allow an evaluation of success as discussed at Chapters 5, 6 and 7.

Ultimately the question must be whether the legislation affects all equally or are some individuals or categories harmed by the regime? Is the balance right here between intervention, to the benefit of the majority, whilst causing only minor cost to others? Economists would stipulate that a policy is efficient where 'the gains (to whomsoever) exceed the losses (to whomsoever)'.[58] A cost-benefit analysis might be used to measure the success of seemingly paternalistic legislation. Costs associated with regulation can be divided into administrative costs, compliance costs and indirect costs.[59] Administrative costs include costs for those agencies which enforce compliance and firms responsible for compliance. So, the Pensions Regulator might be such a cost as it monitors and enforces compliance with AE. Additionally, the employers and product providers involved in implementing AE will also bear the administration costs of the regime. Compliance costs would also include employer contributions, investment in payroll software to comply with AE and ongoing compliance costs. Marginal costs may vary depending on the size of employer for example and this leads to indirect costs which can be difficult to identify and value. The costs of opting-out of AE appear to be very small but a further question is whether those for whom the legislation is not required will properly identify themselves as such and opt-out. What if they stay in – will they be worse off? The costs may also relate to default contributions and funds for those who stay in. It might be true that initially all benefit from an increase in pension saving but there may be a point where the individual might have made different and better choices had they not been defaulted into the workplace pension at a set contribution. This might be described as the opportunity cost of meeting contribution obligations. My empirical study considers how pension decisions are made and valued by the affected individual. Benefits are described as 'any reductions in the losses which would have accrued from unwise decisions made by the relevant individuals if the law had not induced them to an alternative choice'.[60]

[57] Dworkin, 'Paternalism', (n 1) 184.
[58] Ogus, *Regulation: Legal Form and Economic Theory*, (n 40) 25.
[59] ibid, 155.
[60] Ogus, 'Paradoxes of Legal Paternalism', (n 56) 69.

Generally, benefits are described as being more difficult to value than losses. This could be because the causal link between the regulation and benefit is complicated or disputed or because of the extended timescale for the accruing of benefits, such as the case with pension benefits accrued under AE.[61] Benefits including 'non-market goods' such as 'trust' and 'investor confidence' are particularly difficult to value.[62] Using the cycle helmet example, Ogus describes a process of averaging the difference of financial losses between those wearing and not wearing helmets and multiply this by the number of estimated accidents involving cyclists who would not have been wearing helmets had the law not required them to.

For AE this could be the difference between an individual spending all their wages now as opposed to using some to pay minimum pension contributions under AE. There are a number of difficulties in calculating the costs and benefits of this. First of all, no one can say what the individual would do with their money if they still had it all to spend. They might just spend it all or might have invested it in something that far outstrips pension fund performance and would give liquidity of their assets, capital and pension provision. Even if you were able to calculate the benefit to the individual, the costs are very difficult to ascertain. The obvious cost is the level of contributions paid by the employee, employer and tax rebate relinquished from the state. However, added to this would be the additional costs of administration undertaken by the employer for administering the new regime and the ongoing costs to the fund saved. Many argue that paying a minimum level of contributions to the scheme is so low that the pension benefit to be expected is negligible. If the benefits achieved at the end are so small as to be insignificant to the individual this may negate the value of the paternalistic intentions.

Additionally, we need to consider the costs to those who do not benefit from the regime. At the most crude level, benefits to the recipient of the policy intervention should exceed costs.[63] This goal, referred to as 'optimal loss abatement' by Ogus requires regulation to be 'set at a level at which the total benefits exceed the total costs by the greatest amount'.[64] Chapter 5 considers whether some individuals benefit more than others from the regime and whether the marginal costs of compliance are higher for some, described by Ogus as indirect costs.[65] It can also be argued that the net benefit of AE might be so difficult to prove or be so subjective that AE would have to be justified on paternalistic grounds rather than on a pure cost-benefit analysis.[66] Those in favour of nudge or soft paternalism, would argue that the retention of choice makes soft paternalism easily reversible and, consequently very low cost.[67] However, it is clear from the data that, even where

[61] Ogus, *Regulation: Legal Form and Economic Theory*, (n 40) 156.
[62] JC Coates IV, 'Cost Benefit Analysis of Financial Regulation: Case Studies and Implications' (2015) 124 *The Yale Law Journal* 882, 894.
[63] Ogus, *Regulation: Legal Form and Economic Theory*, (n 40) 153.
[64] ibid.
[65] ibid, 155.
[66] DH Cole, 'Law, Politics, and Cost-Benefit Analysis' (2012–2013) 64 *Alabama Law Review* 55, 57.
[67] Sunstein, *Why Nudge?* (n 24) 151.

reversibility appears easy in theory, it may be different in reality. Parliamentary intention of the legislation appears paternalistic, although it seems unlikely that it will be clearly identified as such.[68] In examining the range of choices preserved for the individual (choice architecture) and the reality of this choice. It will be demonstrated that there are presently insufficient safeguards within the AE regime.

Burrows describes an alternative evaluation of policy based on efficiency.[69] Success of intervention can be demonstrated where there is a potential benefit and the legal system has identified the conditions under which such a benefit would exist. For a variety of reasons, the individual would not otherwise choose to make the beneficial decision themselves but when they look back at the result of the policy intervention they accept it. Whilst they might think they are opposed to the change at the time, they will prefer the new arrangement after the policy change and would not choose to go back to the old regime. In the area of investment and finance it has been argued that the ordinary user does not have the knowledge, ability or interest in fully managing decisions and that rather than patronising the individual, paternalistic legislation supports individuals who might choose inefficiently and make bad decisions for their long-term financial health. There is an element of speculation involved in this process.[70] 'What would the party have done if' is a question which goes beyond that of redistribution. This is more about redressing the balance rather than identifying what individuals really want or might want if they had all the facts. Distributive motives generally improve the position of one party or class of individuals. Efficiency motives would not generally alter the balance and could be seen to benefit all participants. Both parties know where they stand and how the risk is apportioned and benefit from certainty of contract and reduced negotiation costs. This is distinguished from paternalism because the second guessing is seen as necessary because of some imperfection in the market and will not be pursued if the beneficiaries do not want it.[71]

It may not always be clear what was intended by a policy and what the consequences are. Considering the imposition of the minimum wage, it might be seen as being motivated by efficiency as it saves potential costs of industrial action over pay and provides certainty of costs to the employer and of pay to the employee. However, if the economic situation and climate before the intervention is such that there is an oversupply of labour then it might be perceived as a rebalancing of bargaining positions to cede the power of the employers for the benefit of poor workers – distributive. If the effect of the new law is that workers earn less money in total because employers reduce overtime, we might say that certain workers would have preferred not to have the law but that the state thinks it is better that they are paid more to work less even if that means they earn less overall.

[68] Ogus, 'Paradoxes of Legal Paternalism', (n 56) 63.
[69] Burrows, 'Analyzing Legal Paternalism', (n 16) 495.
[70] Kennedy, 'Distributive and Paternalistic Motives in Contract and Tort Law', (n 54) 573.
[71] ibid.

The workers might still choose to go back to the old situation if they were given the choice – paternalism. Some workers might lose their jobs completely because of the change or employers go out of business if they are no longer profitable – side effect of paternalism. This oversimplified example shows how difficult it is to categorise the motivation and effect of legal intervention. It may be possible to identify the key effects and motivations and thereafter classify the other effects as side effects. The state might try and demonstrate that the law is efficient as it is merely then operating as a facilitator of what was demanded but having removed some of the 'transaction costs'.[72] Transaction costs are described as all those additional costs that should be factored into transactions where contracts are inefficient. This might include extended negotiations, legal costs, costs of disputes arising from the contract, uncertainty costs which can all impact on the bargain which exists before legal intervention. For implied terms, these costs are reduced as the parties cannot negotiate these away, have certainty of the effect of contractual terms and are free from the threat of litigation arising from such provisions.

A further loss is in the exercise of choice and freedom itself, but it may be impossible to value the loss of autonomy to make personal financial decisions. What is the value of being able to make choices which is lost to paternalism? The value might be that the increased range of options makes it more likely that the individual will benefit and there is a greater chance that his desires will be satisfied. Dworkin describes this as an 'instrumental value' of choice.[73] Essentially the more choices there are the more likely it is that the individual will get something they want. Some individuals might enjoy the fact that they have a choice and this creates the additional satisfaction of being able to choose. An alternative argument might be that there is an intrinsic value in choice itself. This leads us back to the question: is it better to have a choice than to make a bad decision? AE appears to offer the best of both by retaining choice but having the beneficial position as a default or fall back. Defining 'beneficial' and maintaining genuine choice are at the heart of the justification for the policy.

Burrows weighs the potential gains in efficiency against the loss of free choice considering whether free choice has an intrinsic value.[74] If an intervention is deemed efficient then it might be the most politically acceptable model of all. It is seen as making most people better off without taking sides and without intervening unnecessarily in the lives of its citizens. Is there really a value that can be attached to developing personal decision-making skills and feeling good about having made a decision for yourself and how can this be valued against the fact that this may result in the individual being worse off as a result of the choice? Is it a choice between liberty and the efficiency gain that could be achieved by limiting liberty in some respects? In the case of AE, the individual is enrolled into a pension

[72] ibid, 587.
[73] G Dworkin, 'Is More Choice Better than Less?' (1982) 7 *Midwest Studies in Philosophy* 47, 58.
[74] Burrows, 'Analysing Legal Paternalism', (n 16) 495.

scheme and has contributions to the scheme deducted from pay by her employer. However, she may choose to opt-out of the arrangement. Those in favour of paternalism might argue that the individual has their cake and can eat it as well. She benefits from intervention as she is enrolled into pension saving as a default option. This prevents procrastination, misinformation, deliberation and short-term needs influencing her decision to save if that is her long-term intention, but she can choose to leave if she wants. The difficulty is that from what we know of decision making, the intervention may cause the individual to disengage from making further decisions and this is explored throughout my thesis. Therefore, the process which requires the individual to consider this 'decision' made on their behalf should be considered further.

Considering what the individual might have done had there been no intervention asks whether there is a net benefit and will this be the same for all individuals or does this depend on knowledge, salary scale or personality? It is difficult to see how it is possible to value the bargain that might have been and Kennedy suggests efficiency arguments 'could justify almost anything'.[75] In relation to implied terms, a number of factors might improve efficiency. It may be possible to imply terms such as fiduciary duties into the AE relationships which will negate some of the difficulties of the regime. In AE, there is asymmetric information concerning the suitability of the financial product which might be rectified for those affected individuals by the inclusion of a term to make the seller liable for loss in prescribed circumstances.

In the case of the introduction of AE, the pensions industry is responsible for promotion to some extent. The reported data considers the role of the industry in the creation and distribution of employee information and whether there is adequate oversight. The state may create added benefits by requiring schemes to be used for AE to meet certain minimum requirements and closely restricting charging. This may create efficiencies to the point that the consumer would have demanded the pension product had such limits been in place before (there is added value to the bargain). However, if the employee cannot afford the pension they may choose to opt-out. In that situation the employer has incurred the costs of administering a scheme that is rejected by the employee anyway.

VIII. Conclusion

This chapter has considered the tension between individual freedom and the role of law. Some believe that the law should only intervene to protect harm to others and this is the basis of the criminal law. However, paternalism describes the situation where law intervenes to protect the individual from harming themselves and this is more difficult to justify and assess the consequences of. Legal paternalism

[75] Kennedy, 'Distributive and Paternalistic Motives in Contract and Tort Law', (n 54) 600.

also exists in various forms ranging from prohibitive hard paternalism to softer nudging paternalism. This chapter has set out the principles which indicate that legislation is paternalistic namely:

- legislation intervenes with individual free choice;
- this intervention is either against the wishes of the individual (hard paternalism) or temporarily against the will but which may be changed back by the individual (soft paternalism);
- the reason for the intervention is predominantly to benefit the affected individuals (as defined by the legislator).

Any imposition of law represents a restriction on personal autonomy, but it is the intervention for the purpose of improving the wellbeing of the affected individual which makes paternalism more difficult to justify than laws which intervene to prevent harm to others or for the purposes of redistribution of wealth. Such an intervention requires assumptions to be made by the lawmaker about what the will of the individual is and in defining what constitutes a benefit to the individual. The example of implied contractual terms was explored to illustrate that, whilst freedom to contract may be desirable it should be recognised that this can lead to negative consequences in some cases, where the bargaining position of the parties is unfair or where errors are made by one party. In such negative cases the individual should be able to rectify those negative consequences or be compensated appropriately. It can be difficult to demonstrate benefits and costs from a policy intervention and this will be explored further throughout this book. It appears that the AE regime is paternalistic although the effects of implementation could further define the classification of the policy.

Assuming that the main policy intention was paternalistic, to benefit the individual, the next chapter will consider the form of AE used and how that impacts on the effects of implementation, in turn impacting on the justification of the policy intervention. Chapter 5 contains the findings of my empirical study which also considers the issue of identifying net benefits in order to further justify the regime. Soft or liberal paternalism is justified on the basis that the individual can still choose to go back to the pre-intervention position and so this might be a preferable justification for the policy than demonstrating a benefit on a cost-benefit analysis. Consequently, the role of the operation of choice is key to justification for the policy as considered in Chapter 5. If the exercise of choice is compromised then the policy is more like hard paternalism and must be able to demonstrate the value of intervention, on a cost-benefit basis, to a much higher level.

4

The Role of Behavioural Economics in Legal Intervention

I. Introduction

In recent years the work of behavioural economists has been influential on policy and law making both in the UK and abroad. The discussion of the policy in Chapter 2 highlighted the use of defaults to pension saving in Australia and New Zealand but the US has produced a large volume of the literature on using behavioural science to produce different savings behaviours. Policy makers in the UK and internationally have introduced policies to change the way regulation works to be more beneficial and take account of the way individuals make decisions. At the forefront of the change has been financial services regulation where policy seeks to produce better results for investors without too much paternalistic intervention.[1] The literature in this area uses known behavioural traits and suggests alternatives to regulation to produce different results.

This chapter will consider the influence of behavioural economics on the AE regime and whether the execution of the regime, ie the legislative reform, fully considers the issues and lessons to be taken from the behavioural economics literature. The previous two chapters addressed the question 'why do we have AE?' and this next chapter considers why we have this form of AE. What was the policy trying to fix? What particular behavioural traits are targeted and utilised by the regime? How is this done? Is it justified? Does it work? It will consider intention, method, justification and potential for unintended consequences flowing from AE. Following from the general consideration of costs compared to benefits of paternalistic intervention in the previous chapter, this chapter will consider the costs versus benefits of the specific form of AE that has been implemented in the UK. As expressed by Sunstein, 'Do the benefits justify the costs, and, if so, has the agency chosen the approach that maximizes net benefits?'[2] It has been suggested that retrospective analysis of regulatory intervention will help assess what works and what does not and favours the creation of independent review.[3]

[1] See: The Behavioural Insights Team: www.behaviouralinsights.co.uk/.

[2] CR Sunstein, 'Empirically Informed Regulation' (2011) 78 *The University of Chicago Law Review* 1349, 1387.

[3] ibid, 1391.

In considering the justification for introducing AE and then comparing the consequences to intention, using empirical data, the analysis of the AE intention will suggest possible improvements.

II. Behavioural Economics

This chapter will explore the cognitive biases described as being a cause of past poor retirement saving and consider how the AE legislation is designed to correct them. 'Any suggestions of new regulation to counter investor cognitive biases must be based on concrete evidence of the debilitating impact of such biases, which the specific piece of regulation seeks to remedy.'[4]

Regulation which does not actively spur deliberation also raises special concerns as 'deliberation-promoting nudges' are more easily accepted than those that 'seem to work more subconsciously'.[5] UK pensions legislation has, in recent years, protected the notion of individual choice whilst securing basic protections relating to accrued rights. The demise of the final salary/DB schemes has shifted the burden of investment choice and performance further onto the individual who will ultimately underwrite the cost of their own retirement. Behavioural economics challenges some of the assumptions made about the individual's ability to make these decisions and in some instances, this now influences law and policy.

Traditional economic principles assume that individuals are fully rational and 'have well defined preferences (or goals) and make decisions to maximize those preferences'.[6] In a pensions context this was considered in Australia in the review of Superannuation policy. Previous policy was based on the assumption that 'super fund members should be treated as rational and informed investors, with disclosure and market conduct controls being the main regulatory instruments with which to oversee the industry'.[7] However, assumptions about regulatory protections, financial literacy and motivation which would allow individuals to make optimal decisions have been proved wrong and, where the system is compulsory, as it is in Australia, this creates a significant volume of unintended consequences of the policy.[8] Behavioural economics challenges these old assumptions and uses the work of psychologists and economists to consider how cognitive shortcuts create anomalies. This is then reflected in economic planning and policy making. Implicit in this is the belief that these anomalies are not in the interests of the

[4] Avgouleas (2006) 'Cognitive biases and investor Protection regulation an evolutionary approach', 8. http://ssrn.com/abstract=1133214.

[5] CR Sunstein, *Why Nudge?* (Yale University Press, 2014), 150.

[6] C Camerer et al, 'Regulations for Conservatives' (2003) 151 *University of Pennsylvania Law Review* 1211, 1214.

[7] Australian Government, Cooper, *Super system review: final report* (2010) 8. https://treasury.gov.au/sites/default/files/2019-03/R2009-001_Final_Report_Part_1_Consolidated.pdf.

[8] Ibid.

individual and so policy making might be permitted to be paternalistic to protect against these anomalies.

> In a sense, behavioural economics extends the paternalistically protected category of idiots to include most people at predictable times. The challenge is figuring out what sorts of idiotic behaviours are likely to arise routinely and how to prevent them, while imposing minimal restrictions on those who behave rationally.[9]

Four broad categories of behaviour relevant to policy making are described as: inertia and procrastination; framing and presentation; social influences; and difficulties in assessing probability.[10]

A. Inertia and Procrastination

Default rules can be very important because of inertia. People tend to have a strong bias towards the status quo anyway and if you add to this a lack of understanding or complexity then this increases the power of inertia where people stay with what they know. Individuals also place too much emphasis on the instant moment and discount the value of the future. A simple example might be the desire to have more spending money available to go shopping now rather than putting money into a pension plan to spend in 40 years' time. A source of this status quo bias is loss aversion, where individuals place a greater negative value on losses than a positive value on gains.[11] This loss aversion is linked to the endowment effect,[12] whereby 'The maximum amount a person would be willing to pay to acquire a good is often significantly less than the minimum amount she would be willing to accept to sell the same good.'[13]

For pensions this might operate to reduce the contributions the individual is willing to make for their retirement pension. Another bias which enhances the status quo bias is the tendency to care more about errors of commission than omission. The regret caused by one's own actions seems stronger than that resulting from inaction.[14] This is often linked to procrastination, where the individual intends to do the right thing but finds excuses not to, or overconfidence where the individual believes they will be the exception or will buck the trend. Policy attempts to intervene to correct these biases by specifying a default outcome. The powerful effects of inertia may be the very reason that the UK has introduced AE as studies show that employees fail to self-enrol into pensions themselves when they have a choice. Inertia may not be the only problem as, even if employees do

[9] Camerer et al, 'Regulations for Conservatives', (n 6) 1218.
[10] Sunstein, 'Empirically Informed Regulation', (n 2) 1350.
[11] Camerer et al, 'Regulations for Conservatives', (n 6) 1224.
[12] RH Thaler, *Misbehaving: The Making of Behavioural Economics* (Penguin Books, 2015) 18, 131.
[13] Avgouleas, 'Cognitive Biases and Investor Protection Regulation', (n 4) 16.
[14] Camerer et al, 'Regulations for Conservatives', (n 6) 1225.

decide to make a change, procrastination may operate to delay the completion of forms etc. In this respect, automatically enrolling employees harnesses inertia in favour of all employees being in a pension, with the choice to opt-out being too difficult a decision to make where inertia favours staying in. The inertia bias will still exist after the intervention of AE so the choice of any default is very important and this is considered later in discussion of choice architecture.

B. Framing and Presentation

This describes the influence of the way that information is presented to the individual. The way that information is conveyed can have a significant effect on the individual. Combined with other bias such as loss aversion, it can be very influential if information is presented in a particular way. For pensions, it is important that communications are clear and salient to ensure that the individual really understands the decision to join which has been made for them under AE. This might mean good use of examples with salaries and contributions similar to those of the employee so that he can relate to the amounts and consider his own retirement plans. Too much technical detail might prevent employees from engaging with the literature and making active decisions but if it is too abstract, maybe using percentage figures instead of actual cash amounts, then employees may not relate the situation properly to their own.[15]

Framing may influence the choice and amount of investments and, for AE, there are specific requirements about the content and frequency of information to be given to employees. Review of the regime considers whether this is adequate to preserve the individual right to choose and whether anything could be done to improve AE communications. If the AE regime is paternalistic then is part of that policy that the information requirements are designed to ensure low opt-out rates? In other words, is the disclosure of information in AE impartial or is it designed to keep people in the default position of saving a fixed amount into the default fund? Is sufficient information provided to allow individuals to overcome their status quo bias and inertia in order to seek advice or engage with active decision making? The data reported in Chapter 5 examines these issues as identified by individuals themselves. Key findings are that many were completely disengaged from the process or only made the minimum decision making required and do not revisit such decisions. The information requirements operate to prevent inducement to opt-out which leads to inadequate generic information being provided. In establishing AE as an employer duty, the work environment also becomes part of this framing and presentation of information as employees receive communications at work from a trusted employer so this may further influence the effects. Those findings demonstrate that the current position is far from perfect and does

[15] Thaler, *Misbehaving*, (n 12) 197.

not encourage active engagement, crucial to the justification of the regime as soft rather than hard paternalism.

Another aspect of this is information asymmetry. This occurs where one party to the bargain either has more information or a greater understanding of the meaning of the information than the other party. When the FCA looks at this concept it is predominantly talking of consumers and selling firms but the same might be said for the situation where an employee is enrolled in an arrangement chosen by the employer at the direction of the legislator.[16] When dealing with the selling on financial products the answer has often been to disclose more information to the consumer but mere disclosure may not be sufficient to correct the misunderstanding if the consumer does not understand or act on the further information. In this situation individuals may then rely on other biases to make decisions, such as trust in an employer or the government or the fact that other workers have acted in a particular way. The lessons of behavioural science tell us that it is not just important that information is given, but that it is given in such a way that recognises the biases or is framed to produce a positive result. Information must be specific enough for employees to be able to identify that it is salient and to know what the choices of action are. It may be difficult to engage workers with the issues. Overdraft fees are one example given for the fact that individuals pay limited attention.[17] It is suggested that when employees are surveyed about such fees then they are less likely to incur them for some time after as the issue has been brought to the forefront of the mind. Are there sufficient salient triggers in the AE regime where employees are enrolled automatically and could such reminders used in overdraft fees be utilised for AE? There is currently no break or review provision to ensure that employees think about the pension or contribution again until retirement and, the decision having been made, employees are unlikely to seek financial help in the future for pensions. When considering the use of AE to counter the biases further consideration is given to the use of education and financial literacy as an alternative to paternalism to counteract bias.[18]

C. Social Influences

This describes the scenario where the individual is influenced by their perception of others. The data reported in the following chapter, contains many examples of this. A recurring theme was that most people believed that colleagues had a better understanding of pension matters than they did and would often go along with what the majority were doing. Sunstein uses the example of self-created communities[19]

[16] M Wheatley, 'Making Competition King – the Rise of Behavioural Economics at the FCA' (Financial Conduct Authority, 25 March 2014) www.fca.org.uk/news/making-competition-king.

[17] CR Sunstein, 'Nudges.gov: Behavioural Economics and Regulation' (*SSRN* 18 February 2013), 5.

[18] Part IV, B, below.

[19] Sunstein, 'Empirically Informed Regulation', (n 2) 1356.

and government campaigns on AE seek to capitalise on this. The UK introduced AE with a campaign using the slogan 'we're all in'. In New Zealand, the information campaign also encouraged people to visit websites designed to improve financial education and understanding.[20] Prospect theory is an example of social influence and occurs where people use external information to make decisions.[21] That might mean they refer to the current position and look at potential for gain or loss but they might look back to last year and notice that the potential gain was much higher then than it is now. An example of this could be the recent property price dip. Prices were overinflated and then fell but are now in recovery. If you know that your neighbour sold at the top of the market for £25,000 more than you have been offered for your house, even if the agent tells you this is £10,000 over market value, you will not feel good about it and may even decide to wait longer to sell. This is also linked to a strong aversion to loss which can result in poor decisions where the net effect is not properly valued. This is sometimes referred to as the endowment effect which can be illustrated by the fact that an individual will value something higher if they own it than if they wanted to buy it. This might result in someone reacting inappropriately to a loss in their pension fund investment over a short period and so careful consideration must be given to how such losses are communicated and dealt with. Pension funds should be invested over the longer term and risk matched to stage of life, so knee jerk reactions to fluctuations in underlying investments is detrimental, ie the older you are the less risky the fund invested in.

D. Difficulties in Assessing Probability

Individuals often feel that they will be above average in their own performance and may discount other evidence to the contrary. An example might be smokers who are aware of the statistical health risks associated with smoking but who feel their own risk is lower than average. This might be described as unrealistic optimism and generally describes the situation where individuals are aware of the facts but feel they will do better than average or will buck the trend.[22] Many consumer contracts have cooling off periods specifically to address the issue of consumers regretting a bad bargain. One concern with pension saving is that consumers may not have the understanding to be capable of regret at a useful point. Individuals may not appreciate that they will not always feel the same as they do now and may underestimate future changes. In AE this might lead individuals to believe that the rate of contribution set at entry level will be sufficient for a good retirement and they

[20] Department for Work and Pensions Research Report No 663, Collard & Moore, *Review of International Pension Reform* 2010, 70 https://assets.publishing.service.gov.uk/government/uploads/system/uploads/attachment_data/file/214434/rrep663.pdf.

[21] Thaler, *Misbehaving*, (n 12) 55, 295.

[22] C Jolls, 'Behavioural Economics Analysis of Redistributive Legal Rules' [1988] *Vanderbilt Law Review* 1653, 1659.

may not reconsider this decision. This might interact with the way information is presented to powerful effect and is described as projection bias. If consumers are presented with choices in different ways or are encouraged to actively choose then this may counter some of these biases. Individuals may further complicate matters by operating under their own system of norms or heuristics, where the most familiar or unambiguous option is preferred.

III. The Influence of Behavioural Economics on Law and Policy

In the UK a Behavioural Insights Team was established to 'find intelligent ways to encourage, support and enable people to make better choices for themselves',[23] which signals the influence of behavioural economics on law and policy in the UK.[24] It is also noteworthy that one of the first actions of the new Financial Conduct Authority was to commission an occasional paper on behavioural economics,[25] which further demonstrates the influence of the work on policy and financial regulation building on previous work of the FSA.[26] The paper sets out the benefits of developing an understanding of the predictable departures from previously accepted behavioural norms and the potential for using these predictions in future regulation.[27] This follows the influence of New Zealand which introduced the KiwiSaver plan in 2007, with the aim of encouraging the long-term savings habits of those who would otherwise suffer a reduction in living standards post retirement.[28] The work is also evident in the revamp of the Australian system and design of MySuper default funds which acknowledges that individuals often stay with default positions even to their detriment. The original system was predicated on the assumption that Superannuation members should be treated as rational and informed investors, with disclosure and market conduct controls being the main regulatory instruments. However, the Cooper Review found that in a compulsory system this also required member interest which was often lacking. When poor financial literacy is added to this the role of defaults becomes much stronger.[29]

Previously, regulators assumed that individuals made rational choices, assessed products and personal needs effectively and chose the best products to serve

[23] The Behavioural Insights Team, 'Annual Update 2010–11' (Crown Office Behavioural Insights Team, September 2011).

[24] As discussed generally in Thaler, *Misbehaving*, (n 12).

[25] K Erta et al, 'Applying Behavioural Economics at the Financial Conduct Authority' (Occasional Paper No 1, Financial Conduct Authority, 2013).

[26] D De Meza, B Irlenbusch, and D Reyniers, 'Financial Capability: A Behavioural Economic Perspective' (Financial Services Authority, July 2008) www.fca.org.uk/publication/research/fsa-crpr69.pdf.

[27] Erta et al, 'Applying Behavioural Economics', (n 25) 4.

[28] The KiwiSaver Act 2006.

[29] Australian Government Super system review: final report, 8.

their needs. One difficulty in assessing the decision making of others is that assumptions must be made. The question here is whether the decisions are, in fact, unreasonable and whether the potential detriment to the consumer should be corrected by intervention. The FCA report recognises this difficulty, highlighting that 'If the FCA mistakenly intervenes to "correct" reasonable consumer choices, our interventions could impose costs for no real benefit, or even make people worse off.'[30] The report further considers that in order to assess what choices are reasonable, we must first understand what consumers really value. Using the example of the failure of self-enrolment in pensions, it might be logical to put off joining until debts are paid off but if procrastination occurs after the debt is paid this becomes an error.

'Individualised risk, responsibility and choice are at the heart of the [defined contribution] model, yet inertia and low levels of personal saving suggest that individuals have difficulty making appropriate decisions' for their own good.[31] This is a theme of my empirical research which considers the individual's experience of workplace pensions, understanding of any changes and perception of the information they have been given about pensions by employers or the government through media campaigns. Only by taking the opinion of those expert in personal benefit and detriment (the affected individual) can we understand whether intervention is justified either in the nudging way as described by the FCA or the more formal basis prescribed by the AE regime. Financial services products may be more susceptible to behavioural traits than other areas because of a number of factors, namely:

- the complexity of the products and pricing/costs;
- information asymmetries mean that the consumer may have less information than the vendor of the product or may understand less of the information;
- individuals find it difficult to evaluate short- and long-term interests and exercise self-control;
- elements of uncertainty inherent in many financial products are off-putting to consumers;
- consumers may go with instincts rather than reason when deciding what to do; and
- longer-term products, such as pensions, are more difficult for the consumer to evaluate and often the success or failure will only be revealed after a long period of time. This limits the opportunity to challenge the quality of the product or learn from mistakes.

[30] Erta et al, 'Applying Behavioural Economics', (n 25) 19.

[31] K Straus, 'Re-engaging with Rationality in Economic Geography: Behavioural Approaches and the Importance of Context in Decision Making' (2008) 8 *Journal of Economic Geography* 137, 138.

The FCA is particularly concerned with the way products are sold and whether intervention is required to address the newly identified consumer biases and reactions to improve the more traditional disclosure of information regime. In a similar way to government policy, the FCA is looking at ways to utilise the lessons from behavioural economics to nudge better decision making which is 'less interventionist [and does] not constrain consumer choice'.[32] The difficulty with any nudging is identifying the failing behaviour and demonstrating that the intervention causes a better outcome. To this end the report supports empirical evidence to establish true preferences and improve nudges. It is also a real concern, where you have legal intervention, to ascertain which of the various behaviours and biases are predictable. Whether the intervention is deemed to be hard or soft paternalism or a nudge, there is still an intervention which requires objective justification. If you cannot predict behaviour you do not foresee the full consequences of intervention. Policy makers have developed a checklist when making policies designed to influence behaviour and good policies should reflect this:

- individuals are heavily influenced by the individual who communicates information;
- responses to incentives are shaped by mental shortcuts, eg loss aversion described above;[33]
- individuals are strongly influenced by others;
- individuals go with the flow on defaults;
- attention is drawn to novel and relevant material;
- action is often influenced by sub-conscious clues;
- emotional associations can powerfully shape action;
- individuals seek to be consistent with public promises; and
- individuals act in a way that allows us to feel better about ourselves.[34]

IV. Regulatory Intervention and Choice Architecture

In considering how to respond to these behavioural biases, policy makers had a range of options available to them, including the use of paternalistic legislation. Traditional economic theory assumes that individuals have the 'cognitive ability to solve the necessary optimization problem. … [and] that the households also have sufficient willpower to execute this optimal plan'.[35] For retirement planning,

[32] Erta et al, 'Applying Behavioural Economics', (n 25) 9.

[33] At paragraph A.

[34] Institute for Government, 'Mindspace: Influencing Behaviour through Public Policy' (Cabinet Office 2010) www.instituteforgovernment.org.uk/sites/default/files/publications/MINDSPACE.pdf, 8.

[35] S Benartzi and RH Thaler, 'Heuristics and Biases in Retirement Savings Behaviour' (2007) 21(3) *Journal of Economic Perspectives* 81, 82.

households seem to base contribution amounts on a benefit comparison of spending the money now versus saving for retirement. According to life cycle theory, in their younger years workers 'borrow from the future by means of debt to boost current consumption; middle-aged individuals become net savers … and enter accumulation phase … then de-cumulate or draw-down their assets to finance old-age consumption'.[36] However, behavioural traits may prevent the effective accumulation of assets:

> Individuals have cognitive biases that lead them to act in systematically irrational ways, such as that they act against their own self-interest; and … [that] policy makers should use choice architecture – that is, they should organize the context in which people make decisions – to minimize the negative impact of those cognitive biases.[37]

Lack of self-control is a key instigator as it seems that individuals often have an awareness that they are not saving enough but are unable to take action. If the individual commits to saving into a retirement plan then they cannot easily access the savings and are committed to a certain amount of saving. The question here is whether policy makers should legislate to ensure that the default position is that employees are committed to saving in a pension plan or whether the approach should be to educate individuals to ensure that they undertake such commitments themselves. It is difficult to see exactly what biases are targeted by the AE policy and which are ignored and some would argue that the use of choice architecture is not connected to specific biases the policy maker is trying to correct.[38] Consequently there will be externalities as a result of the policy which will affect those with differing biases to produce varied results.

A. Policy of Legal Paternalism

A policy of legal paternalism assumes that imperfect choices can be improved by policy. It is argued that it is 'legitimate for private and public institutions to attempt to influence other people's behaviour even where third-party effects are absent'.[39] This type of paternalistic policy supposes that consumers are divided into those who are fully rational and those who suffer bounded rationality. By implementing a paternalistic policy this might impose costs to those who are fully rational. An asymmetrically paternalistic policy operates to create 'large benefits for those

[36] OS Mitchell and SP Utkus, 'Lessons from Behavioural Finance for Retirement Plan Design' in OS Mitchell and SP Utkus (eds), *Pension Design and Structure: New Lessons from Behavioural Finance* (Oxford University Press, 2004) 5.

[37] AC Desai, 'Libertarian Paternalism, Externalities, and the Spirit of Liberty: How Thaler and Sunstein are Nudging Us toward an Overlapping Consensus' (2011) 36 *Law and Social Inquiry* 263, 265.

[38] ibid, 270.

[39] CR Sunstein and RH Thaler, 'Libertarian Paternalism Is Not An Oxymoron' (2003) 70 *The University of Chicago Law Review* 1159, 1162.

people who are boundedly rational … while imposing little or no harm on those who are fully rational'.[40] If the policy is designed to counter inferior decision making, then it must be clearly identified at the outset which traits are targeted and how the policy will work. For AE, it has been argued that the policy is designed to harness inertia to ensure that the default is a savings decision. However, it is important to recognise that the bias which creates inertia and pulls the individual towards the status quo will still exist within the new policy regime and the consequences of this need to be considered carefully for policy interventions such as AE. An integral part of the success of such policies is that there should be a low implementation cost and cost to the rational individual. AE is described as soft paternalism and an option which will make mistakes less likely.[41] It is the exercise of choice which is seen as the legitimising action in paternalistic legislation as it allows the individual to return to the previous position. However, nudge or soft paternalism may not be clearly visible. No-one is confused or fooled by prohibitions of hard paternalism but there is a danger that nudges will not be visible and fail to be scrutinised.[42] One reason for my research and interviewing individuals was to ask whether the individual feels the benefit of the intervention and what their views are on their own position, now and in the future. There are other forms of intervention such as requiring an active choice by the individual and these are preferable to those which operate 'behind the back of the chooser'.[43] Chapter 2 describes the paternalistic intention and justification for AE which represents a change in direction for pensions' regulation.[44]

B. Choice Architects

This kind of policy intervention can be described as 'Choice Architecture' with AE having a greater effect than significant economic incentives.[45] From what is understood of decision making, the individual tends towards the status quo and so the default rules, established under AE, will be significant. Sunstein identifies three main contributing factors: inertia and procrastination, implicit endorsement and reference points.[46] In order to overturn the default position, the individual must make an active choice. They might consider that they will stay with the default as it must have been created for a good reason using the default as a reference point when deciding whether to change. However, it has been argued that AE only addresses the status quo bias of those who are otherwise aware of their savings needs and in fact AE does not really match cognitive bias in other respects.

[40] Camerer et al, 'Regulations for Conservatives', (n 6) 1219.
[41] Erta et al, 'Applying Behavioural Economics', (n 25) 47–48.
[42] Sunstein, *Why Nudge?* (n 5) 147.
[43] ibid, 149.
[44] Erta et al, 'Applying Behavioural Economics', (n 25) 47.
[45] Sunstein, 'Nudges.gov', (n 17) 7.
[46] ibid, 23.

For others, the 'solution circumvents the problem rather than attacking it directly', and AE simply replaces one bias for another and ignores the bounded rationality problem altogether.[47] If a person suffers from bounded willpower but not status quo bias, they might opt-out of AE as they overcome the default because they do not have the willpower to save and AE is not a solution. AE may offset problems with complexity but does not solve them as it does not allow people to understand their needs better. A generic default is substituted which may be an improvement but is not a solution.

The policy maker may lack skill and expertise to create good policies to counter human bias without significant external effects or unintended consequences.[48] A distinction between AE in the UK and the US is that the state has intervened in the UK to require all employers to enrol employees, whereas in the US the policy of AE only exists where individual employers choose to implement it, without regulatory compulsion. This is an important distinction as it brings a third-party interest into the decision-making process. It may be more difficult for the individual to make a clear decision with the influence of employer and state which may not be fully aligned in interests; or may even have conflicting interests with the employee. As the government has introduced the legislation to set up AE and is visibly backing the policy with a media campaign this might further influence individuals to stick to the default as they believe that it must be in their best interests. There is some research which found that lack of financial sophistication might lead individuals to believe that they were being advised by their employer in relation to the default as there was an assumption that the default must be in the best interests of the employees.[49] There is also evidence of this in my empirical study, discussed in Chapter 5. This fails to consider any conflicting interests such as those of the employer.

It must also be recognised that the policy maker, be it the government implementing the AE legislation or the employer implementing the specific choice architecture of its particular pension scheme, may also be subject to the same behavioural bias as the individual. The policy maker has political will as well as obligations to support the policy with tax incentives which are a cost just like the employer's costs.[50] There is also a tendency for over simplification of underlying theory to make more definite policy recommendations and any policy maker must choose amongst competing preferences and accounts to form a clear policy.[51] The 'veneer of scientific objectivity' in this process leads to a slippery slope to harder

[47] Desai, 'Libertarian Paternalism, Externalities, and the Spirit of Liberty', (n 37) 237.

[48] MJ Rizzo and DG Whitman, 'Little Brother is Watching You: New Paternalism on the Slippery Slopes' (2009) 51 *Arizona Law Review*' 686.

[49] J Beshears et al, 'The Importance of Default Options for Retirement Saving Outcomes: Evidence from the United States' (September 2006) www.nber.org/programs/ag/rrc/F6%20Beshears%20Choi%20FINAL.pdf.

[50] O'Connell, Institute of Policy Studies, 'KiwiSaver: A Model Scheme' (2009) 36 *Social Policy Journal of New Zealand* 130, 137.

[51] Rizzo and Whitman, 'Little Brother is Watching You', (n 48) 712.

forms of paternalism.[52] Policy makers may also be influenced by other factors such as industry bias or immediate political concerns which might give 'fully rational policy makers an incentive to discount future consequences'.[53] The full effects of AE will not be known until the first employees start to retire by which time the policy maker will no longer be in government or accountable. Policy makers may also suffer from the same narrow framing bias as individuals, choosing ad hoc solutions to particular problems. It has also been argued that policy makers are affected by the framing of information and accept the new paternalists framing of 'what form of paternalism shall we have' rather than considering whether paternalism is desirable at all.[54] The seeming inevitability of paternalism of some form creates a framework within which more and more policy making will operate.

It may be that there is really no alternative to paternalism or choice architecture as some 'organization or agent must make a choice that will affect the behaviour of some other people'.[55] In the case of a workplace pension then the employer might choose whether to offer a pension and on what terms, but it might also be argued that such terms are subject to contractual negotiation and will be agreed between the parties rather than being imposed as they are under AE. Even after the intervention of AE legislation, the employer retains almost full autonomy in respect of designing the pension plan to be used for compliance with AE and so influences the range of choices open to the individual employee. This argument has been made in terms of various policy interventions including those designed to better an individual's health. The example of healthy food choices and restrictions of these choices in a work cafeteria may be quite easy to demonstrate health benefits but it is a completely different matter to demonstrate the universal benefit of requiring all employees to be enrolled into a pension plan of the employer's choosing. It is not clear that all will benefit in the same way and this next section will consider the particular form of AE that we have in the UK and how this interacts with the behavioural bias described above. Perhaps this limited paternalism, whether described as libertarian, asymmetrical or nudge is simply a compromise to induce agreement between liberal and paternalistic pressure groups.[56] In seeking agreement from such polarised positions the resulting compromised policy may be too generic to be useful. This can be described as a best guess or majoritarian default and the success of any such policy intervention will depend on particular default positions.[57]

[52] ibid.
[53] ibid, 724.
[54] ibid, 728.
[55] Sunstein and Thaler, 'Libertarian Paternalism is not an Oxymoron', (n 39) 1164.
[56] Desai, 'Libertarian Paternalism, Externalities, and the Spirit of Liberty', (n 37) 286.
[57] Camerer et al, 'Regulations for Conservatives', (n 6) 1226.

C. Alternatives to Soft Paternalism/Choice Architecture

It has been argued that a pure paternalistic response with no opt-out would be preferable to AE. If you compare AE to a form of second state pension then it is easy to see how this could work, with the government collecting contributions like taxation thus preventing the need for welfare payments to top up pensions in the future. The Australian Superannuation scheme is a useful comparison with compulsory employer contributions. This reduces the externalities associated with future generations having to support those who have made the choice to opt-out now. In establishing NEST, the government has created a compliant scheme but not all employers can or will use this for all employees. If the government had, instead of making employers responsible for implementing AE, undertaken the administration of AE and operated it as additional NICs or a single approved pension scheme then there would be no role for the employer in choosing the scheme and default positions. Benefits would be similar for all employees and the potential for conflicts of interest reduced, as employers would have no role in scheme design and the role of the financial services industry would be very limited. However, this option restricts freedom of choice and the opportunity to invest in a competitive free market viewed as an added layer of taxation and was clearly politically unacceptable.

Employers rely heavily on the financial services industry in the creation of AE compliant schemes and there are clear potential conflicts of interests between the parties. Many employers lack qualified staff to deal with pensions whereas the expertise already exists within the government pension departments which could oversee a standalone scheme. However, it seems that no matter whether it is the government or a private employer, some agent has to design the plan and so choice architecture issues remain.[58] A difficulty in choosing the design is that it will inevitably affect those other than the direct subject of the nudge and these externalities have to be weighed carefully against the social gains.[59] For example, if people are encouraged to save more then they will not be able to spend as much which can be harmful to the wider economy.

One way to avoid paternalistic intervention with varying consequences for different individuals is to require individuals to make a choice themselves. The requirement to choose negates the effects of inertia but may be costly and time consuming, particularly in light of the other difficulties exhibited by individuals in processing information and screening out irrelevant information. However, it does cater for the individual much better than the one size fits all approach of the default. Where there is no default and employees must choose then they must actively engage with the process. 'In this active decision regime there is no default

[58] R Bubb, P Corrigan, and PL Warren, 'A Behavioural Contract Theory Perspective on Retirement Savings' (*SSRN*, 3 July 2015) https://papers.ssrn.com/sol3/papers.cfm?abstract_id=2626069.

[59] Desai, 'Libertarian Paternalism, Externalities, and the Spirit of Liberty', (n 37) 279.

to fall back on because employees are not allowed to remain passive; they must explicitly declare their enrolment preference.'[60] Active decisions have been shown to increase employee contributions much faster than they would under AE.[61] However, although this removes the government influence to some extent it can be difficult to enforce. It is unlikely that direct penalties will be imposed for failing to choose and it must also be recognised that the choices offered are also restricted and forcing choice may be just as unpalatable as strict paternalism. However, the act of choosing operates as 'an indispensable safeguard against erroneous purchases and thus is in the interests of those who might be denominated purchasers (by default)'.[62]

Financial education has also been suggested as an alternative to AE on the basis that if individuals understand their financial position and pension better they will make good choices themselves.[63] Chapter 2 also described the importance that legislators placed on financial education at the inception of the AE policy. The Australian Government also recognised the difficulties of reliance on the financial services industry for this and the limits of disclosure of information as a form of engagement.[64] Financial Literacy was allocated AU$20 million to improve education and understanding of financial matters, including pensions.[65] My empirical research explores the role of information and understanding on the operation of choice and it is clear that mere disclosure of information itself does not assist in the process of financial education to create positive action. Framing should be considered in the creation of information used to educate employees on their pensions to ensure it must be based on how people actually digest information. In other words, 'In order to be effective, any effort to inform people must be rooted in an understanding of how people actually think.'[66] Thaler and Sunstein have argued that education itself is inadequate but there may be other reasons to educate rather than relying on some form of paternalism.[67] Education may assist the individual to form a preference and choose. A key finding of behavioural economics is that framing affects choice but this may affect preferences as well.[68] AE makes a selection of choice even before the individual develops a preference and education may

[60] GD Carroll et al, 'Optimal Defaults and Active Decisions' [2009] *The Quarterly Journal of Economics* 1639, 1639.

[61] ibid, 1642, 1652, 1655.

[62] CR Sunstein, *Choosing not to choose: Understanding the Value of Choice* (Oxford University Press, 2015) 125.

[63] RP Larrick, 'Debiasing' in DJ Koehler and N Harvey (eds), *Blackwell Handbook of Judgment and Decision Making* (Blackwell, 2004) 112.

[64] Department for Work and Pensions Research Report No 663, 69.

[65] OECD/IOPS global forum on private pensions: *Private pensions and government information campaigns: lessons from OECD countries* October 2008, 12: www.oecd.org/finance/private-pensions/41531982.pdf.

[66] Sunstein and Thaler, 'Libertarian Paternalism is not an Oxymoron', (n 39) 1182.

[67] RH Thaler and CR Sunstein, *Nudge: Improving Decisions about Health Wealth and Happiness* (Yale University Press, 2008).

[68] Desai, 'Libertarian Paternalism, Externalities, and the Spirit of Liberty', (n 37) 281.

be useful to 'help people decide not only what to do but also, more important, what they actually want'.[69] Whilst form of information is considered as part of AE, I do not believe that it is effective in all cases and should be reviewed. Information 'must be both available and easily processable to be used effectively'.[70] Large amounts of information act as a barrier and result in consumers failing to read or consider their options under the product.

V. Auto-Enrolment as Choice Architecture

In choosing a particular type of pension plan which employees are defaulted into joining, a number of decisions and features of the plan are agreed by the employer and the product provider. This particular combination of features, such as contribution levels and default investment funds, creates a choice architecture which can significantly affect the savings behaviour of the individual.[71] In this respect, the employer affects the policy making of the legal intervention. Whilst AE specifies broad compliance, a large amount of discretion is left to the employer to implement the regime. This question of how employers design their plans is under researched with more emphasis on the effects of competing design plans or worker savings behaviour.[72] It has been argued that the employer and employee's interests are aligned in respect of pension plan design,[73] but there is a growing body of work which demonstrates that there are potentially negative effects and that the employer may even exploit the behavioural biases of its employees.[74]

A. Auto-Enrolment

Prior to the introduction of AE, where employees were offered membership of employer sponsored pensions, it was on a self-enrolment basis. Research in the US found that switching from self-enrolment to AE significantly increased pension plan membership.[75] As well as increasing participation it was found that

[69] ibid.

[70] R Bollen, 'A Case Study of Bounded Rationality in the Market for Superannuation Products' (2007) 4 *Macquarie Journal of Business Law* 49, 64.

[71] Bubb, Corrigan, and Warren, 'A Behavioural Contract Theory Perspective', (n 58) 3; Sunstein and Thaler, 'Libertarian Paternalism is not an Oxymoron', (n 39) 1174.

[72] Bubb, Corrigan, and Warren, 'A Behavioural Contract Theory Perspective', (n 58) 4.

[73] Z Bodie, 'Pensions as Retirement Income Insurance' (1990)28 *Journal of Economic Literature* 28, 37.

[74] Bubb, Corrigan, and Warren, 'A Behavioural Contract Theory Perspective', (n 58) 6.

[75] BC Madrian and DF Shea, 'The Power of Suggestion: Inertia in 401(k) Participation and Savings Behaviour' (2001) 116 *The Quarterly Journal of Economics* 1149, 1159; Beshears et al, 'The Importance of Default Options for Retirement Saving Outcomes', (n 49) IIA.

AE equalises participation across employee demographic groups. The operation of inertia is said to be working in favour of maintaining a position of saving rather than the previous position of not joining the scheme voluntarily. However, there is only a specified minimum criteria for compliant schemes under AE which can lead to varying benefits and consequences as a result of the policy intervention and much of the discretion lies with the employer. The consequences for the individual will depend on the structure of the defaults and communication of this to employees.

B. Opting-out

In AE, the employer will provide the employee with basic information and will often rely on the product provider to send key pension features and information about opting-out of the pension. As outlined in the previous chapter, the low opt-out rate has been used as support for the success of the policy intervention, but this does not address key questions such as whether the individual understands choices and engages with the literature and whether the decision to stay in the plan is a conscious or positive one. Indeed the freedom to choose is one of the main justifications for the regime and is often considered in terms of the cost of exit without considering 'who imposes the costs and how'.[76] It has been argued that there is no procrastination in the decision of whether to opt-out of AE because the decision to opt-out is not complicated.[77] However, other factors and biases may affect opt-outs, as evidenced in my empirical study. Some individuals 'may procrastinate in their decisions to opt-out of the default'.[78] It might also be the case that the endowment effect operates so that individuals value the benefit of membership more after they become members than they did before, although this is difficult to measure and because the pension is not a tangible item the endowment effect may not be as strong as when other goods are held.[79] It is difficult to identify whether inertia or acceptance of the position is the true reason for lack of opt-outs. Perhaps 'workers are not suddenly discovering, to their dismay, that they are saving more than they had wanted' but it can also be said that low opt-out is no indication that workers actively choose to stay in the plan.[80] Externalities, misunderstandings and other heuristics may influence the behaviour of individuals still and lack of opt-out should not be taken as acceptance of the benefit of the AE intervention.

[76] Rizzo and Whitman, 'Little Brother is Watching You', (n 48) 698.

[77] Madrian and Shea, 'The Power of Suggestion', (n 75) 1179.

[78] Carroll et al, 'Optimal Defaults and Active Decisions', (n 60) 1642.

[79] J Arlen, 'Comment: The Future of Behavioural Economic Analysis of Law' (1998) 52 *Vanderbilt Law Review* 1765, 1778.

[80] Benartzi and Thaler, 'Heuristics and Biases in Retirement Savings Behaviour', (n 35) 83.

C. Defaults

In designing a default we assume that it will reflect what the majority would choose if they made the decision. The default will act with inertia to prevent individuals moving from whatever default is set:

> In view of the fact that many people do not opt-out even when it is simple to do so, a self-interested or malevolent government could easily use default rules to move people in preferred directions. If we accept very strong assumptions about the likelihood of government mistake and about the virtues or private choice (uninfluenced by government), we might regard opt-out as an illusory safeguard and for that reason reject some forms of soft paternalism.[81]

My empirical study demonstrates that default contribution levels and employer matching of contributions can be a strong pull. Evidence suggests that, whilst AE may increase overall participation in a pension, this may lead to individuals paying lower contributions than they would otherwise have paid if they had joined voluntarily at a later date.[82] Research from New Zealand also indicates that AE might lead to a shift in savings patterns rather than actually increasing savings levels[83] or at least that alternative saving is significantly reduced by the KiwiSaver membership.[84] Some research shows that the net wealth accumulation of members is negatively affected by KiwiSaver membership, with only five out of 28 cases showing a positive outcome in terms of net accumulation of wealth.[85] If the UK policy of AE does not lead to an increase in overall saving then it fails to meet the intended aims of improving living standards. It also appears that AE results in 'passive' saving with employees doing nothing to move from default contribution rates which may be the result of status quo bias or procrastination.[86] This might be attributed to the cost of gathering and evaluating the information needed to effect a change or the complexity of the decision, which is often a reason for sticking with the default investment option. In AE the default investment option will remove the need to consider fund selection but the individual then relies completely on the default fund as appropriate to their needs; which it may not always be.[87]

[81] Sunstein, *Why Nudge?* (n 5) 153.

[82] Madrian and Shea, 'The Power of Suggestion', (n 75) 1165.

[83] Department for Work and Pensions Research Report No 663, 50; New Zealand Treasury Working Paper 11/04, Law et al, 'KiwiSaver: An Initial Evaluation of the Impact on Retirement Saving' 10 https://treasury.govt.nz/publications/wp/kiwisaver-initial-evaluation-impact-retirement-saving-html#section-8.

[84] Law 'KiwiSaver: an evaluation of a new retirement savings scheme' (2017) 51(3) *New Zealand Economic Papers* 262, 277.

[85] New Zealand Treasury Working Paper 14/22, Law & Scobie, KiwiSaver and the Accumulation of Net Wealth, 12: https://treasury.govt.nz/publications/wp/kiwisaver-and-accumulation-net-wealth-wp-14-22-html.

[86] ibid, 1177; JJ Choi, 'Saving for Retirement on the Path of Least Resistance' (2004) National Bureau of Economic Research: https://scholar.harvard.edu/files/laibson/files/saving_for_retirement_on_the_path_of_least_resistance.pdf.

[87] H Cronqvist and RH Thaler, 'Design Choices in Privitized Social-Security Systems: Learning From the Swedish Experience' (2004) 94 *American Economic Review* 424, 425.

Caps on charges and fees for default funds may have the effect of making the default more appropriate for the majority of workers, negating the need or desire for active choice in investment for many but does not solve the problem of individuals sticking with low default contributions. There will also be externalities where those who would be better moving from the default position stay as enrolled; possibly because they perceive it as a recommendation.

The initial level of default contribution is very important. In New Zealand, the initial employee default was set at four per cent although employees could choose eight per cent. The year after the KiwiSaver was introduced, the minimum default was reduced to two per cent because of concerns about affordability. However, most employees stuck with the original default of four per cent.[88] The introduction of AE by private companies in the US has also been considered paternalistic but if this actually causes a reduction in the total value of contributions then the intention, or the consequences at least, must seem more difficult to justify. There is a:

> Particularly powerful impact of defaults on individuals with low human capital [which] implies that variation in defaults across decision domains may cause these individuals to exhibit seemingly contradictory preferences. Policy makers may wish to keep these individuals in mind when setting defaults.[89]

US research confirms that, in practice, employees do not know how much salary should be contributed, use arbitrary figures, rely on default levels and then do not adjust these as the affordability of paying more increases.[90] This is confirmed by the data from my research. Clearly for those who contributed nothing before, the introduction of AE and mandatory contributions seems positive but the 'sticky' nature of the default means that those who would have joined the scheme later but paid higher contributions will no longer do so. For those employees, AE actually reduces retirement savings.[91] Employers might consider increasing contributions for those with longer service but must be very careful not to breach age discrimination legislation and so often just fix the default contribution rate for all employees.[92]

The cynic might argue that employers may even choose a default contribution rate that minimises employer contributions and 'This behavioural contract theory perspective thus explains the pattern of low default contribution rates combined with matching that employers in fact commonly choose.'[93] Employers have already

[88] Department for Work and Pensions Research Report No 663, 45.

[89] J Beshears et al, 'The Limitations of Defaults' (2010) www.nber.org/programs/ag/rrc/NB10-02,%20Beshears,%20Choi,%20Laibson,%20Madrian.pdf, 12.

[90] P Secunda, 'The Behavioural Economic Case for Paternalistic Workplace Retirement Plans' (2016) 91 *Indiana Law Journal* 505, 516 & 528.

[91] R Bubb and RH Pildes, 'How Behavioural Economics Trims its Sails and Why' (2014) 127 *Harvard Law Review* 1593, 1618.

[92] Equality Act 2010.

[93] Bubb, Corrigan and Warren 'A Behavioural Contract Theory Perspective', (n 58) 38.

moved from providing defined benefit to defined contribution plans which shifts performance risk from the employer to the employee but this may have been possible because employees failed to value the defined benefits properly and agreed to contractual changes which were not beneficial. In the UK reports identify a downward trend for defined benefit and hybrid schemes. These schemes are reported to have gone from being used in 24 per cent of AE declarations to the Pensions Regulator in 2014 to just three per cent at the end of 2016–17.[94] Clear evidence of the unintended consequence of a levelling down of pensions as a consequence of the introduction of AE. The low default option in AE was perhaps designed to take account of those with 'low capital' but I am interested to know what effect the setting of a low default rate has on others with higher capital. Further research is needed on how employees choose to fix contribution levels and this forms part of my empirical study.

Defaults are described as 'sticky' because the operation of the status quo bias means individuals will find it difficult to change from the default position. Research from New Zealand indicates that most savers do not move from default contributions or funds.[95] Other research from the US indicates that the success of AE, heralded by the transformative figures of those in pensions, simply highlights difficulties with opting-out.[96] These findings are equally applicable to the UK regime. It can be difficult to create a default which accommodates all as there will be differences in disposable income and priorities and equal treatment legislation may prevent a distinction being made between different elements of the workforce. This results in a one size fits all default – normally at the lowest common denominator to prevent mass opt-outs. The study finds that active decision making increased both enrolment and the level of contributions paid by employees much quicker than on standard AE.[97]

Matching contributions are often set up in a way that employers will match the employee contributions up to a maximum amount and this can be tied to age or years of service provided that the AE minimum contributions are paid. Whatever level is set as the maximum match can act as an anchor to the individual when choosing contribution amounts and it may even work with behavioural biases to produce negative consequences for some. It has been argued that employers exploit these biases in designing their pension plans.[98] In other words, the choice architecture of the plan design shapes the employee decision making.[99]

[94] The Pensions Regulator Automatic enrolment Commentary and analysis: April 2016–March 2017, 21.

[95] Department for Work and Pensions Research Report No 663, 89.

[96] Carroll et al, 'Optimal Defaults and Active Decisions', (n 60).

[97] ibid, 1642.

[98] Bubb, Corrigan and Warren, 'A Behavioural Contract Theory Perspective', (n 58) 7.

[99] ibid, 8.

D. Auto-Enrolment and Behavioural Bias

Critics argue that the defaults do not specifically address behavioural traits and are not intended to change the biases.[100] Instead the 'Defaults are generally designed to match what the choice architects believe to be the choice most people would have made had they made a choice at all.'[101] For pension planning it is difficult to see any consensus on what this is as some would pay higher contributions than others. The result is setting defaults at the lowest common denominator. For AE this has resulted in a minimum total eight per cent contribution rate. Of course, some employers may pay more but employees are only required to pay the minimum amount, which equates to a four per cent contribution (including tax relief). If AE is successful simply because it increases the numbers of savers, then the lack of opt-outs to date can be seen as validation; but if the total value of saving does not increase then success of the regime is more doubtful.

It may also have the negative unintended consequence of creating further inequality where the tax and other benefits of the policy are enjoyed more by a non-target group than by the target group. For example, research in New Zealand suggests that KiwiSaver benefits are unequally distributed and contribute to greater inequality in some cases.[102] Males over 55, especially those with a higher education, and high income earners received a disproportionate share of the incentives because of their ability or motivation to access them.[103] US, research also supports this finding that a significant percentage of tax benefits for DC plans accrue to the highest-income earners.[104]

Intervention in one area may create an incentive for further intervention, for example where the policy goal remains unachieved.[105] For example, with AE one downside to the increases in enrolment levels may be that the actual contributions made are lower than individuals would have chosen if required to choose a rate themselves.[106] This might lead to increases in minimum contribution levels in future. Sunstein suggests that the advances in technology should be harnessed to allow defaults to be further tailored to individual needs to reduce negative effects using 'People's own choices and situations [which are] likely to be far more accurate than more general ones.'[107] It is interesting that he identifies a tipping point where inertia is no longer effective and other impulses will be stronger forcing the

[100] Rizzo and Whitman, 'Little Brother is Watching You', (n 48) 706.
[101] Desai, 'Libertarian Paternalism, Externalities, and the Spirit of Liberty', (n 37) 271.
[102] Gibson et al 'The Distributional Impact of KiwiSaver Incentives' (2009) 36 *Social Policy Journal of New Zealand* 111, 118.
[103] ibid, 119.
[104] Burman et al The Urban-Brookings Tax Policy Center (2004) 'Distributional Effects of Defined Contribution Plans and Individual Retirement Accounts' 2: http://webarchive.urban.org/UploadedPDF/311029_TPC_DP16.pdf.
[105] Rizzo and Whitman, 'Little Brother is Watching You', (n 48) 707.
[106] Madrian and Shea, 'The Power of Suggestion', (n 75).
[107] Sunstein, 'Nudges.gov', (n 17) 25.

individual to act. Indeed it might be a valid design strategy to set a higher default, described as an offset default, which encourages some rapid opt-outs but which maximises the welfare of those who stay in.[108] A study considering the operation of defaults finds that higher employee contributions set as a default may result in higher numbers of leavers but that lower income individuals are more susceptible to following the default rules.[109] In this particular US study, three quarters of employees opted-out of the plan within the first year where the default was set at 12 per cent. The study suggests it might be better to start off lower (six per cent) and increase contributions. This idea was used in the AE design starting at an initial one per cent contribution by the employee rising to four per cent. However, the default might be too low and not progressive enough for many.

Beyond that specified as a minimum to comply with AE, the employer decides what default contributions to set, to what extent these will be matched by the employer, chooses the pension provider and default investment fund. What if the employer and providers use what is known of behavioural economics to design a plan which is most efficient for the employer but which 'fails to effectively address the basic retirement savings problem'.[110] If employees are rational then they may prefer a lower employer contribution and a higher salary because it allows them flexibility but also allows them to save for retirement when they can afford to. If contributions are matched for all employees, then this will normally require a corresponding adjustment to salary to reduce the overall cost to the employer. This is detrimental to the rational worker as they would have preferred the higher salary and would have saved enough for retirement. However, we know that many individuals do not behave rationally for a number of reasons. Irrational myopic workers are described as having two distinct classes; those who are aware of their self-control problem and those who are not. Naïve myopic workers are described as those who believe they actually will choose to save more tomorrow and trust their 'future selves to do the right thing by their current selves'.[111] There are also 'inattentive passive workers' who will save a fixed amount for retirement without considering other savings or choices within their pension plan. In light of all these differing and competing behaviours it is clear that a one size fits all AE plan will not correct each behaviour and so some must be preferred over others by the policy intervention.[112] A plan which offers employer matching contributions will be viewed favourably by the naïve and rational workers producing differing end consequences. Naïve workers may overvalue the value of the matching when agreeing the employment contract but will then choose to save less because they overvalue present consumption.[113] The rational workers also value the matching

[108] Carroll et al, 'Optimal Defaults and Active Decisions', (n 60) 1666.
[109] Beshears et al, 'The Limitations of Defaults', (n 89).
[110] Bubb, Corrigan and Warren, 'A Behavioural Contract Theory Perspective', (n 58) 22.
[111] ibid, 25.
[112] ibid, 26.
[113] ibid, 27.

but will actually get the benefit of matching as they will ensure they benefit from the full matching amount. It is possible that in this way the naïve workers cross subsidise the rational workers who in effect receive more total employment benefits than the naïve workers.[114] In other words, there is a redistribution of wealth from the naïve group to the rational group. This may operate to the employer's advantage as the naïve employees' value the package highly because of the matching but the employer is not required to fund the matching as the naïve employees will not pay enough contributions to benefit fully from this. The inattentive passive workers may instead ignore the pension contribution entirely and will favour a compensation package with higher wages and so they are likely to simply take up the minimum required.

There is some evidence in the US that the consequences are that lower income, younger workers are less likely to join plans without AE and it has even been argued that libertarian paternalism is actually motivated by 'an unstated egalitarian impulse'.[115] However, not all will benefit equally depending on particular biases and other financial pressures. A useful example is that of the airline employee who is permitted to fly first class on any flight if there are vacant seats. Whilst all employees can benefit from the free seats, the additional costs associated with the trip, such as hotel and expenses, mean that more of the highly paid employees will benefit from the scheme than lower paid workers. This is also described as 'leakage' in analysis of the KiwiSaver[116] which identified that the policy was only modestly successful in reaching the target audience of the legislation. With the policy intention of assisting those who would suffer a lifestyle reduction on retirement the research identified that for every person in the target population another 14 people saving in the plans are not the target population.[117] This means that the tax savings and incentives are being applied widely in an unintended way, which results in a subsidy for those who don't need it by those who do. If the money used to fund the tax savings and incentives was applied directly to the intended recipients this would reduce leakage so we can see how important the choice architecture is, both in terms of the consequences for the individual and the policy.

In relation to choosing where to invest contributions, the same biases will operate. Whilst the opposite may be the prevailing view, more choice is not necessarily a good thing, as evidenced by US research.[118] Increased choice may contribute to the welfare of individuals by satisfying their desire for choosing but only to the extent that the choices offered meet the desire of the individual. If the individual

[114] ibid, 28.

[115] Desai, 'Libertarian Paternalism, Externalities, and the Spirit of Liberty', (n 37) 279.

[116] New Zealand Treasury Working Paper 11/04, 22.

[117] ibid.

[118] M Bullard, 'The Social Costs of Choice, Free Market Ideology and the Empirical Consequences of the 401(K) Plan Large Menu Defence' (*SSRN*, 12 May 2013) https://papers.ssrn.com/sol3/papers.cfm?abstract_id=2263353; P Secunda, 'The Behavioural Economic Case for Paternalistic Workplace Retirement Plans', (n 90) 505.

has very specific wants, then the choices offered may fail to satisfy the individual and they will not appreciate the range of choices offered. It is the recognition of the fact that the individual may want to have a choice which is important.[119] This may be why, for example, AE compliant schemes are required to join employees without individual choice of investment. The result is that all employees are defaulted into saving into the low risk fund but can choose to change investment fund if they would like to. A similar system operates in Australia where default funds depend upon the industry related to the individual's workplace.[120] Some employees may even believe that the nomination of a default fund is 'implicit advice from the company'.[121] This might be an example of the 'Messenger' effect where the relationship between employer and employee is such that the employee trusts the employer with their pension fund.[122] This is evident in my study which describes employees agreeing to change provider because they trusted the employer's decisions. This default fund is now 'stickier' than before as a result of new caps to charges which only apply to the default investment fund.[123] This may result in fewer employees choosing to move funds, even if this would be beneficial. This can be viewed as an attempt to prevent cross-subsidisation by the boundedly rational employees of the more proactive employees. The theory is that employees should only pay fees for services they will use. More consideration should be given to producing better defaults for a smaller group of individuals to produce better results rather than the current one size fits all approach. There must be a balance in this default setting policy as too much choice may also cause equally unfortunate consequences for some, as in the case of 401k plans in the US.[124]

A further improvement might be to have a range of default options triggered by age/stage or salary of the employee. This scheme described as 'Save More Tomorrow' is an interesting mix of default and active choice where the employee is presently paying a set default amount but agrees to increase this to a particular amount at some defined point in the future.[125] In this US study this plan is effective where it is tied in to a pay rise so that the employee does not suffer the sense of loss with the increased contributions (to combat loss aversion) and the change will be automatically in place at the set time (to combat inertia and procrastination). This might appeal to the employees who know what they should do and also recognise that when tomorrow comes they will not have the willpower to do what is required. They can therefor contract to commit themselves to do what they know they should to counteract: 'The very inertia that explains why automatic enrolment

[119] G Dworkin, 'Is More Choice Better than Less?' (1982) 7 *Midwest Studies in Philosophy* 47, 58.
[120] Department for Work and Pensions Report No 663, 88.
[121] Carroll et al, 'Optimal Defaults and Active Decisions', (n 60) 1667.
[122] Institute for Government, 'Mindspace: Influencing Behaviour through Public Policy' 19.
[123] As discussed in ch 2.
[124] Secunda, 'The behavioural economic case for paternalistic workplace retirement plans', (n 90), 523.
[125] RH Thaler and S Benartzi, 'Save More Tomorrow: Using Behavioural Economics to Increase Employee Saving' (2004) 112 *Journal of Political Economy* 164.

increases participation rates [which] can also lower the savings rates of those who do participate.'[126] This would be an improvement to the current AE model which has no incentive to increase contributions. Without incentive, participants will stay with the default option. This can be illustrated by the way that members respond to fund selection in pension arrangements with the Save More Tomorrow study finding that more than half of all members did not change from the default fund position throughout the duration of membership of the scheme.[127]

As well as the 'sticky' nature of defaults, any rules relating to contributions or investment strategy may provide an anchor or starting point.[128] Employees and employers may use the minimum contribution levels as an anchor which fails to consider the sort of income that the contributions might generate as a pension at retirement. Not all AE plans will operate on the minimum compliance level and some may create anchors based on the level at which the employer offers to match contributions and so sometimes anchoring might be beneficial as it encourages higher savings. For investments this might mean that individuals stick with the default investment strategy even if this is not the most suitable for them. Individuals might even perceive the default investment as some form of advice from the company 'on the best allocation of one's retirement assets'.[129] A difficulty for AE as a policy is the disparity of consequences for affected individuals depending on the choice architecture used by their employer. The discretionary nature of implementation allows for winners and losers of the policy which casts doubt on the success of the regime.

E. Framing and Disclosure

Existing tools employed in protection of investors of the wider financial markets may still be useful: disclosure, simplifying choices and paperwork, increasing salience of information and promoting social norms. The way that information is received can be influenced by a range of individuals' preconceptions and so any disclosure 'should be based on an understanding of how people actually process information'.[130] This will require consideration of the salience, simplicity and situation in which the information is given. How and not only whether is important here.[131] People should be able to take the information and understand the consequences of one course of action versus another. Even the way that information appears on the page can influence choices with some research finding that the number of lines on a form affected the number of funds invested in

[126] ibid, 169.
[127] ibid, 168.
[128] Madrian and Shea, 'The Power of Suggestion', (n 75) 1181.
[129] ibid, 1182.
[130] Sunstein, 'Nudges.gov', (n 17) 11.
[131] Sunstein, 'Empirically Informed Regulation', (n 2) 1369.

for self-selection investment pensions.[132] It is questionable whether there are sufficient controls on the type and method of providing information to employees to properly meet the goals of the AE legislation. It seems that individuals are drawn to things that they can understand and are 'much more likely to be able to encode things that are presented in ways that relate directly to our personal experiences than to things presented in a more general and abstract way'.[133]

The type and quality of information given to individuals in relation to pension saving is important as even 'highly educated policy experts and government officials – would not absorb all the information we had sent them and thus would fail to arrive at decisions that maximized their self-interest'.[134] The government recognised the importance of information prior to the introduction of AE but this has been lost in implementation.[135] Pension statements can be difficult to read because of the long-term nature of the products but statements should be clear and avoid the use of jargon and contain salient illustrations.[136] There is some evidence, for example, that presenting statements with a monthly income figure rather than a total account balance would be useful and may increase individual contributions.[137] It should also be remembered that individuals demonstrate strong loss aversion and so may react strongly to short-term losses where these are disclosed.[138] This requires a careful balance in annual pension statements to ensure that individuals are given sufficient information to make decisions but recognising that they may also use the information inappropriately.

There is also some research from the US which indicates that the 'rich save more' and are more likely to seek financial advice.[139] Related to this is research from New Zealand which found that members with higher levels of education were more likely to contribute higher levels of salary to the KiwiSaver plan.[140] Where schemes are set up with a significant tax advantage or other incentives these groups are more likely to take full advantage of these than the target group.[141] The data, discussed in Chapter 5, also considers the situations where employees look for advice and the role of professional advisors for pensions. There is some research which indicates that those who take the advice of a professional will

[132] Benartzi and Thaler, 'Heuristics and Biases in Retirement Savings Behaviour', (n 35) 88.
[133] Institute for Government, 'Mindspace: Influencing Behaviour through Public Policy' 23.
[134] RH Thaler and W Tucker, 'Smarter Information, Smarter Consumers' (*Harvard Business Review* January/February 2013) https://hbr.org/2013/01/smarter-information-smarter-consumers.
[135] Department for Work and Pensions, *Automatic Enrolment- Information for Workers Qualitative Research* (DWP Communications Research Report 2, July 2011).
[136] LA Fleishman-Mayer et al, 'Designing Better Pension Benefits Statements: Current Status, Best Practices and Insights from the Field of Judgment and Decision Making' (*RAND*, April 2013) www.rand.org/content/dam/rand/pubs/working_papers/WR900/WR951/RAND_WR951.pdf, 5.
[137] Thaler and Tucker, 'Smarter Information, Smarter Consumer', (n 134) 48.
[138] Benartzi and Thaler, 'Heuristics and Biases in Retirement Savings Behaviour', (n 35) 94.
[139] KE Dynan, J Skinner and SP Zeldes, 'Do the Rich Save More?' (2004) 112 *Journal of Political Economy* 397, 438.
[140] New Zealand Treasury Working Paper 11/04, 12.
[141] ibid, 18–22.

contribute more but advice could be tied to a commitment to pay more in the future, like the Save More Tomorrow plan,[142] to increase the numbers of workers accepting professional advice.[143]

VI. Conclusion

The work of behavioural science has challenged many of the accepted economic norms, particularly when ordinary individuals are dealing with complex financial products such as pensions. This work suggests that individuals can be expected to demonstrate behavioural biases and traits in a predictable way and policy makers now attempt to frame policy in a way which anticipates these and corrects them. The UK has accepted that behavioural insights should inform policy and legislation and has introduced AE as a consequence of this. It has been argued that AE is soft paternalism and is the best type of policy intervention as it changes default positions whilst retaining individual choice. Whilst the legal regime specifies much of the detail of intervention, a crucial element, the actual pension plan design, is largely left to individual employers to determine. This adds a further layer and complexity to the policy as the choice architecture, or design of the range of choices available, is then created both by the legislators and the individual employers required to effect AE. Policy makers may themselves be subject to the same behavioural biases that the policy attempts to correct in individuals so this can result in varying consequences for the intended recipients of the intervention.

It has been argued that someone will always have to define the range of choices available and so to some extent soft paternalism and choice architecture are inevitable, but this does not mean that the AE legislation necessarily does at it was intended. It is important to consider the alternatives which were rejected, such as financial education, active choosing or an entirely paternalistic alternative where contributions are deducted like taxes and administered centrally by the government in evaluating the success of the AE policy.

Having decided to use choice architecture and introduce AE there are many unspecified elements in the legislation and it is not always clear which behavioural traits are targeted by AE and whether there are side effects or externalities. The policy of requiring default enrolment results in more people being members of a pension plan but the default options for contributions and investment may result in some individuals paying in less than if they had voluntarily joined the plan at a later date. Considering the justifications for legal intervention discussed in Chapter 3, it is necessary to consider whether individuals are better off, in their own opinion, as a consequence of the intervention. Whilst we can see the

[142] Thaler and Benartzi, 'Save More Tomorrow', (n 125).
[143] Benrtzi and Thaler, 'Heuristics and Biases in Retirement Savings Behaviour', (n 35).

benefit of increased numbers of savers, the costs are more complicated than the identified low cost of choosing to leave the scheme. Many of the behavioural traits remain and individuals become passive savers without making decisions for themselves. If this is the case, then it goes against the justification of the regime with reference to the preservation of choice. There may be additional associated costs such as over-reliance on defaults resulting in lower than expected savings. There is also evidence that the intervention may result in unintended consequences and inequalities where the non-target group for the policy reaps most reward.[144] These issues are explored in the next chapter which contains the findings from my qualitative empirical study and demonstrates evidence of some real costs associated with the form of AE implemented in the UK. Improvements to the regime might include a promise to pay more tomorrow or more effort to communicate effectively with employees to promote more active engagement and understanding of the choices available under pension plans and this is also considered in the next chapter.

It seems quite clear, however, that AE was introduced as a part of a general policy to help people to help themselves to save more for retirement. The underlying assumption is that by automatically enrolling people into a default saving plan, inertia will work in favour of saving but free choice will be preserved by the right to opt-out. However, the other identified behavioural traits may prevent operation of active choice and the default positions are inadequate to prevent harm to some individuals. If individuals are saving in greater volumes but save less than they would if they had made an active choice, then this must suggest that the policy could be improved. The next chapter will also consider what behavioural biases are in evidence when people discuss their workplace pensions, which should provide a greater understanding of the interaction between the AE policy intention and free choice.

[144] Gibson et al 'The Distributional Impact of KiwiSaver Incentives', (n 102) 128.

5

Empirical Research Findings

I. Introduction to the Research

This research considers the way that AE has been implemented in the UK. Low opt-out rates have resulted in the legislation being classed as a success, but I would argue that it is insufficient to evaluate the regime simply by considering the opt-out rate. This does not get to the root of whether inertia or active choice is the reason for current rates. Instead my work considers how this law is interpreted, applied and experienced and is focussed on the specific issues of implementation of AE. Previous chapters have identified the AE regime as paternalistic and reliant on the affected individuals identifying that they benefitted from the regime or exercising their free choice decisions preserved within the particular design of the scheme. Chapter 4 considered the use of choice architecture and the influences of default positions on choices. It was suggested that default positions would be difficult to move from and I have questioned the use of preservation of choice as a justification for the regime if people do not really understand that they have choices or make active decisions. The findings of my empirical study add to the evaluation of the true impact of AE on those most affected by it and identify whether costs exist beyond the intended small cost of having to opt-out if the worker does not like the policy. If AE intervenes with free choice, can we see how people act in response? The retention of the opt-out has served as justification for the regime and been referred to by the Department for Work and Pensions (DWP) as evidence of the success of the regime – as opt-out rates are low.[1] However, my work is more interested in whether active thinking and choices are being made as this is at the core of the justification. Opt-out rates might be low because individuals do not make active decisions and this might lead to unintended consequences. Consequently, the success of the regime might be limited if individuals do not actively make choices about contributions and investments and there may be negative consequences if individuals do not engage with the workplace pension as they would with other financial assets.

In discussing the regime with those affected by it, practical insight is gained into the legislative reality of the policy intention. My research also identifies potentially

[1] Department for Work and Pensions Automatic Enrolment Review 2017: Maintaining the Momentum Cm 9546, 29.

negative and unforeseen consequences. For example, there is some concern that the form of implementation of AE leaves too much discretion with the employer and that the default positions will be a strong influence over employees. This may result in a false sense of security where employees mistakenly believe that they are saving enough and do not seek further advice or engage with other options available to them.

This empirical research evaluates AE in a different way to the government's approach to review.[2] The government research focus has been on 'the context and constraints in which successes are achieved' and on timely delivery of the regime, operation of NEST, employers understanding of duties and to what extent saving is increased by the introduction of AE.[3] There is recognition of the need for engagement but this is largely focussed on information and messaging.[4] The current low opt-out rates have meant that the research focus has been to monitor the trends in saving and participation rather than examining how and what people choose – other than if they choose to opt-out. Essentially, whether AE increases pension participation and how this affects employers.[5] The right to opt-out is highlighted as preserving individual responsibility for the decision but the focus is on why individuals make the choice to opt-out and the role of information.[6] More recent evaluation[7] places more emphasis on the adequacy of saving but this does not address the difficulties of setting defaults as a replacement for thinking and the way this results in some employees paying in less than they would if they made more active choices. Some qualitative work has been undertaken to consider employers' views on AE and the reasons why employees had chosen to opt-out from those employers.[8] The specific research aims were focussed on those who had chosen to opt-out and in identifying how the decision to opt-out had come about.[9] The research questions were designed to 'support the DWP in creating policy that succeeds in changing retirement savings behaviour'.[10] This research used qualitative interviews with employers and those employees who had chosen to opt-out as well as analysis of data provided by the employers. It was large scale and followed earlier qualitative research with large employers with a similar focus.[11]

[2] Department for Work and Pensions Long-term Income and Evaluation Team, *Workplace Pension Reforms Evaluation Strategy* (Research Report No764, Department for Work and Pensions, July 2011).

[3] ibid, 7.

[4] Maintaining the Momentum (n 1), 75–77.

[5] Department for Work and Pensions, 'Official Statistics on Workplace Pension Participation and Saving Trends of Eligible Employees: Broken Down by Sector and Other Characteristics' (October 2014); Workplace Pension Participation and Savings Trends of Eligible Employees Official Statistics: 2009 to 2019 (June 2020).

[6] Department for Work and Pensions, *Automatic Enrolment Evaluation Report* (Research Report No 887, November 2014) 27.

[7] Department for Work and Pensions Automatic Enrolment Review 2017: Analytical Report December 2017, 69; Maintaining the Momentum (n 1), 30.

[8] Department for Work and Pensions, *Automatic Enrolment: Qualitative Research with Employers Staging in 2014* (Research Report No 889, January 2015).

[9] ibid, 27.

[10] ibid, 28.

[11] Department for Work and Pensions, 'Automatic Enrolment Opt Out Rates: Findings from Research with Large Employers' (August 2013) https://assets.publishing.service.gov.uk/government/uploads/system/uploads/attachment_data/file/227039/opt-out-research-large-employers-ad_hoc.pdf.

The findings reported here are instead focussed on the whole experience of implementing pension change and, in particular, how employees deal with information and choices. In speaking to employees who are still in a workplace pension as well as those who have opted-out, there is a wider scope to consider all of the engagement and decision-making process. To opt-out you must have engaged with the literature or information on some level, but my focus is on how pensions are considered by employees in the workplace, what choices are being made and why. My data shows that many employees do not engage on any level with their workplace pension, may not even be aware that they are in a pension, how much they pay or that they can choose to opt-out. This goes to the heart of the justification question 'If AE is justified by the preservation of choice is this recognised and effective for those affected by the regime?' To fully evaluate the regime it is necessary to try and understand what people think about their pensions and how decisions are made or not, rather than just look at those who have already made a choice to leave and assuming that the others have chosen to stay. The employer's experience is also important as this directly impacts on the employees' experience and the relationship, so the research includes data from an employer perspective from medium-sized employers. This also led me to conduct interviews with product providers and financial advisors as their role is not always clear but might directly impact employees' decision making as well. Examples of the relationships between information, understanding and decision making are explored in my work. To obtain this information, qualitative rather than quantitative research was most appropriate 'to identify the perspectives of research participants'.[12] The data I wish to consider is also not readily available presently and must be created through qualitative methods. I can contrast this to the situation where research focusses on what happened rather than why.[13]

II. Research Design and Methodology

The research aims to explore the justification for the introduction of AE and a key part of this is whether the individuals involved legitimise the paternalistic intervention by agreeing with the change. The only way to obtain employees' views, and an understanding of how decisions are made and the implementation received, is to talk to the employees. The question of justification for paternalism, the reasons given during development of AE and the role of behavioural economics were considered in conducting and analysing the data. This work does not claim to be a population representative sample but when considering sampling I asked

[12] S Milikene, I Gaizauskaite and N Valaviciene, 'Qualitative Interviewing: Field-Work Realities' (2013) 12 *Social Work* 49, 50.

[13] G Shah Goda, D Jones, C Flaherty Manchester, 'Retirement Plan Type and Employee Mobility: The Role of Selection and Incentive Effects' (National Bureau of Economic Research Working Paper No 18902, March 2013) www.nber.org/papers/w18902.

'what are my cases and what do they represent?'[14] My cases are evidence of the interplay between employees, employers and advisors in relation to workplace pensions in the context of AE. As my work aims to evaluate the implementation of AE considering some real life accounts, it is not necessary to show that the majority of the population agree with those reported here as I can demonstrate that the data produced from those sampled is of good quality and depth and reflects their views. I used purposive sampling to build on data as it was collected allowing me to test and consider developing themes and issues arising from earlier chapters and to compare data within groups and against other groups. This forms part of the category of theoretical sampling as developed by Glaser and Strauss,[15] but which has been applied beyond this to 'Select cases or case groups according to concrete criteria concerning their content instead of using abstract methodological criteria. Sampling proceeds according to the relevance of cases instead of their representativeness.'[16]

Having identified that I would like to speak to workers with different jobs, age and gender I tried to add to my sample where I identified gaps. Purposive sampling within this frame of gradual selection was used to consider implementation of AE, choosing particularly successful or unsuccessful cases to study and analyse. My medium sample is sufficient to compare responses between groups and identify links between emerging themes.[17] I arranged to speak to a number of individuals involved in human resources roles (HR) or management functions at medium-sized employers with employees in Scotland and England. I gave each an information request which was sent out to employees and I conducted interviews with those employees who responded at their workplace during working hours. There was an element of snowballing as, in some cases, an interview respondent recommended me to someone else who I then contacted and they agreed to speak to me. Most of the interviews were face to face and some were over the telephone. Some employees gave me copies of pension scheme information which allowed me to compare the factual situation to individual perception, as described during the interview. Some employees also brought in pension documentation which I read and added to interview notes. The main interviews took place over the period 2014 to 2015. I spoke to individuals of different ages and genders working in different roles, in different sectors across different parts of Scotland and some in England. The data from these interviews provided a broad range of opinions from employees of different ages and skills. As well as speaking to employees, I interviewed employers, HR professionals, financial and legal advisors involved in implementing and providing advice on the regime. Not all of the employees I spoke to had

[14] U Flick, *An Introduction to Qualitative Research* 4th edn (Sage, 2009) 404.

[15] B Glaser and L Strauss, *The Discovery of Grounded Theory: Strategies for Qualitative Research* (Taylor and Francis, 2000).

[16] Flick, *An Introduction to Qualitative Research*, (n 14) 121.

[17] SE Baker and R Edwards, 'How Many Qualitative Interviews is Enough? Expert Voices and Early Career Reflections on Sampling and Cases in Qualitative Research' (National Centre for Research Methods Review Paper, 2012) 9.

been auto-enrolled but all had to make decisions relating to a workplace pension of one sort or another. I also reviewed materials provided by employers and some of the employees in order to compare these to responses by employees about what information they were given, which adds some element of triangulation. Further verification was achieved by comparing responses by employees and employer representatives from the same organisation.

Semi-structured interviews were recorded and the audio recording was used to produce detailed transcripts.[18] Whilst I have been as consistent as possible in my method of collection, analysis and reporting I acknowledge that social life cannot always be fixed to rules and, that participant accounts, however transcribed or reported, may not be accurate.[19] People like to please and will give the most interesting aspects of their life and so analysis must account for this.[20] I have tried to address this by asking all participants to reflect on how the experience of speaking to me has made them feel about their pension and reported on this in my findings. I have also tried to focus on actions and decisions rather than opinions about abstract concepts. As with all qualitative research my analysis was conducted on an ongoing basis on different levels. The data was reduced in the process of transcription and notes, described as I added headings and summaries and created initial codes. The coding was refined continually as I collected and analysed more data. I used thematic analysis to interpret the data that was generated.[21] Attride-Stirling suggests that presenting data which has been thematically analysed, using thematic networks is useful for presentation and developing the analysis further. This seeks to 'unearth' themes at different levels and enhance the reader's understanding of the data and where the researcher's findings come from and how these relate to each other.[22] This approach involves identifying basic themes, then organising these into larger groups known as organising themes and then deducing the global theme.[23]

III. Findings

Thirty-eight semi-structured interviews of a qualitative nature were conducted. This included employees, employer representatives, providers and advisors. At the first stage of analysis I set up nodes or themes based on my research questions as I assumed that I would have some data relating to these themes given the questions

[18] M Hammersley, 'Reproducing or Constructing? Some Questions about Transcription in Social Research' (2010) 10 Qualitative Research 553.

[19] WS Knapp, 'On the Validity of Accounts about Everyday Life' (1981) 29 *Sociological Review* 543.

[20] S Halliday and P Schmidt, *Conducting Law and Society Research, Reflections on Methods and Practices* (Cambridge University Press, 2009) 22.

[21] K Roulston, 'Data Analysis and "Theorising as Ideology"' (2001) 1(3) *Qualitative Research* 279–302, 279.

[22] Attride-Stirling, 'Thematic Networks' (2001) 1(3) *Qualitative Research* 385–405.

[23] M Nind et al, 'Methodological Innovation and Research Ethics: Forces in Tension or Forces in Harmony?' (2012) 13 *Qualitative Research* 650.

I was asking. Further coding was added as I progressed to deal with data which did not fit into these themes or issues. I then considered the broader themes that were supported by the data and have illustrated this using a technique of 'thematic networks'.[24] This process involved going through all of the coded text and identifying issues discussed under each node and then condensing this into summarised themes of the discussion. These themes are described by Attride-Stirling as 'basic themes' which are then organised into larger 'organising themes'.[25] Using this I have identified five broader 'global themes' which describe the data[26] namely:

(1) Action.
(2) Barriers to Decisions.
(3) Intervention and Implementation thereof.
(4) Engagement and Understanding.
(5) Trust.

Figure 1 Thematic Networks from the Data

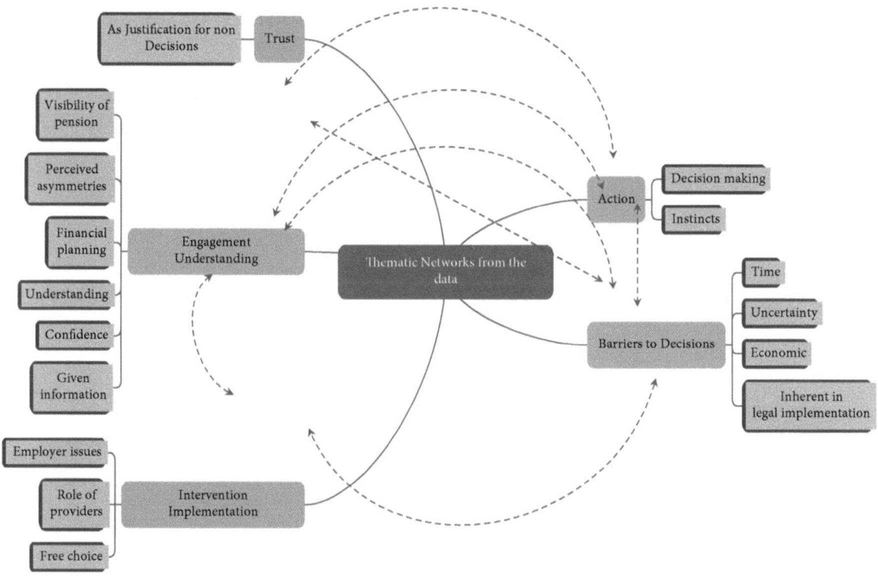

My findings are reported from the perspective of these five themes, which are reported under separate headings, rather than describing responses from employees versus employer's perspective. In this way I can consider the issues as they arise from all angles and allow the reader to consider the data for themselves in its coded form.

[24] Attride-Stirling, 'Thematic Networks' (n 22).
[25] ibid, 392.
[26] See figure 1.

A. Action

Following the justification for the introduction of AE discussed in Chapters 2, 3 and 4 (preservation of choice), I thought it was important to ask individuals about actions they had taken, not taken and perceived as being taken by others. If individual free choice legitimises the policy, then I was interested to understand how people act in relation to workplace pensions and what influences this action. The question of individual autonomy is central here and this data has clear links to the rest of my work. When discussing pension scheme actions, my respondents discussed: the level of contributions, extra member contributions, the question of joining the scheme or not, pension transfers, investment of fund choice, staying in or opting out of auto-enrolment, salary sacrifice arrangements, checking payments and seeking advice. This global theme[27] describes how interview respondents discuss their own action or inaction relating to pensions. Two main strands of discussion took place: those relating to instinctive action and those describing what influenced the decision-making process. This links to behavioural economics, discussed in Chapter 4, and the question of autonomy versus paternalism, discussed in Chapter 3.

Figure 2 Global Theme: Action

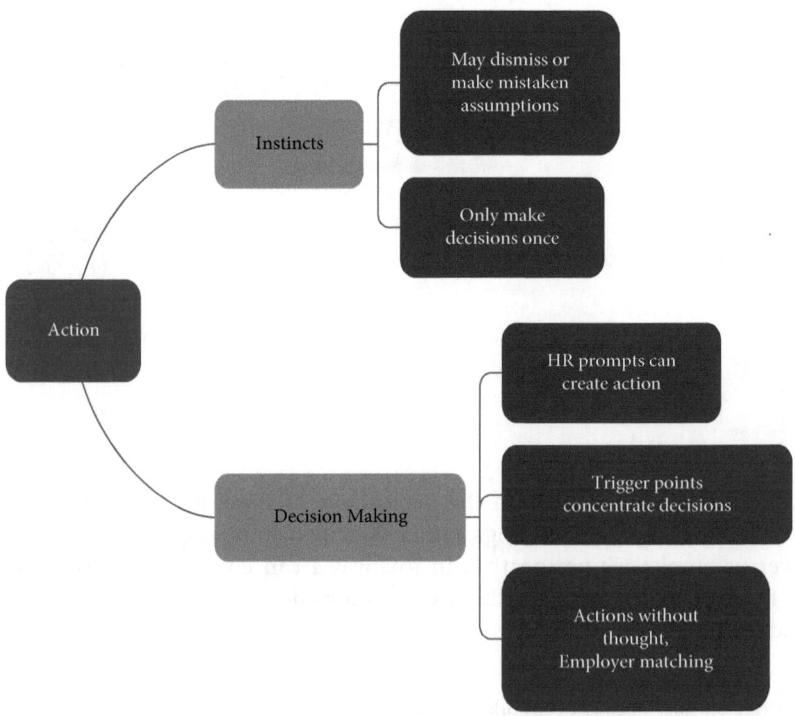

[27] See figure 2.

Considering first of all the decision-making process it is clear that sometimes a 'choice' is made without any action by the individual. Many respondents reported paying contributions at the default contribution level. One company had a policy of a minimum three per cent salary contribution by both employer and employees which the employer would match up to six per cent. When I discussed choice of contribution level with employees of the company, many respondents knew that the company would match their contributions but were unsure what percentage of salary they actually paid, how much that was in monetary terms or what the maximum matching percentage was. One individual who had been auto-enrolled had chosen to pay three per cent of salary in contributions on a matching basis but was considering getting an increase to get the benefit of employer matching up to six per cent. Another confidently stated that they paid one per cent over the matching amount but were less certain what that translated to as a percentage of salary. This illustrates the anchor effect, discussed in Chapter 4, where the setting of a minimum level acts as an anchor with the matching maximum also operating as a ceiling. Others simply picked a number explaining 'I didn't do any research or if I put this I'll get this amount …. perhaps I should have. But I only just thought oh I'll just double it to an affordable amount …' This clearly illustrates a number of behaviours prioritising affordability now without considering what value this creates in retirement and also a lack of engagement with illustrations and other literature that was provided to assist in the process of establishing a good contribution level.

It also seems that employees' inaction may result in more changes than simply being auto-enrolled. For practical purposes, pension benefits are often not described in the contract of employment but by reference to the benefits handbook. This makes updates easier if the handbook is changed without requiring a contractual change to the employment contract, but it also means that changes can be effected without action or agreement of the employee. For example, this might be to increase contributions if the AE legislation subsequently requires it or to change the definition of pensionable pay. Such changes would still need to be communicated to the employees but they would not need 'Action.' This practice was described by HR professionals and product providers. When I asked about the process of having forms returned one advisor replied that 'If we go back to the retrospective exercise then that [information of changes] just gets sent out and saying this is now part of your terms and conditions … you don't have to sign anything.' This was described as preferable to the process of getting forms signed and returned as that can be difficult but it does highlight the scope of possible action without engagement by the individual.

Another example of inaction was described by one HR manager when discussing seasonal summer workers who had all been auto-enrolled and stayed in the pension. The explanation given by the HR manager was that they had not read any of the information they had been given about it. She described how employees got online payslips every month which they had to open as a document. This contained the information about pension contribution deductions.

The HR manager described how she had to open these online payslips for employees when they came in to see her with queries as the employees did not realise they had them or at least had never opened them. In this situation, summer student workers might have decided that they wanted to stay in the pension but it is also possible that they had not opened the given information and were not aware that they were in the scheme until they left employment at the end of the summer or at a later date.

This may result in individuals having multiple pension pots which they lose track of. Whilst deferment might be used by employers to avoid this issue for summer students and those on short-term contracts initially, employers may be prohibited from applying a further deferment to the same individual if they are employed again the following year as this might be considered part of an ongoing contract of employment. Each case will depend on its own facts and employment law advice is generally needed in these circumstances to clarify whether the individual can be subject to further postponement. This is also the case for agency workers who might be employed on multiple short-term contracts. One employer that I spoke to acknowledged the difficulties of dealing with the shorter term agency workers. Often a postponement period is used for those workers as this allowed the agency to identify whether the agency worker would stay on the placement or not. Further research on the impact of AE and the decision-making process for short-term workers would be useful.

One interesting theme coming from the data is that people seem to view action as something which is final and does not need to be revisited. This is an example of status quo bias which was discussed in Chapter 4. One respondent illustrates: 'Yeah, I pretty much made the decision then and haven't looked at it since … I think it was just the knowledge of you have a pension and that was that.'

Another on the question of investment of fund choice said 'I forgot that I was in the low risk until I was talking to you now.' This illustrates that if the individual cannot remember what decisions have been made, they are unlikely to revisit them because they have changed their mind. Some kind of trigger, intervention or prompt is needed to encourage ongoing dynamic decision making. Intervention by HR or trigger points such as receiving information can prompt further action and so this might be something that could be implemented as an improvement to the policy. Even something as simple as a twelve-month review and affirmation of decisions might promote more engagement and active decision making. One respondent, who had such a review, explained that he was going to change the contribution level and investment fund at their review if he could: 'They must contact you somehow after 12 months and … there must be a window that I can make a change.'

This individual, whilst sketchy on some of the detail knew that there was a trigger point coming and was considering how to respond. Not all employers will have a formal review process but this might be something that should be required to ensure that employees revisit previous decisions or lack of action. Employers introducing higher contributions or matching was also reported as something which prompted action:

> Maybe the matching only came in at that point … That might be what triggered me to go and speak to the pensions advice guy. There must have been some reason because I am a little bit lazy.

Some employees described actions without any real thought. One respondent described the basis of current contributions to pension:

> as simple as that's what the company was going to match … so it was more just to get the benefit out of the company but it does leave me a bit concerned if I actually sat down and thought is that going to leave me enough at the end. That probably would have been worthwhile doing.

Matching seems to produce a strong anchor with respondents perceiving matching as a reasonable contribution level. Several respondents indicated that they would increase contributions if the employer did as well, even if it was a high level. As one respondent commented: 'I thought eight percent … so that was quite a lot you know … but then if that's the rules then you sign it and that's the end of it, you just get on with it.'

Action also occurs where no real decision making has taken place but an instinctive response chooses action. This can be a positive thing where the individual believes pensions are a good thing but it can also cause the individual to make a choice without really considering it. One individual was in a low risk fund although they were young and might have been better off choosing a higher risk fund, like a colleague who was also risk averse but had taken advice. Anchoring effects were also observed with some describing the fund chosen as the default as they are risk averse and 'the high risk was too much for me'. This assumed that the default was most suitable for them irrespective of age, fund size or years to retirement and assumed that anything else was high risk. Others describe fund transfers as automatic: 'well it was sort of done for us, we got it done automatically … because it happened to everybody'. A respondent from the same company described the same event but explained that they had been asked to choose whether to switch to the other provider. Why would both employees have a different view of the circumstances of change of pension provider? The answer may lie in lack of understanding or lack of engagement by the first respondent or maybe an instinctive decision was made as she assumed there was really no choice to be made as her employer was presenting the new company as better value. This also ties into the question of making decisions and then forgetting them. Other respondents made assumptions that AE did not affect them and therefore ignored all the information they were given, even though some of these assumptions were wrong. There is a strong connection between action and engagement and understanding. A recent report in the US demonstrates that such poor judgements might mean that individuals end up working longer than they expected.[28] This is a clear cost to the individual if a default position prevents active engagement and leaves the individual disappointed in years' to come.

B. Barriers to Decisions

This theme[29] explores the question: if actions are limited to instinctive or default decisions what are the barriers which prevent individuals making decisions for themselves? Many reasons were given for individuals remaining in default funds or contribution levels or otherwise failing to make active decisions in relation to their pension. Four broad sub-themes were identified as barriers: inherent legal requirements, time, economics and uncertainty.

Figure 3 Global Theme: Barriers to Decisions

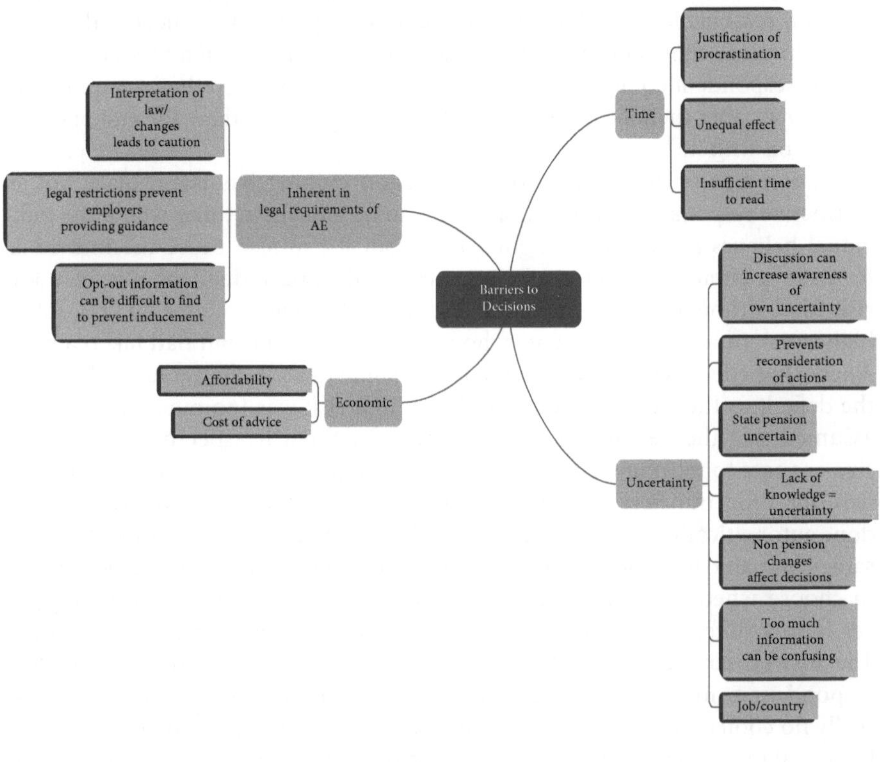

[28] S Banerjee, *The Gap between Expected and Actual Retirement: Evidence from Longitudinal Data* (Employee Benefit Research Institute, November 2014).

[29] See figure 3.

i. Inherent Legal Barriers in the Regime

The sheer volume of pension changes and legislation was mentioned by some as a reason for uncertainty. One respondent explained:

> In my head the problem is the Government keeps changing … they seem to change the rules all the time … I am very confused … I guess I am a bit sceptical as to what I'll actually get in the end because the rules will have changed by the time I retire.

Legal requirements may also prevent understanding. The Employment Rights Act 1996 requires employers to provide information on pensions in the written employment contract and to provide AE information to third parties, including personal data. So, whilst AE might be seamless if pension changes are effected through benefit booklets, contractual changes might still be required to ensure compliance with other parts of the employment law regime including consent to disclosure of personal information under AE. This adds to the layers of information given to employees about change. To protect jobholders from attempts by their employers to influence their decisions, a jobholder can only obtain an opt-out notice from the scheme into which he has been auto-enrolled. This is usually the pension provider rather than the employer to ensure that the employer does not induce employees to opt-out of AE. Employers are also prevented from providing what can be construed as financial advice on such matters. As a consequence, employers may err on the side of caution when providing written communications or discussing directly with employees to prevent enforcement action by the Pensions Regulator. This can pose difficulties for the relationship and prevent decisions being made. One respondent reported:

> I just found out how to opt-out actually yesterday when I tried to find more email and I found the assessment letter that was sent to me and it was like the end of the pages, five pages where they are so the only place I can see how do I opt-out … but it is just it was inside the attachment of the email which I wasn't that aware and I had to find out. I mean they don't really highlight how do you opt-out within the email. I wish it could be easier to find.

A representative of the HR team from the same company said:

> The interview pack has information and they get an email with their personal details and they need to log in and try and find the opt-out information. It's not easy to find – I was looking for it and it was difficult to find. Lots of people may not know that they can opt-out and won't look for it and many won't even have logged on.

One advisor also admits that 'Unfortunately from my perspective rather than trying to help with engaging people it is just a compliance issue making sure that the employer doesn't fall foul.' Another member of HR explained:

> Even just trying to get the letters back from people was tricky … they thought if they didn't sign it they didn't have to be auto-enrolled … We are not allowed to advise people what to do so it's quite a tricky situation … So I had several people and every week

> they would come up and try – can I come out of it yet? -. No you can't because we need to auto-enrol you first and then you'll get the comms and it will tell you your options … but we could not do anything beyond that because we are not meant to be advising people to come out of it.

Some HR employees believed that this will result in people failing to opt-out but will instead stop making payments sometime after the opt-out date. This will make the administration process more difficult for employers, who must keep accurate records, and will result in increasing numbers of small pension pots. My research demonstrates that an element of knowledge is required for individuals to know that they have a choice to opt-out and that they should look for the way to do this. They also need to be proactive in this and I will discuss this later in relation to knowledge and information generally. The third aspect here is that a usual source of assistance, the HR department, feels constrained in helping employees in this situation should they later be accused of providing financial advice or inducing opt-outs in breach of legal requirements.

The administration of the enrolment and opt-out being with the product provider rather than within the control of the employer might also pose issues relating to lack of awareness. One HR respondent explained:

> We've had some anomalies but probably the most significant one so far has been people on the leadership team who have reached their lifetime allowance … So we basically had to put their pension contributions to zero so they would not exceed their allowance and then with auto-enrolment coming in we've had problems because the system wants to enrol them again and if it does that and shows a contribution then they've obviously exceeded their allowance.

This refers to employees with protection from the lifetime allowance cap on pension funds. In this case anyone identified as potentially at risk of losing the allowance was referred to the financial advisor who came into the place of work which allowed the employer to stay out of danger of the inducement prohibition but ensures that employees are made aware of the issue. However, not all employers will have resources to provide such financial advice or the technical expertise to identify such issues and protect valuable allowances.

A further issue arising from compliance is that some individuals may be contractually enrolled at the point of joining service. Contractual enrolment can be used by an employer to avoid the administrative burden of continually assessing the workforce to ensure that individuals are auto-enrolled at the point they satisfy the trigger conditions. It works by amendment to contractual terms so that employees must join a qualifying pension scheme on commencement of employment. In this situation, the pension is seen as a condition of employment and the opportunity for decision making is diminished as the right to opt-out does not exist. The individual may choose to leave under the scheme rules and has the right to cancel the contract during the statutory 'cooling-off' period in accordance with FCA rules but action in this situation is dependent on the employee reading the information given to them about the pension.

ii. Time

The organising theme of time came up in my research in two different ways. Time was used by respondents as a justification for indecision or putting off revisiting decisions as many felt that they had so much time before retirement that the issue was not immediate or pressing. The fact that the benefit is so far away allows all sorts of variables as to what might happen to come into consideration:

> I mean let's be honest, we don't know whether I'm going to get a pension or not. Whether I'll be alive at that point or not, whether the pension age might have been increased to 70, because previously it was 60 and now it is 65.

Access to the pension at a particular time of life is also important to some and influences saving 'So they've allowed me access to that when I'm fifty five' which was important to this individual who wanted to use the money for a special holiday at that stage in life. The motivation to be able to spend money on a holiday at this stage also motivated this respondent to understand the pension policy, funding and access issues. Another comments that 'with TESSAs and ISAs if you had a little bit of capital you would put it in there … but I don't want to put it in that [pension] because I actually want to put it into something I can see, I can feel'. Another respondent comments on the value of advice in the future saying:

> Advisors are people who are trained by other people and the market changes, advice changes, thinking changes and I really think it's a load of old rubbish, frankly … The people delivering it are always sincere … but that does not mean that it will continue to be the truth.

Another time factor relates to the theme of understanding, as many reported that they did not have enough time to read the information given to allow better understanding of their pension and the issues and choices they had. One said, 'I haven't entered in yet not because I don't want to it's I just haven't had time to read all the information and make a decision yet.' This individual works for an employer about to go through AE so the procrastination of joining will not work for long but they may not get around to reading the AE information either. This is strongly related to the form of information, financial education and the individual's perception of themselves, as some individuals perceive that it will take a very long time for them to understand their position and that they do not have the free time to allocate to that task. An individual who reported to be happy with the information given said, 'It is the sort of thing you know at some point in the next few years I should sit down and spend a day you know looking at it and making more informed decisions.'

Another also commented that they 'don't really want to spend two hours doing such a thing [reading pensions information pack]'. This brings us back to the behavioural biases described in Chapter 4 and particularly the tendency for individuals to procrastinate and the importance of framing information. Procrastination was one part of the reason for the introduction of the regime, as described in Chapters 2 and 3, and here we can see clear evidence that the introduction of AE makes procrastination work differently. However, it does not necessarily mean that this is better for the individual but that the default position imposed by AE replaces the individual's previous default position. This research attempts to consider whether the default could be further improved by encouraging positive action.

Another interesting discussion related to the fact that there is no point spending any time thinking about a pension until there is a reasonable sum in it. This was reiterated by financial advisors:

> you're not going to be overly motivated if you're saving £20 per month into a pension saying I don't know if I need to speak to someone but you'll be very motivated if you've got £100,000 in a pot going what am I supposed to do with this … I think it is just down to the numerical amount and the pension and of course the imminent issue.

Effectively there is no point thinking about the investment until it has been going for a while. Employers must also spend time in order to implement AE and the amount of time available may vary the consequences for employees. Some of the larger employers with more time or manpower might make more effort on information sessions where others may only be able to provide the statutory minimum which may again impact the individual.

iii. Economics/Financial

The economic barriers and influential factors discussed under this heading included: the seeking of financial advice and who would pay for it, tax incentives, affordability of contributions, debts, employer matching and other financial priorities. Affordability will override many other considerations: 'I didn't do any research … perhaps I should have. But I only just thought oh I'll just double it to an affordable amount.'

Mortgage and student loan debt was also viewed as a priority to be paid before any (let alone extra) contributions were made to a pension. Some individuals might be better off seeking professional help to discuss overall finances rather than simply paying the maximum affordable pension contribution. It may be better to pay off expensive debts first and reducing pension contributions in the short term, but individuals are not keen to seek this sort of advice. Even where individuals have an understanding of interest, inflation and risk/return this may not encourage them to consider financial planning for retirement.[30] Some providers acknowledge the issue: 'It would be foolish to solely consider your pension savings when you've clearly got other immediate debt problems.'

The same can be said for those with a large pension pot value who have protected the 'pot' against future reductions to the lifetime allowance for tax purposes.

[30] Crossan et al 'Financial literacy and retirement planning in New Zealand' (2011) 10(4) *Journal of Pension Economics & Finance* 619, 634.

When such an agreement is in place with HMRC the individual cannot make any further pension contribution or the protection is lost and so the onus is on the individual in this situation to ensure that they are not prejudiced by AE. Employers are cautious about prompting employees to check this for fear of breaching the inducement provisions. However, with the retail distribution review and upfront payment for financial advice, the cost of advice can no longer be absorbed within pensions and for many the fees will be too great. This results in wealthier individuals, such as higher rate taxpayers and employers, being advised on their financial needs but the lowest paid workers are without any advice. Research from abroad supports this, indicating that the poorest workers expecting to have the state funded pension as a main source of income or those with poorer health are unlikely to seek advice.[31]

More general financial considerations aside, you might think that it is always good to be contributing to a pension but financial advice might help the individual have a more realistic expectation and perhaps encourage action to increase contributions over the years. Financial advice may become more important to employees as retirement approaches when a pot of cash has been saved but it is too late to change the size of the pot significantly at this stage. Anchors also come into play here as many individuals refer to the employer matching amount and base their own contributions relative to this without further consideration as to personal circumstances and the appropriateness of the amount paid. Advice is considered again under part D, Engagement and Understanding, below.

iv. Uncertainty

Respondents described uncertainty about many aspects of their pension arrangements. It seems that discussing past decisions (even those made quite recently) can increase the individual's awareness of his uncertainty, too much information can be confusing and lead to further uncertainty, changes (even if they appear not to directly relate to pensions) can cause uncertainty which can prevent pension decision making and the unpredictable nature of the state pension sometimes causes confusion and concern about private pension arrangements as well. One individual explained:

> Can I be completely honest with you and because of what has happened with pensions and this increase in pensionable age and when you can retire and with the economy I do very much wonder why I am bothering to pay quite a large chunk of my monthly salary into a pension that ultimately might only be worth pennies in 25/30 years' time.

The question of what or whether the individual would get a pension was mentioned by other respondents. Another talked about the changeability of life and the world and how this meant that advice is not durable or worthwhile, no matter how well intentioned the advice. Another mentioned the recent global financial crisis and

[31] New Zealand Treasury Working Paper 11/04, Law et al 'KiwiSaver: An initial Evaluation of the Impact on Retirement Saving.'

how the banks had not managed well so what would happen to pension companies if a similar thing impacted them? Tax restrictions and changes about how much pension could be taken when were also a source of some confusion although those most motivated to benefit from tax reliefs are higher rate taxpayers and may be more inclined to seek advice. Some reported uncertainty about the constantly changing pension policy as a reason not to trust that the pension was worth relying on:

> At the moment the problem, in my head the problem is the government keep changing. I don't know how much it affects them, whether it affects my pension but they seem to change the rules all the time and bringing in new things or taxing it differently and I am very confused about how things are taxed .... I guess I am a bit sceptical as to what I will actually get in the end because what rules will have changed by the time I retire and what the government will have dreamed of or decided to let us have and that will change so many times in the next 30 years.

Respondents were often uncertain about the level of contributions that they paid, whether transfers had been completed, who to ask for further information or the charges that applied to their pension fund. Security of funds was also an unknown being described as a gamble by one respondent. Uncertainty about the current factual position can lead to individuals failing to reconsider decisions, such as the level of contributions. For example:

> Well to be honest I thought I was paying five per cent ... so I had to query that because it came back and said it was 2.2%, I was thinking why on earth would I suggest 2.2% but anyway that's what they said so ....

Here a lack of certainty led the respondent to leave the position unchallenged. Another reported, 'I actually don't know at the moment whether, I'm assuming that it's not up and running because I haven't investigated things' and another noted that, 'Yes you have to decide, or well maybe they pay into it automatically and I have to decide whether I want to pay in I think that's maybe what it is.'

Here the link between uncertainty/assumptions and inaction can be seen clearly. This will be elaborated further when considering the question of engagement. In some cases of uncertainty the respondent will, instead of checking the position, convince themselves that a particular version of events is true rather than admit the uncertainty and try and resolve it. This exchange illustrates the point:

> Interviewer: And so what percentage of contribution do you pay?
> Interview Respondent: I can't remember.
> Interviewer: Can't remember.
> Interview Respondent: I think it's the maximum that I can.
> Interviewer: Okay.
> Interview Respondent: It's the equivalent to what is now mandatory, as far as I understand.

Here the individual does not know what percentage of contributions they pay but convinces themselves that it is the maximum that they can be so no further action is needed. Uncertainty about the state pension was also reported as motivational by some encouraging the individual to contribute to the private workplace pension. However, misunderstandings about the difference and interaction between state and private pensions and retirement ages was also problematic. One respondent talking of a workplace pension confused its rules with the state pension system: 'But realistically by the time I'm 67, it is probably going to be 76 [when we can retire]. We'll be working until we die.'

Others simply expressed a hope to get something whilst some were heavily reliant on the state pension. The state pension has undergone a significant and public change as part of the policy of pension changes generally and so it is, perhaps, unsurprising that most respondents see it as 'uncertain'. Individuals were also uncertain about the implications of contractual changes that they had consented to in some cases. For example:

> Interview Respondent: We now get the, I can't remember what it is called, something to do with the tax and NI.
> Interviewer: Salary sacrifice?
> Interview Respondent: I think the company now pay the equivalent of that to your pension as well.
> Interviewer: Yes.
> Interview Respondent: I can't remember exactly how it works but we get the benefit of it.

In this example, the contractual change to effect salary sacrifice had been agreed and the individual was uncertain of the details but instinctively thought it was for their benefit and did not need to consider it further. This might also imply an element of trust in the employer to implement beneficial changes. Other uncertainties which prevented decision making was reported relating to job security and whether the individual would remain in the UK for their careers. Often respondents were uncertain about the charges and costs associated with their workplace pension or whether the financial advisor who came to speak to them was independent or not.

C. Intervention and Implementation

This global theme[32] deals with discussion of the practical aspects of implementing the regime and how the intervention is perceived. There were three subthemes which emerged under this global theme namely: employer issues, the role of product providers and the question of free choice.

i. Employer Issues

Some employers are seeking professional help to ensure compliance with AE but not all employers have the same resources available to apply to the task

[32] See figure 4.

Figure 4 Global Theme: Intervention/Implementation

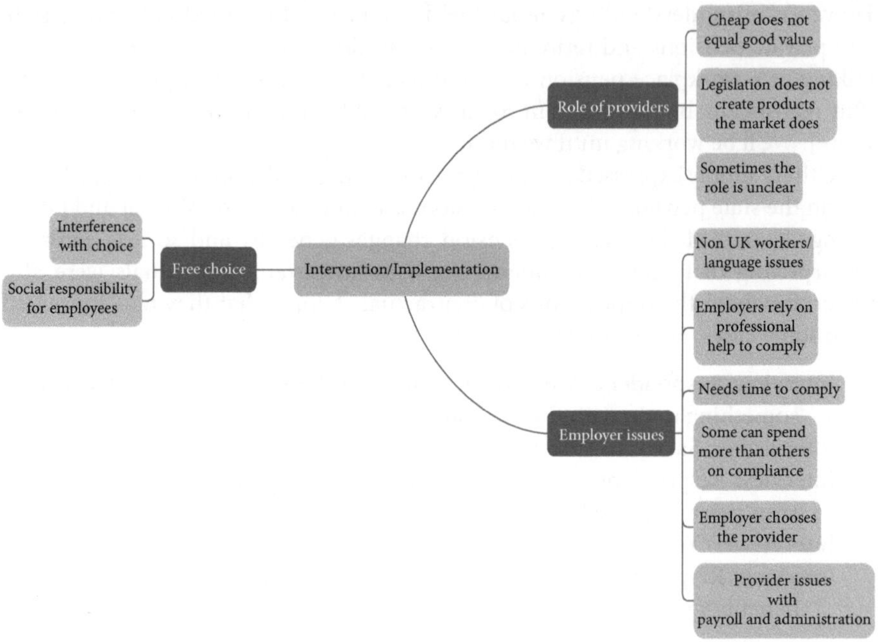

of implementation. For example, one employer representative described putting together a team to deal with AE where one of the HR team spent 50 per cent of her time dealing with AE in the seven months leading up to introduction. Employers and providers need time to work out issues but this may not always be available as Pensions Regulator sanctions are a real concern. Management of employee data can also be time consuming to ensure compliance with data protection requirements and to ensure that the various administration systems accept the form of data.

As described by one product provider:

> I've got a lot of sympathy for them [employers] because they have really been reliant on these payroll companies saying look this is what we need from you and … it's the employer's responsibility, the employers duties … but they've been told by their Payroll company that they will have this information in the format that [provider] require by this date then they've got no reason to doubt that until we got to the real staging months … When it became clear that the data wasn't in the format … That's at the point they were let down.

Employers listed a number of issues related to AE compliance: creating communications, organising and hosting briefings, checking the payroll and other systems and testing them pre-staging, overriding problems with incompatible systems and identifying problem areas or groups of individuals needing extra attention. Some were concerned that providers are not fully functional for AE and worried about the continuous three-year re-enrolment. Employers rely on product providers to deal directly with their employees but problems are often brought back directly to the HR department at the employer as they are easy to access. One employer talked about an employee who came in with documentation for two policies that had been created for him in error and wanted HR to fix it. Someone had to engage with the provider to sort it out and ensure one was properly cancelled and no contributions held for it but the HR representative felt that they could not get involved as the mistake was between the provider and the employee. As indicated above,[33] employers find it difficult to tread the path between providing information and falling foul of the inducement to opt-out provisions of the legislation.[34]

Not all employers will have the resources available to stay on top of compliance and the increased labour costs will affect some more than others. One legal advisor commented on inducement provisions and difficulties where contractual changes are needed:

> I think lots of employers don't know they exist as they are more concerned with putting the contributions in … I hope people are sitting down and having sensible conversations about it … I think people are getting advice from payroll specialists and accountants rather than lawyers.

Lack of expertise can be particularly difficult where there are non-standard situations such as foreign workers who need more support to understand the process and options. Many UK employers will have many staff where English is not their first language and so this additional barrier operates alongside the other behavioural barriers. One employer commented that:

> I think yes they are not reading it. Also they have a lot of overseas employees so I think people from the UK would have a better grasping of it whereas we've got lots of different nationalities … so even the concept of a pension or contributions … it's done obviously completely differently.

There was also a reported lack of clarity on non-standard enrolment. Issues such as maternity pay and salary sacrifice payments often needed bespoke solutions which were not included in the administration offering by providers and required checks and workarounds which is labour intensive. Employers also felt that there was a lack of guidance on payroll issues and seemed worried about this as the Pensions Regulator has issued a number of enforcement notices, mostly related to problems with administration and payroll. The employer will choose the provider but there have been issues with administration and it seems that the employer will retain ultimate responsibility for these rather than the provider, because of contractual exclusions and Pensions Regulator guidance. Some respondents described changes from salary related pensions to money purchase schemes or salary related schemes on a lower basis of pensionable salary.

[33] Part B, above.
[34] Pensions Act 2008, s 54.

Where employees have specific provisions in their contract of employment then these may need to be changed if a new pension scheme is required to implement AE. This can cause issues where there is a contractual commitment to pay a fixed percentage into a named personal pension plan where it is not possible to agree with the provider of the plan that it can be converted into a qualifying scheme for AE purposes. In this situation the employer has both the existing contractual commitment and a new obligation to pay into an AE compliant scheme for that individual. It can be difficult to reach agreement with employees in this situation. Some smaller employers and those in the charitable sector reported difficulties meeting financial business needs, complying with AE and maintaining good employee relations. Conversely if the pension clause in the employment contract is more generic and refers to current information or the employee handbook, it is easier for employers to make changes to allow for implementation of AE but the employees may not be as aware of the changes as discussed below.[35]

Implementation may also impact different businesses in different ways. For example, in recruitment agencies, different types of contract are used depending on the duration of placements. One respondent described a lot of 'churn' in the short-term, lower paid placements and the impracticalities of providing pension benefits from day one as placements may not last long. The process can be quite complicated and labour intensive and is passed on to the ultimate placement client. It may not be worthwhile if the placement is only for a few days and so postponement is often used to avoid having to enrol under AE straight away. However, postponement but may not always be permitted if the individual is deemed to have continuing contracts which can be considered together and, in that case, the agency employee would need to be enrolled. For one HR recruitment person I spoke to it was 'the last straw' and means that they are no longer growing that part of the business but concentrating on the longer-term placements.

In general terms AE can impact on the employer/employee relationship and needs some extra attention from the employer to ensure that employees understand AE and their choices. Employers also expressed concerns about the false sense of security it might instil in employees paying in small amounts. The impact on the employer generally and on the employer/employee relationship can be said to be costs of AE but are difficult to quantify.

ii. Role of Providers

The role of providers is sometimes unclear and there was a feeling that a cheaper product does not necessarily equal good value to employers and employees. There was also some criticism that the industry had failed to be ready for AE with functionality not being good enough for active conditions. This required HR to monitor everything and then do a manual fix when it went wrong. In many cases, providers

[35] Part D, below.

are engaged to provide the full service in relation to opting-out and this is checked by the employer to ensure that accurate data is used but employers do not have any control over the process. However, as discussed previously, sometimes the basis of the relationship and responsibility is unclear and this could lead to gaps where employees fall between areas of perceived responsibility:

> Providers thought they were ready but it was much more complex, payroll let it down – they were all pointing fingers at each other, payroll was so late in coming to it they caused major issues. It's still an ongoing problem.

Payroll providers blame product providers and vice versa:

> It would have been an interesting observation had the payroll providers been on the hook … if the Pensions Regulator said we're going to be looking at payroll providers, they are part of this. Then it would have been interesting to see if they would have changed their tack.
>
> I often find that one says one thing and one says another and it is difficult to know what I am meant to be doing.

When I asked about recourse in the provider agreements, I was advised that the agreements are drafted so broadly that most of the responsibility still rests with the employer even where it is a provider issue. It may also depend on which individual the HR person contacts within the provider as to whether they get 'advice' or simply 'information'. In one case the product provider had a problem with contributions so that employees could not see them on benefit statements. HR explained:

> Well we [employer] paid them but the employees couldn't see them so we had loads of queries about that and there was an acquisition of the company as well and when the payments couldn't be seen some were worried about the company cash flow.

This problem highlights the difficulties that some employers have experienced and also the impact that AE has on wider business issues. Employers need to get compliant products for AE but NEST may not be suitable so employers must deal with private product providers on the provider's terms. It is important to recognise the role to be played by the financial services industry in the provision of compliant products. One advisor commented:

> Having legislation to allow flexible retirement does not facilitate flexible retirement … that's ludicrous we've constrained it to the extent that nobody can make any, make a profit so it has to be outsourced abroad … And just because, they are focussing on the horrendous charges … now that is cheap as chips but it is not suitable for everybody.

This is particularly interesting as almost everyone I spoke to had no idea what costs or charges were associated with their pension. This lack of engagement means that a cheap compliant product may be chosen without considering genuine suitability and the effects of defaults and lack of engagement mean this will not be apparent until it is too late.

iii. Free Choice

Interference with choice and social responsibilities were also mentioned by respondents. One respondent reported that receiving the AE information made her 'scramble to join' on a voluntary basis. Some that I spoke to were unhappy that the regime interfered with a graduate cash alternative that they had been getting prior to the introduction of AE and that they now felt that it was like they were 'getting a higher rate of tax' between the students loans, pension contributions and loss of the cash alternative to employer contributions. They felt that they lost out as a result as previously they would have been getting the six per cent employer contribution as a cash sum to pay off student debt. Now they had to pay into the pension and could only afford to pay at three per cent contribution, so not only did not get the cash alternative, but they did not get the six per cent employer matching contribution either as three per cent was all they could afford to pay. The opt-out does not help them as they cannot have the cash alternative reinstated as it would breach the employer inducement provisions so this is another externality or cost on this group.

A non-UK national thought that AE was an interesting approach and explained that in France there would be state intervention and higher taxes but that it seems that this is not acceptable in the UK. I asked about this idea of higher NICs rather than AE but most respondents had not thought about it and preferred the situation where you can still choose to opt-out. One respondent reflected:

> If the government is going to start interfering where the money goes they need to outlaw the fact that people can spend more than they earn and live on credit card debit and live a lifestyle they can't afford … now it's harder to get a mortgage than it used to be …. So I think there's other things that should be sorted out before pensions.

The question here is really whether intervention in one aspect of the individual's financial decisions will lead to further limitations or whether it can be justified at all. If the justification is that it will benefit the individual and that they have choice, then do both elements need to be present? The question of benefit is difficult to assess and choice is not always active, as discussed above.[36] Any intervention represents the preference of a particular choice and this may not objectively be the best financial course for all, but free choice is difficult to value. However, there may be a social moral responsibility which needs to be shared between employers and employees to ensure that everyone has enough to live on in retirement. As one stated, 'I don't want to be the one funding everybody else.' Some felt it was more for the employer to pay in but the employers believed that they were already having to absorb enough additional cost in terms of time to implement the project, ongoing compliance issues and increased pension costs. Other respondents felt that the starting point was too low describing it as 'sweetie money'. Several respondents

[36] Part A, above.

noted that it would be better if you could choose your own provider and plan which is not how AE works as discussed in Chapters 2 and 4. In many respects the varying views about the acceptability of the intervention demonstrate that the regime does not affect everyone the same way and so collective acceptance on the basis that there has been no mass opt-out is not a safe assumption to make. For all the other reasons discussed here, individuals may choose to opt-out initially or at all, but that does not imply active reflective decisions are being made.

D. Engagement and Understanding

This is the largest global theme[37] and explores data concerning the relationship between understanding and engagement (which leads to positive action or decision making). There are six subthemes feeding into this: emotional ownership of pension, perceived asymmetries in power and understanding, pension as part of financial planning, understanding and education, confidence and information provided by employers and providers.

Figure 5 Global Theme: Engagement/Understanding

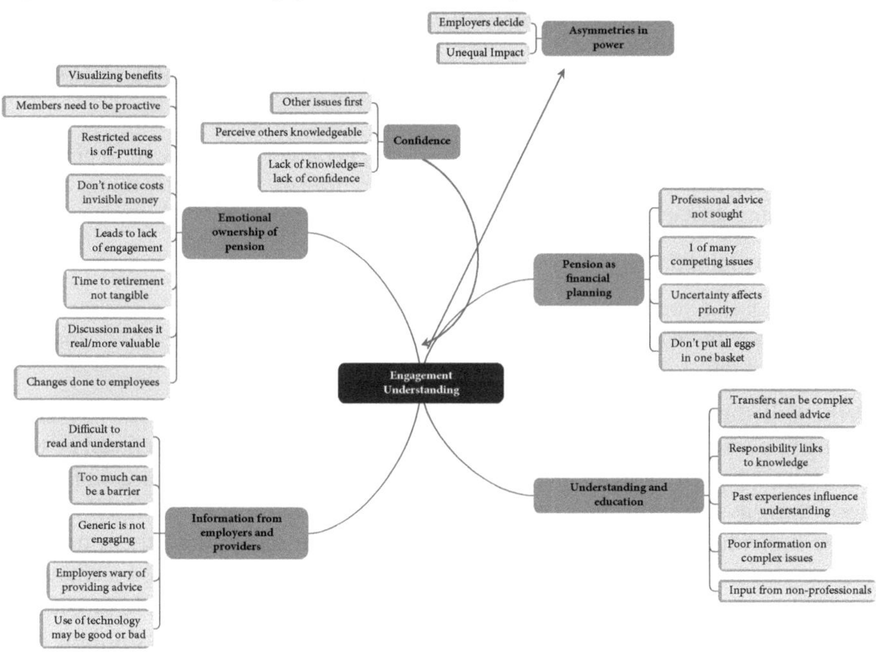

[37] See figure 5.

i. Emotional Ownership of Pension

Individuals reported that they were not aware of the cost of pension contributions but also reported lack of certainty. Decisions were then forgotten so the pension becomes invisible in some respects. One respondent said, 'It's so, you know, in the background of my everyday life that I kind of ignore it.' Some respondents did not relate to their pension as being their own asset and restrictions on accessibility make this worse. The period between paying contributions and taking benefits out are a mental barrier to some who cannot visualise the benefits in real, tangible terms. One respondent described how they had intended to opt-out but that they got a salary increase at just the right time so did not really notice the deductions. This is a good example of how the 'Save More Tomorrow' scheme, discussed in Chapter 4, might work in practice if the individual does not suffer financially as a result of paying in more. A negative aspect of not noticing the contributions, however, is that the individual often then does not see the pension as their asset in the way that they would see a car loan, which they know comes off their salary every month. There is no emotional ownership or connection to the asset. Those who felt older were more aware of their pension answering that they paid in extra 'cos I'm old'. However, the same individual whilst appreciating that she should do something, was unaware of the status of pending transfers in from other small pots or the actual percentage level of contributions she paid. So feeling older is not a magic bullet for engagement and ownership of pension and related decisions. The lack of accessibility is also difficult for some:

> I don't know if I want to put it in that [pension] because I actually want to put it into something I can see, I can feel … we want all our nice cars and our play things and our nice things that go with it I suppose people maybe don't look at it if it's not tangible.

Another explained:

> I guess just if you suddenly want to go on holiday or you've got kids and something came up with them and you needed to loan them a lot of money, you can't do that with your pension … like emergency funds.

Perhaps if there was some limited access this might encourage greater levels of saving in pensions. For example, access such as in the KiwiSaver which can be used for a house deposit, or in financial hardship.[38] Others see the lack of accessibility as a good thing as it prevents them spending the money because of a lack of self-control. Some individuals see changes as being done to them rather than them having a role to play in deciding what is to happen. One respondent discussed a change of provider and when asked if they had transferred their fund from the old provider to the new one replied: 'I must have done. I assume it was automatic, but thinking back now, I'm sure we had a choice and I did, yeah.' This shows the full cycle going from initially thinking it was just done to reflecting and then ending with some certainty

[38] KiwiSaver Act 2006, Sch 1, KiwiSaver Scheme Rules.

in what they did as a result of recognising their own uncertainty. This is also an example of an individual simply deciding what the facts are where they are not sure – up until this point the respondent felt that it must have been done without their choice. These factors can lead to disengagement with all pension decisions as the individual does not view the contributions as real money that they have control over.

Some issues will require proactive decisions – for example, transferring multiple small pension pots into a more efficient fund or ensuring that a lifetime allowance is protected. One individual discussed a recent transfer that they had had to chase for. She explained that she did not really know what the transfer in would do for her, explaining 'It's probably my fault for not chasing … if you don't chase you don't get answers – people won't deliver unless you keep on at them.' A key consideration of this research is to consider what will make individuals engage with choices relating to level of contributions and investment choices especially when they are in a default position. Disengagement is a major problem as this often prevents the individual considering matters further or taking any action.

Discussing the various elements of pensions seemed to make it seem more real and valuable to individuals, but it is not clear how long this effect lasts. As part of each interview I asked each respondent to consider whether the conversation with me had made them feel differently about anything. Many reported that the knowledge that we were going to have a conversation about their pension made them look at documents or have a conversation with someone beforehand. Many reported that they did not realise how little they knew about their decisions or choices:

> Probably shaming me into the fact that I haven't paid attention … It's only because I knew I was having this interview I started thinking about it … I might actually go and look at [this] now … I think I should get off my backside sort of thing and sort out the fact that I've got the three [pension pots] … Maybe … get an appointment with a pensions' advisor … I'm not sure it influenced anything although it might have made me realise that I do have an opinion about it. To be honest, I forgot about the whole thing … Yes … which I will do after this [check if missed contributions now up to date] now that you have made me think about it.

Having a simple conversation about pensions might be an easy and cheap way to encourage engagement with pension choice and may encourage individuals to check their current position. This is less onerous than the 'Save More Tomorrow Plan'[39] as it simply commits to a conversation. However, employers are unlikely to do this because of fears they will breach the inducement provisions or are seen to be providing advice. Perhaps if the provider was required to ask the individual to confirm certain decisions or have a check-in conversation at specified intervals this would be an improvement.

[39] RH Thaler and S Benartzi, 'Save More Tomorrow: Using Behavioural Economics to Increase Employee Saving' (2004) 112 *Journal of Political Economy* 164.

ii. Perceived Asymmetries in Power and Understanding

Some respondents reported that employers make all the decisions to pensions: asymmetrical power. Others reported that not everyone is affected the same way by the pension: asymmetrical effects. AE leaves the employer to set up the plan, choose provider and make decisions about categories of employees and contribution levels. Many reported the employer changing product provider before or in relation to AE and employees seemed to accept this as almost automatic and without choice reporting that 'it was sort of done for us'. This was the case even where the plan was a group personal pension and the individual had control of the policy and the decision of whether to transfer it or not. Employers may also see provider choice or benefit structure as entirely their prerogative, particularly where it must change schemes to meet the AE quality tests. These factors can also lead to disengagement if the individual feels powerless anyway. One respondent reported a change from a final salary scheme to a money purchase arrangement and described the consultation process surrounding the change. He said, 'I think with all these things usually the mind is made up before all that and sometimes if you are in a business where they know the unions aren't that strong it's a foregone conclusion.'

From an employer perspective there was frustration that changing legislation and removal of tax benefits had led to the situation where the defined benefit scheme was too much of a liability to continue but uncertainty over the introduction of AE led to delay in creating new schemes:

> We closed it to a majority of members in 2006, now at that point the government were threatening to install auto-enrolment within two years and we've then decided well there's not much point in doing something else … [but there were delays with the introduction of AE so] we had in 2013 possibly two or three hundred people in a scheme but twelve hundred not in a scheme, it got more and more embarrassing. When we looked at what was compulsory [under AE] I mean it's just ridiculous … so we said that was absolutely rubbish and worked out our own scheme.

Other issues which came up related to transfers being done automatically, when in fact the individual had to agree to any transfer and just could not remember. Also, the introduction of salary sacrifice arrangements seemed to cause confusion, even where changes were contractually varied. Some changes are effected by making changes to employee handbooks rather than agreed contractual variations.[40] One provider described the issuing of employee letters for those who had previously been scheme members after the implementation of AE to the effect of 'do you know your contract has changed?' In this situation the new terms might simply be sent to the individual which may add to this sense of having change imposed on

[40] See Part A above.

them. Post-AE contracts may become more generic and bound to the legislation to allow increases in employee contributions without further agreement, but this might also allow other scheme changes.[41]

iii. Pension Financial Planning

The individuals I spoke to largely rejected financial planning advice for pensions even when it was provided free at the place of work by the employer. The financial advisors reported that they only advise the employers on AE and had not seen any increase in take up of advice by individuals. One described the introduction of the Retail Distribution Review (RDR),[42] as marginalising the man in the street because advice now must be paid for up front rather than it being included as commission. 'The people who need it most are the ones who understand it least, that are unable to get the advice.' Even where advisors are available free at the place of work it seems that some individuals will not take this up. Some feel advice is pointless:

> Pension advice is like advice on food. Edwina Currie once said go to work on an egg and lost her job because of that. Because of the salmonella. Eggs are good for you, eggs are bad for you. Eggs are sometimes good for you.

This interesting analogy describes cynicism about the value of advice very well and most simply discussed matters with friends or relatives if at all.

A pension is seen as one of many competing priorities but uncertainty about the value of a pension affects where it is placed in the order of priorities. One individual felt that he would always take life assurance over a pension. It is difficult to disagree with this where there are dependents and a mortgage, but he had thought about this in a way that some had not. Without professional advice, the individual looks elsewhere to satisfy concerns about uncertainty but will still want to diversify and 'don't want to go ploughing everything into a pension'. Some reported that they did not see their pension as their only planning for retirement, citing other investments in property. This is linked strongly to the individual's perception of time. Financial planning is often seen as something for the future or for getting a mortgage 'I might think about this if I am looking at my planning in the future.' Some were inclined to see financial planning as project based and for dealing with particular issues. Others simply felt that 'advice might be worth nothing in 20 years' again emphasising the time difference between realising pension benefits from other financial products.

[41] Subject to the duty to consult employees in prescribed circumstances. Pensions Act 2004, ss 259–261. The Occupational and Personal Pension Schemes (Consultation by Employers and Miscellaneous Amendment) Regulations 2006 and the Occupational Pension Schemes (Consultation by Employers) (Modification for Multi-employer Schemes) Regulations 2006.

[42] See Financial Conduct Authority 'Post-implementation review of the Retail Distribution Review' – Phase 1 (December 2014).

An interesting discussion with one individual who had spent most of his life working in the US caused me to reconsider differing attitudes to finance and investments here in the UK to the US. He described the crippling cost of medical care and explained how it was difficult to save enough money to be able to pay for healthcare in retirement in the US and consequently he and others he knew were much more inclined to look to riskier investments such as direct equity investment. It has made me reflect on whether part of the apathy for saving in the UK is subconscious reliance on the welfare state generally even if the state pension is poor. The whole pension system is in a state of reform including the state pension. This effect is being monitored but it would be interesting to see if changes to the National Health Service (NHS) would result in changing attitudes and more engagement with retirement planning. Attitudes towards AE pensions in the US are also different with US savers not being required to save by the state. Employees in the US also value pension benefits as significantly less valuable than healthcare.[43]

Those individuals who were knowledgeable about their pension also seemed knowledgeable about tax planning and other financial products, but many had extraordinarily little knowledge. The first chapter describes the parliamentary discussion of the importance of advice and the need to ensure individuals are financially literate. This is partly met by the creation of the Money Advice Service but, where an individual needs specific advice on more complicated decisions, this service may be inadequate. Employers are cautious to ensure that they are not seen to be giving advice. The employer's advisors must also consider who they act for and consider potential for conflicts of interest if they advise both the employer and the employee. This may lead to more generic information being offered to individuals by the pension broker or advisor as described by one employer:

> When, a few years ago we used to do it [pay for their Independent Financial Advisor to see employees] and if individuals wanted they could have a one to one meeting with him and he would you know answer any questions that they had and it was something that was started with the best of intentions but … he said I really don't think that this is a good idea because you know they are looking for financial advice, you know they are seeing me as somebody that can say to them well you know it's in your best interests to do this … So we don't have one to one sessions anymore.

Past mis-selling and other scandals have created an environment where financial advice is not valued highly which means that decisions are being made on the basis of the individual's understanding of given information. This may lead to poor management of pension expectations and other financial priorities with only the

[43] P Fronstin and R Helman, 'Views on the Value of Voluntary Workplace Benefits: Findings from the 2014 Health and Voluntary Workplace Benefits Survey' (Employee Benefit Research Institute, November 2014).

wealthier individuals and employers receiving full advice. The requirements for disclosure of payments for advice may also have the effect of restricting the market, which may be further restricted by the requirements of AE compliant pensions. Put simply it may not be as profitable for the industry and so it may focus on other products. AE pensions were envisaged as simple products not requiring advice but it seems that the lack of members' understanding can lead to disengagement and poor decision making. The cost of advice is weighed as expensive but the cost of failing to get any advice could be just as costly, although not immediately apparent.

iv. Understanding and Education

Some pension transactions are complex and may need professional advice, for example pension transfers. Many individuals I spoke to did not seek this advice and consequently did not address the issue of having multiple small pension pots. Some reported poor available information on complex issues, such as transferability of pensions between EU states. Employers reported difficulties in ensuring they provided accurate information to those workers who would be likely to leave the UK and EU area or to those who have come into the UK from another country with existing pension arrangements. The employees I spoke to with non-UK nationality or previous pensions felt that it was difficult to understand their situation. Employers and employees both reported cultural differences in attitudes to finances and the role of the employer and how it was difficult to use the same information for foreign workers. Many individuals relied on conversations with non-professionals or experience of friends and family when making decisions:

> A colleague pointed out that it was like taking a cut in salary by not taking the employer contributions and when I looked at it that way it seemed absolutely daft that I wasn't contributing.

and:

> I did think about paying in more but I discussed it with my husband and we decided not to.

So whilst information has an important role, the way it is used is just as important. The question of education rather than just providing information was also raised during interviews. Some suggested the government had more responsibility to educate generally on financial matters. Where individuals do not understand the issues then decisions are not made and the question of responsibility is strongly linked to understanding, which can be variable depending on the form of communication used. Where an individual has no understanding of how much a pot of £100,000 will buy in terms of future income then they don't know what they really need and have no motivation to save a bigger pot as £100,000 may seem like a large nest egg. Individuals who have a good understanding of their own position tend to place more responsibility on the individual, where those who have less grasp will blame themselves to some extent but also want the employer or state to take more responsibility for them. When faced with uncertainty some individuals will rely on the employer and trust their arrangements:

> There was a plan charge and individual charges and I am not clear about the charges multiplied over different products and it was not clear at the outset. It was easier to go with that one though as the employer had brought in the broker.

It is also clear that some individuals draw on experience to form a view on future decisions which is an example of prospect theory, discussed in Chapter 4. For example, reference was made to the global financial crisis and uncertainty over currency and inflation and how past issues can impact on a future pension: 'I'd probably save things elsewhere, I am still a bit sceptical about pensions. I just don't understand them and there seems to be, just a lot of bad press at the moment.' Others admitted they were good with numbers, being engineers or bankers, and so they understood quite clearly the way the information was presented. This does not seem to relate to particular employments as several engineers who work with complicated numbers, were as confused by pensions as others. As indicated above, where an individual fails to understand the given information, they will make assumptions and may not realise that they have choices at all.[44] Individuals often seem to move from a point of uncertainty to deciding that a certain position is correct and then do not check this. For example an HR manager reported: 'I think maybe they don't understand that they can opt-out – I had a senior manager say she wasn't allowed to opt-out and I said that you could.'

v. Confidence

From the conversations I had it seems that individuals often lack confidence in their own understanding of their pension and feel that others understand it better, even if they are no different to themselves. In this situation they are more susceptible to social influences and may do something because 'everyone else was doing it'. This acknowledged lack of understanding then leads to lack of confidence in making decisions. Confidence in the employer/employee relationship also means that employees may prefer to address other issues which they are more confident about rather than ask the employer about pensions.

vi. Information Provided by Employers and Providers

Many of the individuals I spoke to expressed information itself, or rather too much of it, 'a massive package' to be a barrier. Even HR personnel spoke of

[44] At Part B(iv) above.

bombarding employees with lots of letters and terminology as part of the compliance process:

> Interview Respondent: Well we send so much at the start of the contract, as you get more stuff through, it's hard enough to get them to accept the contract, get bank details and get them onto the system so they are paid I think they just think oh my goodness there is more paper.
>
> Interviewer: So do you think people complete what you chase for?
>
> Interview Respondent: Yes and because we are not chasing for the pensions documents – they are in anyway. I mean some people when they get their pack through the door, it's a big massive thick pack you know and they've got to sign it and it's amazing how many times they'll get reminders that they've got to sign it and if they've not signed it by a certain date then its deemed to be accepted, but you know and then they'll come and say to you I've got this thing through the door what does this mean and I am thinking well you got that about 8 weeks ago.

It was reported that the packs sent out were too large and difficult to read or understand. One describing a transfer of a fund to a new provider described 'a lengthy process with all sorts of paperwork coming and it was a bit confusing to be honest'. Some HR managers reported having to 'target' certain sectors of the workplace and arranging one to one meetings with financial advisors to ensure that sufficient numbers engaged in the process but not all employers have such resources available and then more generic, less salient information will be the standard. Generic information provided by product providers was found to be a barrier. It is difficult to get more specific information from employers who are concerned not to breach the employer inducement provisions[45] and do not want to be held responsible for providing advice. As described by this HR manager:

> We also had quite a few people … coming up to us and trying to come out of it before they had gone in. So I had several people and every week they would come up and try can I come out of it yet? And I would say no you can't because we need to auto-enrol you first and then you'll get the comms … but we could not do anything because we are not meant to be advising people to come out of it.

And another:

> It's difficult when somebody comes down … we've got it all online on HR link you know your first port of call is to recommend that they visit that page, show them the page … and then they say what would you do, so you know I say well sorry I'm not allowed to discuss it any further with you, you know I don't want to do that, I don't want to give you anything that's going to be construed as advice.

[45] Pensions Act 2008, s 54.

Another says:

> We have to be completely on the fence … if they have got a query they have to deal with it directly with [provider].

One financial advisor comments:

> You give them an illustration and it means nothing … and we've got a default fund for investment [an AE legal requirement] but nobody ever goes beyond the default fund because they don't know or don't think.

Some respondents wanted personalised figures based on comparison to existing lifestyle. There is also the question of the cost of providing the information and responsibility which is discussed above.[46] Advice can be costly and is prohibitive for many. It is difficult to see a solution to this dilemma – employees want more personal guidance, but employers cannot give it. The data also shows that, whilst technology may be a good way to ensure compliance with the information requirements, it may not encourage engagement and may act as a barrier to decisions in some instances. One good example is the case of two employees in the same organisation with access to the same modelling information which would have allowed them to see what effect adjustments to pension contributions would have. One did not know it was there and indicated this might be the sort of information that would make her change her contributions but the other used it and often made changes to investment and contributions based on this. It may not even be the technology that is the barrier but just awareness of its existence. How can we explain the different result when they have both been given the same facts and information? One respondent discussing missed contributions said, 'I think you can go online and see how it all looks with projections and things. I hadn't realised any of this until recently when a colleague mentioned it and told me.'

Another individual described:

> We have an online thing called [provider brand] where you can log in and see your account, it must be pretty up to date but I did set it up but I don't think I have ever logged back in.

An HR professional from the same employer explained:

> They need to log in and try and find the opt-out information. It's not easy to find – I was looking for it and it was difficult to find. Lots of people may not know they can opt-out and won't look for it and many won't even have logged on.

It seems that the link to online information may be lost amongst the other information sent in the pack: 'The online tool is very useful but that information got lost in the rest of the paper in the pack with 60 other pages.' It might be an improvement to drip feed information or at least send links to online tools multiple times

[46] See Part C above.

or in multiple mediums – paper, e-mail, presentation slides etc. The problem of communication versus compliance is acknowledged by employers and product providers, but responsibility is not always clear. There may be a gap in terms of ensuring individuals understand their position in order to act on it. Employers can feel burdened by the legislation and are keen to ensure compliance but may lack the skills or expertise to deal with pensions which can be complex:

> I'm no pensions expert … all the documentation came from [provider], I put all the details onto the actual system that they have and letters were generated automatically and are branded with our logo but it was [provider] documents.

This may result in over reliance on advisors or product providers to deal with employees but may result in gaps or mistakes over responsibility. Contracts between the providers and employers will often contain an indemnity by the employer whereby the employer is responsible for properly distributing information given and ensuring accurate data is provided to the provider. However, the relationship between HR, product providers, payroll providers and intermediaries is often closer in practice than appears on paper. Employers I spoke to reported that they often rely on advice from contacts at the product provider, even where contractually the advisor intends to provide information not advice. Fears over responsibility may result in employers being over cautious and employees getting more generic information rather than the more salient information and advice they are looking for. It may also mean that it is difficult to get any party to provide answers to employees as each party may feel that it is not their responsibility to respond. One HR professional put me in contact with her product provider who she saw as her advisor, explaining that he had been so helpful in advising and keeping her right through the implementation of AE. When I discussed the provision of information and advice with the provider contact, he stressed that he did not provide advice but merely information. When discussing the provider role, he stressed that the company provided written and online information which was useful but that 'We don't advise anyone.' He acknowledged that the company can tailor information depending on the employer, but it is the employer's responsibility to ensure that they do it right although:

> It's not just go and help yourself [to the information/communications] … we will definitely shape that. It just depends whether the advisor is still involved or not. If the advisor is still involved he'll probably want to have an element of control of that because that will be part of the services … that he is charging for.

So here the employer is deemed responsible for the communication, but the provider still wants to shape the information process depending on input from an Independent Financial Advisor (IFA). This relationship might look advisory, but the Pensions Regulator is likely to find the employer remains responsible for any failures, as discussed in Chapter 2. Often the contracts between the provider and employer are standard forms issued by the product provider and difficult for the employer to vary. The employer seeking to comply with AE may agree to purchase the group personal pension on certain terms but the person dealing with the product provider for implementation may not be aware of the terms and responsibilities. The dilemma for the HR person is clear:

> People are getting more engaged but they're relying on their employer a lot more to give them that sort of, that information and that's their first port of call and that's why we have designed our, all kinds of information and tools and comms campaigns to try and help these members.

In the next chapter the complexity of this relationship is considered further but there are at least three parties with overlapping roles and responsibilities:

(1) The employees look to the employer who has provided them with the scheme for advice and information.
(2) The employer refers them to the product provider as their individual pension policy is with them and not the employer.
(3) The provider has contractual arrangements with the employer, to provide access to the group personal pension to comply with AE, and with the employee, as a member with an individual personal pension with the provider.

If the employer also has an intermediary or IFA then they may also be engaged to provide information to the employee but they advise the employer and not the employee. The relationship may be further complicated where an external payroll or administration provider is also involved as there have been many issues between employers, payroll and provider causing errors in AE. Taking the example of opt-out forms, the employer will engage the provider and will use the provider information to send out letters to employees and will give the provider the employee data to allow them to process it. The provider will send out welcome packs with the opt-out information which the employer does not want to discuss with employees for fear of breaching the inducement provisions:

> I understand why employers wanted a slick process because … the people who were pretty militant and anti-pensions who would definitely want to opt-out … which has been a big pain for a lot of employers, they can't get their head around that.

This provider had significant dealings with employers and indicated that the experience of the employers I spoke to was common. This is further complicated if there is a further intermediary or IFA contracted to provide the opt-out information instead, but they advise the employer and have no real relationship with the employee. The provider needs the opt-out information to ensure that they fulfil their obligations to the employer but this may be out of their control and so what is the relationship between IFA and provider here and who has responsibility for ensuring that the employees have the information they need and that they can choose to opt-out if they want? If there was to be a charge as a result of an opt-out error causing a member to lose their lifetime allowance[47] protection,

[47] The lifetime allowance was introduced by the Finance Act 2004 to limit the total savings made to a registered pension scheme. Individuals with enhanced lifetime allowance (under s 218) could protect

where does the responsibility lie? With the member who should have read the information and ensured that they opted-out in plenty of time? With the payroll who failed to action instructions or the provider? Where administration issues cause a late payment of contributions where the employer has paid these on time who is responsible? Further clarity of the roles is needed – especially where staff dealing with implementation of AE may not be involved in the decision-making process regarding appointment of advisors and providers. No one party is taking responsibility for advising the employee but simply for the provision of information. Should any of these parties take responsibility for ensuring that the employee has engaged, understood or takes action? Should the product provider be clearer about their role with the employer to prevent misunderstanding? This is discussed further in the next chapter. It seems easy for misunderstandings to arise where a provider will 'help shape communication' with an employer but does not believe this is advice. HR professionals dealing with this find it difficult as the following exchange discussing resolving difficulties highlights:

> Interviewer: So is that your financial advisor or your contact at [provider]?
> Interview Respondent: Both actually, I've got both of them. And various e mails, I often find that one says one thing and one says another and it is difficult to know what I am meant to be doing.

From this evidence it is not surprising that employees sometimes feel they do not understand and are not sure where to go for advice. Many employers will also rely on the information and templates provided by the Pensions Regulator which will result in more standard and less salient information in contrast to the tailored, salient information which behavioural economics informs us will have the best results. The role of the Pensions Regulator in bringing enforcement action will also be discussed in the next chapter. There is little case law at present but as the number of fines and Regulator interventions continues to rise, employers may gain more confidence about what is acceptable in the debate of information versus advice.

Another issue raised was that, whilst opt-out rates are currently low, this might be because individuals did not choose to stay in but failed to engage and at a later stage just stop paying. Leaver rates are variable but appear higher for those employers with casual workers and it is important that these rates are monitored alongside opt-out rates. For example, Scotland appears to have higher rates than the rest of the UK reporting an average of 13 per cent of those automatically enrolled, leaving at some point after the opt-out period.[48]

their fund from the allowance where they do not make any more contributions to their pensions. If the member subsequently makes a payment because of AE their pension will be subject to a significant tax charge (s 214).

[48] Department for Work and Pensions, *Employers' Pension Provision Survey 2015* (March 2016) https://assets.publishing.service.gov.uk/government/uploads/system/uploads/attachment_data/file/584593/rr919-employers-pension-provision-2015.pdf, 53.

> If you are looking at people who are not paid a vast amount of money … they probably don't even notice it's coming out of their wage. When they do it might prompt them to say well actually I could spend this money better elsewhere … But then they've missed the opt-out window by the time that that maybe drips through to them. So we were always keen to look at opt-out versus leaver rates.

An employer makes a similar point when discussing summer student workers who were auto-enrolled: 'Surprisingly the others have stayed in and that's what I say, that's the reason, people don't read, so I mean OK the fund's going to be there for them later on.' Another comments, 'Opt-out is quite low, lower than we thought but I think the cancellations will be higher – you know they will not opt-out in time but will just stop paying it.'

If there are higher leaver rates of this nature this would mean an increase in the number of small pension pots. The complexity of the UK system with a vast range of providers and schemes in use for AE increases the likelihood that people will end careers with multiple pots to deal with.[49] Small pots tend to need positive action by the individual to ensure they are not left or forgotten about and further legislation was considered and abandoned on this.[50] The concern remains that multiple pots are more likely to be forgotten and require engagement and positive action to deal with. Leavers in this situation also add to the administrative burden of employers who may not realise initially that payments have been terminated and who must also re-enrol such employees after three years – when they may or may not opt-out again. In Australia automatic consolidation applies where there is a minimum balance and it has been suggested as a better model for the US as well.[51]

For employees who leave the employer, it is important that they are reminded of their small pot in some way to ensure that it is not forgotten. I spoke to one individual who had recently been made redundant about what information she had been sent regarding the change in contributions etc to her pension. The respondent reported:

> I have not had a letter or anything to say what I can do with it now … It is crazy as it could be forgotten as it is just held somewhere … But I know people with much less in their pot who might not have checked or might forget more easily.

The difficulty of dealing with multiple small pots might impact on women more as they are more likely to have career breaks or leave jobs after short periods when they have children or take on caring roles for the family. One respondent discussed her multiple pension pots with me saying:

> As someone who has had a number of breaks throughout her career for different reasons but the main one being childcare I think it is something that needs to be addressed and its only because I knew I was having this interview I started thinking about it.

[49] A O'Connell, Institute of Policy Studies 'KiwiSaver: A Model Scheme?' (2009) 36 *Social Policy Journal of New Zealand* 130, 134.

[50] Pensions Act 2014, s 33 & Sch 17 not in force.

[51] P Secunda, 'The Behavioural Economic Case for Paternalistic Workplace Retirement Plans' (2016) 91 *Indiana Law Journal* 505, 533.

As a result of her pre-interview deliberations, this respondent realised she had a 'missing' pension pot and started trying to recover it. This was not an easy process and it was ongoing when I spoke to her. A reminder about small pots left behind should be included in the regime as otherwise these might be forgotten. Further research could consider whether this impacts on women more than men. With the introduction of AE, the number of small pots will increase but if awareness of this does not correspondingly increase what will happen to all of these small pots? This must be considered further to prevent negative unintended consequences of AE growing.

Different approaches to education and providing information would likely produce more engagement and better decisions for individuals. Some of the respondents also mentioned pension changes which occurred whilst they were on maternity leave and this meant that they were even less clear about the factual position than otherwise. As well as the mode and volume of information, some reported that they could not relate the facts and figures to their own life and welcomed changes which were going to produce statements in 'today's money rather than projected'. Individuals are not confident about financial products generally and pensions seem to be even more complex. Consequently, anything which will instil individual confidence in their own understanding of what the facts and figures mean for them should help with engagement and decision making.

It seemed clear that physical piles of paper are off putting and many do not read annual statements either but even asking people to attend discussions does not always work. One respondent describes: 'The problem is I think for our HR department is they do set up these optional you know Q&A sessions and because they are optional a lot of people don't go to them including myself.'

I spoke to one respondent who was unaware that he was allowed to opt-out of AE, believing his membership was compulsory. Others from the same organisation were aware that they could opt-out having received the same information and this demonstrates the difficulty of relying on individual choice and action as a justification for paternalism. This company was using a strategy of sending paper, emails and presentations but if the audience is not required to attend they may decide not to. This was confirmed by one of the HR team who advised that for those identified as requiring AE they set up a diary meeting for the individual with the advisor to ensure that they attended something as they knew voluntary sessions were poorly attended. Another HR professional commented, 'They got three different lots of information at different stages and it is clear but the only thing is making people read it but you can't stand over them and make them read it if they don't want to.'

This is the key issue and a difficulty with legal intervention in this area. Whilst it may appear that people have a choice, this depends on them being aware of their choices and making informed decisions: it seems that in the area of pensions this is quite difficult and strategies for communication need to be improved. A financial advisor commented:

> Basically you've got to terrify people … explain the situation so they become terrified. Because the danger is by the time they realise what they are on track for it is too late to do anything about it.

A further complication to understanding as reported by some employers was illiteracy or language barriers. One employer with factory workers mentioned that they have large numbers of foreign workers who come in seasonally. As the work is manual, little English is required and so the process of communicating with these people about AE was challenging. The solution was to engage an existing employee as an interpreter but there is no guarantee that meaning is not lost in this process. The illiteracy of some employees was addressed to some extent by holding small meetings and discussions, but this leaves the individual little opportunity to reflect and consider information, which can sometimes be dense and complicated, without further help. For these individuals it is difficult to establish that they have justified AE by their informed consent. An assumption seems to be made that this is beneficial and therefore no further efforts, to ensure understanding of those subjected to the policy, are needed.

E. Trust

This last and smallest global theme is trust. The question of trust or mistrust was raised by a number of respondents as a justification for not engaging with decisions. Some talked of trust of the provider or employer and mistrust of their own judgement, of the state pension and of the durability of advice: 'Well I think I just, I just trusted [Employer] set up a good scheme and they know what they are doing with the money I suppose so I trust them.'

One individual explained:

> I don't think the information that's given is durable. So you can spend a lot of time really getting into your pension and what it's all about, only to find the pillars of stone, the training, the information that you've been given, that you base your information on, turn to salt …. The world changes … life is so changeable, the world is complex and changeable and it's really difficult.

Some employers reported lack of trust in providers where the administration had been poor resulting in an increased workload for HR.[52] Trust is a key concept for pensions as reliance must be placed in the third party holding the assets for the benefit of the individual: but trust here in some respects replaces individual decision making and action which may result in negative consequences. The employees who trust the employer to set up a good plan and tie themselves to

[52] See C(ii) above.

the minimum contributions may be disappointed when they realise the value of their pension is not as they expected. The employers who delegate responsibility, trusting providers to furnish employees with information and process deductions and contributions, will be disappointed if this is not done correctly and they are held responsible by the Pensions Regulator. The trust relationship exists between the employer and employee and product provider which is why there must be adequate safeguards to prevent trust replacing active decisions. Even very well-educated individuals may replace reason with trust. For example, I spoke to one professional respondent about contributions. There was an administration issue highlighted by a colleague which meant that contributions were deducted but not paid into the pension:

> I know you get paid every month and I check my payslip for contributions. I check that it has gone out but I don't ever check that it has gone in. Talking now that seems daft as I would never do that with a bank or ISA or any other type of finance but that's why it's crazy that pensions seem to be so different.

Perhaps the complexity and general lack of engagement with pensions mixed with the trusting relationship in which workplace pensions are presented create the perfect conditions for this sort of situation to arise. Therefore, the safeguards must do as much as possible to ensure that individuals are prompted to engage and understand their options and make active choices within the plan rather than replace all decision making with trust.

IV. Conclusion

Previous chapters have set out the background to the introduction of AE, including the justification and issues with the particular design of default positions within the policy. This empirical work helps to develop understanding of the practical application of this policy. If the policy justification requires individuals to acknowledge that they benefit from the regime then it is important to understand how pension benefits are perceived. If it is the opt-out and element of engagement and choice which are key to the justification, then this should also be tested to understand what can help and hinder engagement and decision making. Identifying benefits and costs of AE is useful for the overall evaluation of success of the policy when considered alongside questions of the 'benefit of AE' and 'operation of choice' within AE.

A. Choice and Defaults

If all that AE is to achieve is an increase in the volume of pension savers regardless of outcomes, then it may be declared a success. I would, however, suggest that a key component in the legitimacy of the intervention is the operation of free choice.

The choice to opt out is often referred to as the key to legitimising the intervention but if individuals do not make their own active decisions about staying with the default positions then there is a risk that they will have a false sense of security or misunderstand their position. This can be said to be one of the unintended consequences of the regime. This could lead to real costs to the individual if he pays less contributions than he would have under active choice or if he misunderstands the value of benefits until it is too late for him to remedy. It is insufficient then to rely on the low opt-out rate as a verification of the success of AE as there may be thousands of pensioners in 20 years' time who are surprised to find that they have paid too little into a poorly performing pension fund having relied on minimum default positions established by an employer they trust.

It seems clear from my data that many individuals have a very basic understanding of their workplace pension. The data illustrates that contribution levels, fund choices, providers, fund transfers, salary sacrifice arrangements and benefits are often misunderstood. Some individuals did not really know what choices they had but were just relieved to have dealt with it. For example, some who had been auto-enrolled did not realise that they could opt-out and many knew that they were paying into a pension that offered employer matching contributions but had no idea what that meant as a percentage or monetary contribution. In many cases the default position has almost entirely displaced the individuals understanding of their pension or their desire to engage with it. The operation of the defaults, presented by the employer, has a powerful effect on employees who seem to disengage with any other information about the pension or choices. Defaults and choice architecture were considered in Chapter 4 and this data provides supporting evidence that, where the employer chooses the minimum compliance position, the employee may not realise this or may not do so for some time. Most individuals had little understanding of what the pension saving would provide them with in the way of a retirement benefit and had very little idea what the correlation was between increasing contributions/changing investment strategy and the ultimate benefit they could expect from their pension pot.

It seems that individuals sometimes instinctively make a choice without considering it or alternatively remain with the default unless prompted to reconsider the decision. Where the individual is unclear about what decisions have been made in the past this seems to make it less likely that they will review the decisions in the future. For example, I spoke to some people who did not know what their contribution level was but when I asked about future increases they became certain that they were already paying the maximum they could. The setting of default investment and contribution amounts proves a strong anchor for many who do not actively choose.

Another difficulty is that some changes do not require any action by the individual as they are notified by way of changes to staff handbooks and contain a tacit 'consent if you do not respond' mechanism. This would require engagement and understanding and positive action by the individual to prevent or amend changes. Contractual enrolment and salary sacrifice arrangements require an agreed contractual variation[53] but the data shows that even where individuals have agreed to these, they often cannot recall the effect after the event. Individuals also place trust in the employer or product provider and almost remove themselves of decision making responsibility as a result. Some reported transferring pensions and paying certain contributions because of trust either in the employer or provider. For example:

> Interviewer: 'So you really have no idea what effect your transfer in has had or ....'
> Respondent: 'No. Not at all .... I don't know any of that.'

The individual trusts that the employer makes the best decision for them but does not take into account the fact that the employer has its own economic interests to consider as well as having to compromise across a varied workforce whose interests may not all be the same.

B. Understanding

Pensions can be viewed as too difficult to understand and so individuals do not try. Some issues are more complicated, such as transfers between schemes, but individuals seemed unconcerned by their own lack of understanding. As indicated in the data, one individual reported that she had realised, as a consequence of thinking about meeting with me, that she had a missing pension pot from a previous workplace pension. She had difficulty identifying who to speak to about it and then had difficulties arranging for it to be transferred into an existing arrangement. She was assisted by her current employer but even after all the effort in dealing with it, was not aware what the transfer into her existing pension would equate to in terms of pension benefits. She was happy to know that she had found the pot and arranged for it to be transferred but did not then push to understand what this would buy her in benefit terms. The same employee was also trying to find out what had happened to another small pension pot when I spoke to her. The provider had changed and she had been told that the pension was terminated even though she had paperwork saying that they would not terminate it and refund contributions at the point she left the employer. These situations can be difficult and rely on having the correct paperwork to hand and being persistent to be dealt with. This respondent was pursuing the matter as 'a point of principle' but there may be a point where many individuals either lack the understanding or tenacity to ensure that they get what they own. My discussions sometimes seemed to make people more aware of their own uncertainty and in some cases motivated individuals to find out more. An improvement on the current position might be to build in a verification point where individuals discuss their pension with a member of the HR team or product provider at a set

[53] Employment Rights Act 1996, ss 1 & 5; The Pensions Regulator Detailed Guidance for employers, 33.

stage and in relation to considering all aspects of the benefit package. This would allow any misunderstandings to be identified and corrected and promote active decision making.

Some people do understand their pensions and this seems to link back to motivation and making an active choice. Those who linked their pension pot to something specific in their individual imagination and had goals based on a particular income at retirement or cash sums for a special holiday saw it as a more tangible asset and were more engaged. For those who lack this interest or the imagination to see their pension as something real, it is important to try and create this through education or better illustrative pension literature which is salient and speaks to them. It is clear that for many individuals, their pension is a distant intangible thing which they are not inclined to engage with. It is often presented as part of an overall benefits package and only referred to in vague terms in the contract of employment. Changes are often effected through the benefits booklet rather than contractually agreed and this increases the disengagement and feeling amongst employees that the pension is for the employers to make decisions about. Sometimes, employees view the workplace pension as being controlled by the employer or provider and cannot see their own role, with changes in provider being reported as 'sort of done for us'. This trust in the employer can operate to prevent individuals being motivated to understand their position.

C. Information

Individuals process their views on pensions from many sources, not just the information given to them by their employer or pension provider. Despite emphasis on financial education, quality and readability of information at the outset of the introduction of AE, individuals still see the information as difficult to read. Many reported that the volume of information was off-putting and often pensions' information is given at the point of joining a new employer and so is given with other documentation which increases the appearance of this volume. Where a new employee is then given forms which must be completed, for example to ensure that they are paid, then these will be read and dealt with as a priority and the other information will be given less priority. Considering the active choice method of intervention, discussed in Chapter 4, an improvement might be to include a single page with pension key facts and options which the employee is required to read, sign and return with the other forms. Whilst this may not increase the understanding of the benefits hugely it will ensure that individuals acknowledge that they understand they have a pension which they can make choices with. This may be enough to promote more engagement at a future date.

Even using technology to provide easy access to information sometimes proved to be a barrier where individuals did not know it was there or knew that they could access it but had forgotten passwords. Generic information was reported by employees to be less useful, but employers and providers are cautious about being seen to be giving advice or inducing opt-outs and respond by providing increasingly generic information. The information which I had sight of was generic and referred to separate briefings or booklets for further details. The terms and conditions make it clear that the provider cannot give the individual financial advice and the main booklet refers to several other specific booklets for further information on issues such as fund choices, fund fact sheets and guide to pension plan tax. Details of what funds are available, how the default fund is constituted, and actual charges applied are all contained in a separate booklet to the one given to the employee I spoke to. This data and the work of behavioural science, discussed in Chapter 4, makes it clear that this two-stage process for information could be a barrier as well. Whilst it may be beneficial to reduce the volume of paper, this creates a need to look elsewhere for details, thus resulting in individuals giving up and remaining in the default positions as the booklet makes it clear that they do not need to take any action. Information on how the individual can opt-out of AE is provided by the pension provider rather than the employer but employees often look to a member of staff at their employer for guidance on this. This can place a strain on the employee/employer relationship as the employer is reluctant to provide any information which could be construed as financial advice or inducing the employee to opt-out. The employee is then referred back to the pension provider which has stressed that it is not able to provide financial advice and the employee may be left without answers.

Information in itself is not enough to ensure understanding. Individuals often turn to non-professionals for advice or rely on past experiences rather than considering the given information. Those who had a better understanding of their own position seemed to assume more responsibility themselves for their general financial planning. The confidence of the individual is also linked to understanding and it seems that individuals perceive others to have a better understanding than they do which can lead to further indecision. Lack of clarity or understanding prevents individuals making further decisions or questioning what they have done in the past.

D. Individual Perception of Auto-Enrolment

The AE policy is a form of legal paternalism and, as well as being justified by the preservation of choice, may be further justified where the affected individual agrees that they benefit from the intervention. The lack of opt-outs may support the argument and that individuals agree that they benefit from AE and therefore remain in the pension. It is clear from this research, however, that many individuals do not understand their pension choices – even the most basic choice that they can leave the scheme. Whilst individuals may agree in principle with legal intervention this does not necessarily mean that they consider they personally benefit and some respondents reported they had suffered loss as a result of the regime. For example, those who lost a graduate cash equivalent because of AE. Lack of understanding is a key barrier to answering this question of whether people choose to stay or not, as people need to understand what they have in order to decide how they feel about it. Many of my respondents did not have this understanding. Many individuals did not appear to engage with the information given, did not actively take or revisit decisions and stayed in the default position longer than was good for them. So whilst many will benefit from the introduction of AE as it will ensure saving at a basic level, the variation between schemes and minimum default positions will greatly influence the benefits experienced by workers. There is some evidence, explored in Chapter 4, that whilst AE increases the volume of people saving, it may reduce the amount of contributions saved when compared to a self-enrolment position. Some workers would have joined a pension without AE, perhaps at a later stage, but would have made an active choice which is likely to have resulted in higher contributions to the fund. The default positions have been chosen to ensure the lowest number of opt-outs but this may create a lowest common denominator effect for the medium to higher earners who are opted in to saving a total of eight per cent of salary as a contribution when they might have opted for 12 per cent or more on self-enrolment. The question is whether the benefit to the lower earners is sufficient to justify the potential loss to the others. More work needs to be done to make the default positions less 'sticky' as described in Chapter 4, to reduce negative consequences.

E. The Employee/Employer Relationship and Auto-Enrolment

The intervention/implementation theme considers the views of all stakeholders in relation to the introduction of AE. Many employers will need to pay for specialist advice in relation to continuing compliance with AE. Not all employers have the same resources available and so this may result in varying quality standards and experience by employees. In some respects, the restrictions on employers, such as providing information that might be construed as inducement to opt-out, which are designed to protect the employee, actually work against better understanding and put a strain on the relationship. Employees look to the employer for further information but are often referred to a third-party provider. There is at least potential for damage to the relationship given the problems that seem to surround providing information which might be construed as advice or an inducement. Coupled with the difficulties some employers have experienced with their providers, there is then heavy reliance on that third party to get it right and ensure the employee gets the information he or she needs. The provision of information is a key employer requirement under AE but this can result in large volumes of generic information being disclosed. Where information is given in multiple mediums and includes information sessions and group discussions there is also scope for misunderstandings or individuals perceiving the information as financial advice. Employers may also have to consider the needs of employees who are non-UK nationals and may have language or other barriers to consider in providing information.

F. Impact of Gender and Age

Women were aware of the need for pension saving significantly more than men and also discussed the impact of career breaks and multiple pension pots more than male colleagues. The impact of career breaks, part time working and small pots continues to be a significant issue with AE. One female respondent described how she was unsure about some aspects of changes to pension benefits as the scheme had been altered whilst she was on maternity leave. The alternation was to her detriment and she was annoyed as part of the change meant that her salary used for calculating her pension benefits was fixed at a point when she had been part-time as she was looking after a child. She had been on maternity leave when the changes went through and so had not engaged with the information or considered the impact it would have on her in future when she returned to a full-time post. She explained that the change was simply communicated on the intranet at work and she received an e-mail asking her to look at it. As she was not in the office as was on leave this acted as a barrier and she did not fully appreciate the significance of the changes. She potentially had a contractual claim in respect of the change but was happy in her career and job otherwise and so had not raised this as an issue with her employer. Another respondent described how her own position was so different to her ex-husband's even though they both started their professional careers at the same time because of her career breaks to look after children. As identified in Chapter 2, AE may not include part-time workers who do not reach the earnings trigger for each contract and so may still result in these workers, still often women, having no access to a contributory pension. It can be difficult for women to buy back years that they miss whilst performing caring responsibilities and so information on this must be made clear where this is an option. Employers should also consider how they communicate with workers who are not in the office because they are on leave (whether maternity, parental leave or sick leave) as ordinary communication methods may not be appropriate or effective.

G. Negative or Unforeseen Consequences of Auto-Enrolment

This data identifies real costs to individuals which arise as a consequence of the AE policy. The predicted consequences of using defaults, discussed in Chapter 4, are evidenced here in many different examples. Individuals fail to make decisions, ignore pensions, are completely unaware of contribution levels and effects and they do not seek financial advice. Where employees ask employers for advice, they are likely to be referred elsewhere or given more information rather than advice.

This leads to the individual failing to engage with the pension and many will remain in default contribution levels and funds which could lead to disappointing results when the pension is used to create retirement income. As outlined in Chapter 4, using the default design rather than active choice, means that the regime relies on continued inertia and so the plan design process and defaults are crucial to the experience and any negative consequences. Chapter 4 describes the possibility that some employees will pay less in the long term with AE unless they are required to make active choices at some stage and this is supported by my research. If employees are left without the default and must choose or elect to join a scheme themselves then often the employees will choose a higher contribution rate than the minimum contribution they end up paying under AE.

Also, the employer exercises a wide discretion in choosing provider, default plan and the default contribution levels. This is then relied on by individuals who trust the employer to do what is best for them. The lack of advice in the process prevents employees engaging in a meaningful way which either leads to a lack of understanding about the benefits or complete apathy. Whilst this is not an immediately apparent issue, it is likely that in years to come, as individuals become aware of the problem, the issue will become more visible. In creating a situation where employees are auto-enrolled into default positions, with minimum (and inadequate) contributions, AE actually causes detriment to some who would have chosen to pay higher contributions at their own instance at some future date. It may also act as a barrier to considering financial planning advice relating to pensions as it creates a false sense of security for some. This is a direct cost of the regime and occurs as a result of the design or the choice architecture of AE in the UK and the exercise of discretion over individual plan design by individual employers.

This cost, negative consequence or externality could potentially affect large numbers of workers to varying degrees. It might be a relatively small cost for some and a larger cost to others. Any assessment of the success of the policy must therefore consider whether this identified cost has a remedy. If the costs of accessing a remedy are prohibitive or it is difficult for the affected individuals to access sufficient information to identify that they have suffered loss, traditional legal remedies may have limited effect.[54] The following chapter explores whether these costs are recognised in AE legislation or whether there is already an adequate legal remedy available for those who believe that they suffer a loss as a consequence of the operation of AE. This might be that individuals believe they have been mis-informed or advised, placed within a poorly performing pension provider or fund or wrongly accepted contractual changes which were detrimental. All of these consequences might arise from the situations described here in this research where the role of providers and employers is sometimes unclear and employees appear dis-engaged from generic information they are given.

[54] AI Ogus, *Regulation: Legal Form and Economic Theory* (Hart Publishing, 2004) 27.

6

Unintended Consequences: Remedies

I. Introduction

A number of negative consequences flowing from the introduction of AE have been identified throughout this book. The empirical data highlights insufficient protection of free choice under AE and that improvements are needed to default positions. Whilst the opt-out provides legitimacy for the regime, the form of implementation and use of defaults erodes the exercise of choice and there are no provisions to encourage engagement and active decision making by individuals. In addition to this, inadequate advice impacts on the effects of AE for many. The employer retains a large discretion over choice of provider and design of the pension under AE and this could result in poor value for some employees as the parties' interests may not always be aligned. Employers rely on their chosen pension provider to assist in the process of ensuring that employees are given the correct information. However, the data clearly identifies that misunderstandings still occur and could lead to negative consequences or financial loss for some. For example, where information is perceived as advice or is simply misunderstood. As a result of further statutory restrictions imposed on qualifying schemes there is likely to be continuing movement of funds between providers. There can be significant variations between fund costs and provider quality and, consequently, variation between retirement benefits produced even when similar levels of contribution are made. The restrictions on charging might make employers more likely to choose schemes without advice and they may not make the best decisions. Some employers may have to accept more basic schemes from their product provider to maintain cost levels and employees may invest their contributions in unsuitable funds. Employees may not be given information in a form which engages and encourages choice. This could also result in multiple small pots being left in more expensive schemes and being forgotten.

In addition to improvements to default positions, further statutory change may be required to eliminate the negative consequences of AE arising from the exercise of discretion in implementing the regime. It is important to consider whether the private law might already afford a remedy for those suffering loss and so this chapter considers the private law remedies available to deal with detriment resulting from the introduction of AE. If there is a clear remedy available under private law then further statutory change would be unnecessary. This chapter will consider the possible private law obligations in respect of these losses distinguishing fiduciary, agency, contractual and delictual obligations arising from the AE relationship. It will consider in particular:

(1) Whether a fiduciary duty might be owed by the employer or its advisors to the employees who are automatically enrolled into a pension scheme.
(2) Whether there are duties owed by the employer (as an agent) to the employee. This includes fiduciary and non-fiduciary duties.
(3) The extent of duties owed by the employer to employees under the contract of employment. This will consider whether fiduciary duties can arise under this relationship, the consequences of the implied duty of mutual trust and confidence and whether there is an implied duty that the employer must exercise care for the economic and financial well-being of the employee.
(4) Other duties arising under contract or delict to the employee in relation to AE. These may arise under the conduct of investment business rules where an advisor fails in his professional obligations to the employer and/or employees. For contract-based pension schemes, a level of protection is offered by the FCA which requires members to adhere to its conduct of business rules. These rules require business to be conducted with due skill and care, fair treatment of customers, consideration of the information needs of clients, take reasonable care to ensure suitability of advice and to manage conflicts fairly.[1]

II. Fiduciary Duties Owed to Employees

The employer may owe fiduciary duties to the employee in respect of the method of implementing its employer AE obligations, in a similar way to the duties owed to scheme members by occupational pension scheme trustees.[2] However, the position in relation to contract-based schemes, such as group personal pensions, has always been governed by contract and FCA rules. Employers frequently use personal pension plans to comply with AE duties. With AE, there has been a blurring of the lines where the employer chooses a provider, the contractual terms, enrols the employee into the arrangement and then deducts contributions from salary. The employee may change the fund investment, level of contribution or choose to leave but cannot vary the contractual agreement or change provider other than by leaving the plan. Even with employers, the provider will write the contract terms and these are adhered to as they are 'take it or leave it contracts'.[3] Here the employees

[1] Financial Conduct Authority, 'FCA Handbook, COBS Conduct of Business Sourcebook 2, 4 & 9: www.handbook.fca.org.uk/handbook/COBS/.

[2] Pensions Act 1995.

[3] The Law Commission, *Fiduciary Duties of Investment Intermediaries* (Law Com No 350, 2014) para 8.6.

do not choose the pension contracts themselves as the contracts are arranged for employees by their employers under AE. My question here is whether fiduciary duties are owed by employers, product providers or advisors to the employees.

The question of fiduciary duties in pensions was considered in detail by the Law Commission in response to the recommendations of the Kay Review.[4] The Kay Review was critical of the short-termism in the UK equity market and the lack of accountability in investment chains.[5] While the aim of the report was to consider 'how far the law encourages pension funds and others to make long term investment decisions', it provides useful guidance about the nature of the relationships and conduct of business in the pensions industry.[6] Professor Kay reported that participants in the equity investment chain should observe fiduciary standards in their relationships with clients and customers, avoid conflicts of interest and put the clients' interests first.[7] It might then be argued that in exercising discretion and choosing the pension scheme for the employee, the employer acts as a de facto investment intermediary or should at least observe fiduciary standards in their dealings on behalf of the employees. This possibility is a clearly identified obligation in the US. Consequently, many employers do not provide investment education to employees for fear of being labelled a fiduciary.[8]

A. When Do Fiduciary Obligations Exist?

Fiduciary duties and the circumstances in which they arise can be difficult to identify. A fiduciary relationship is said to be 'analogous to that between express trustee and beneficiary, and a fiduciary obligation is a trustee-like obligation exported by analogy'.[9] As such the 'trustee' must promote the interests of the beneficiaries, avoid conflicts of interest and not profit from the trust. However, there can be a 'fine line between worsening a present condition and failing to improve the present condition'.[10] In other words, it can be difficult to determine whether there has been a breach even if the duties are found to apply. Any consideration of fiduciary duties needs to identify to whom the duties are owed, what the duties are and in what respect the breach occurred.[11] There are dangers of extending law by analogy. The 'slippery analogy with trustee' created by the word fiduciary requires careful

[4] ibid.

[5] J Kay, 'The Kay Review of UK Equity Markets and Long-Term Decision Making: Final Report' (Crown, July 2012).

[6] ibid, 2.

[7] ibid.

[8] P Secunda, 'The Behavioural Economic Case for Paternalistic Workplace Retirement Plans' (2016) 91 *Indiana Law Journal* 505, 509 & 520.

[9] P Birks, 'The Content of Fiduciary Obligation' (2000) 34 *Israeli Law Review* 3, 8.

[10] ibid, 19.

[11] *SEC v Chenery Corporation* 318 US 80, 85–86.

consideration of the circumstances and undertakings.[12] The following factors may indicate that a fiduciary obligation exists in relation to a particular matter:

- vulnerability of one party;
- the exercise of discretion by one party;
- management by one party of the affairs of the other party;
- the status or relationship between parties;
- contractual provisions.

i. Vulnerability

In establishing the fiduciary relationship one party is always dominant and another subordinate,[13] and 'Fiduciary Law governs relationships marked by asymmetries of power.'[14] In the employment relationship the employee is less powerful than the employer, traditionally viewed as subservient to the discretionary power of the employer.[15] Finn describes the judicial search for characteristics of fiduciary relationships and finds that vulnerability and reliance in contract may justify supervision of the relationship, but not imposition of the requirement of one party to act loyally in the other's interests.[16] The employee is particularly vulnerable in AE as he has no right to contribute to the process of choosing a pension product or provider. Finn discusses the difficulties with the *caveat emptor* rule in contract and suggests that the results have created an 'emerging trend to insist upon disclosure' where there is asymmetry of information in the contract.[17] Finn argues that this led to an exploitation of fiduciary law to ensure fair disclosure in contracts with courts considering whether to imply terms into contractual performance: 'When we describe a relationship as being fiduciary we are saying not only that it possesses certain characteristics but also that we wish to exact a particular standard of conduct (i.e. loyalty) from one or both parties to it.'[18]

ii. The Exercise of Discretion by One Party

The exercise of power by one party over the other might also define the fiduciary relationship and the exercise of discretion by one party is an indicator of

[12] Birks, 'The Content of Fiduciary Obligation', (n 9) 35.

[13] PB Miller, 'The Fiduciary Relationship' in AS Gold and PB Miller (eds), *Philosophical Foundations of Fiduciary Law* (Oxford University Press, 2014) 73.

[14] ibid, 1.

[15] J Murray, 'Conceptualizing the Employer as Fiduciary: Mission Impossible?' in A Bogg et al (eds), *The Autonomy of Labour Law* (Hart Publishing, 2015) 353.

[16] P Finn, 'Contract and the Fiduciary Principle' (1989) 12 *University of New South Wales Journal* 76, 85.

[17] ibid, 78.

[18] ibid, 83.

such power.[19] 'The fiduciary, by virtue of the power vested in her, stands in substitution for the beneficiary … in exercising legal capacity but the power will only be fiduciary in nature if it is discretionary.'[20] Smith argues that it is more about the exercise of judgement where the fiduciary has discretion and that this requires him to act in the best interests of the beneficiary.[21] Non-discretionary powers are less likely to be described as fiduciary in nature.[22] For example, execution only transactions lack the element of discretion and so will create contractual but not fiduciary duties. In AE the employer has complete discretion in respect of product provider and benefits. This is linked to the duty of loyalty discussed further below, in that the 'Fiduciary owes to the beneficiary a duty to exercise judgment in what the fiduciary perceives to be the best interest of the beneficiary.'[23]

iii. Management of the Affairs by One Party

The issues of trust and confidence and dependency demonstrate the roles of the parties in the relationship. The greater the amount of power delegated to one party to deal with the affairs of the other, the more likely that the recipient of the power will be treated as a fiduciary. For example, an asset manager has a wide degree of discretion.[24] Finn argues that there are many instances of inequality in contractual dealing but that this does not equate to one party owing fiduciary obligations to the other.[25] Fiduciary responsibilities are something more, where one party has relaxed self-vigilance as he believes that the other is acting in his interests.[26] Edelman discusses this suggesting that financial advisors are one of the recognised categories of fiduciary agents but this is because the financial advisor voluntarily assumes the obligation.[27]

In the employer/employee relationship, the employee relies on and trusts the employer to act in his best interests when dealing with the AE pension. Information asymmetries may then lead to the conclusion that the employer owes fiduciary duties to the employee. Such duties might then be qualified or limited by information provided to the employee by the employer. If the employer gives the employee access to information which would make him aware of the limits of the employer's responsibility does this act to limit the fiduciary effect? Financial transactions

[19] PB Miller, 'A Theory of Fiduciary Liability' (2011) 56 *McGill Law Journal* 235, 262.

[20] Miller, 'The Fiduciary Relationship', (n 13) 72.

[21] LD Smith, 'Can We Be Obliged to Be Selfless?' in AS Gold and PB Miller (eds), *Philosophical Foundations of Fiduciary Law* (Oxford University Press, 2014) 158.

[22] Miller, 'The Fiduciary Relationship', (n 13) 72.

[23] Smith, 'Can We Be Obliged to Be Selfless?', (n 21) 148.

[24] D Cabrelli, 'The Liability of Asset Managers in Scots Law' in D Busch and D DeMott (eds), *The Liability of Asset Managers* (Oxford University Press, 2012) 15.10.

[25] Finn, 'Contract and the Fiduciary Principle', (n 16) 94.

[26] ibid.

[27] J Edelman, 'The Role of Status in the Law of Obligations' in AS Gold and PB Miller (eds), *Philosophical Foundations of Fiduciary Law* (Oxford University Press, 2014) 38.

can be complicated and can lead to a finding of fiduciary like obligations being owed by banks to clients where there has been asymmetry in information and some assistance, advice or reliance. This is not a complete fiduciary relationship as the bank or provider still has self-interest in the transaction and so only certain aspects of performance may attach fiduciary like obligations. Finn concludes that 'Fiduciary Law is concerned with an imposed standard of conduct … not suited to the generality of contractual relationships.'[28]

Control of the assets of the other party may be an indicator of fiduciary status and this may arise in a wide range of business contexts, including contractual relationships, which may specify differing terms. Then 'a question arises about the way in which fiduciary obligations may be imposed alongside the obligations spelled out in the contract.'[29]

iv. Status or Relationship

Fiduciary duties are often presumed where a particular relationship or status exists or is implied because this is usual in the industry in which the office or status exists.[30] This approach may have been useful for trustees acting as custodians over property but the law has been extended beyond this holding of property. It now includes many relationships to be fiduciary in nature, whether trust exists or not and leaves us today with the difficulty that fiduciary law is difficult to define, identify and is entirely dependent on the given facts.[31] Company directors owe fiduciary duties to the company by virtue of appointment and so status is key. The duties of good faith, loyalty and duties of skill and care were owed under the common law but were codified by Chapter 2 of Part 10 of the Companies Act 2006. The statutory codification was necessary in part because of difficulties in determining the extent of duties owed which prevented legal certainty. Relationships between lawyers and clients and trustees and beneficiaries are generally thought to create fiduciary duties but academics have questioned this approach of using status to define obligations.[32] It has been argued that, instead of reliance on status, the undertakings of the particular matter should be reviewed to identify whether fiduciary obligations arise. The status of the parties may still provide strong evidence of the nature of such undertakings and 'often the relationship is the reason why undertaken duties are fiduciary'.[33] The effect of the relationship on status is illustrated in a Canadian case which provides that 'Even in the case of a solicitor – client

[28] Finn, 'Contract and the Fiduciary Principle', (n 16) 97.

[29] *F & C Alternative Investments (Holdings) Ltd v Barthelemy (No 2)* [2011] EWHC 1731 (Ch), [2012] Ch 613, 650.

[30] Edelman, 'The Role of Status in the Law of Obligations', (n 27) 30.

[31] J Edelman, 'When do fiduciary duties arise?' (2010) 126 *Law Quarterly Review* 302, 305.

[32] Gold and Miller, *Philosophical Foundations of Fiduciary Law*, (n 13) 3.

[33] Edelman, 'The Role of Status in the Law of Obligations', (n 27) 34.

relationship, long accepted as a status based fiduciary relationship, the duty is not derived from status. As in all such cases, the duty is derived from what the solicitor undertakes.'[34]

Edelman suggests that where duties are undertaken, the status is important in determining the scope but that not every undertaking made by a person in a fiduciary relationship will be a fiduciary obligation.[35] Conversely, fiduciary duties may arise despite the absence of a relationship of trust and confidence.[36] Although Edelman concedes that it is often necessary to consider status to determine the consequences of an undertaking as the law currently stands.[37] DeMott argues that descriptions of fiduciary drawn from contract law principles are mistaken.[38] She describes the historical development of fiduciary law from equity and suggests that it can operate 'precisely in opposition to intention'.[39] Contractual intention is irrelevant: 'Once a court concludes that a particular relationship has a fiduciary character, the parties' manifest intention does not control their obligations to each other as dispositively as it does under a contract analysis.'[40]

The ability to recover from a fiduciary under disgorgement even where the beneficiary has suffered no loss is another clear distinction between fiduciary law and contract. DeMott argues that it is the whole nature and circumstances which will determine whether the relationship is a fiduciary one and then any undertakings are subject to the fiduciary obligations. She gives the example of a designated trustee who has not been given any authority or discretionary power who may not be considered a fiduciary.[41] The law defines the obligations inherent in a particular relationship but the parties define the relationship by their conduct and agreement.[42]

a. Status: Product Provider/Employer's Advisors as Fiduciaries

The question arises as to whether the pension product provider or the employer's advisors owe any fiduciary obligations to the employee. This could be in the act of providing information to employees or otherwise dealing with pre or post contract issues. It seems that the contractual terms are generally agreed between the employer and the provider/advisors and this might lead to an expectation of fiduciary duties owed by the advisor to the employer. Contractual provisions may seek to specifically exclude this and it will depend on the nature of the relationship.

[34] *Beach Petroleum v Kennedy* (1999) 48 NSWLR 1, 188.
[35] Edelman, 'The Role of Status in the Law of Obligations', (n 27) 21.
[36] ibid, 25.
[37] ibid.
[38] D DeMott, 'Beyond Metaphor: An Analysis of Fiduciary Obligation' [1988] *Duke Law Journal* 879.
[39] ibid, 887.
[40] ibid.
[41] ibid, 901.
[42] ibid, 902.

If the advisor or provider engages with the employee this may also constitute a fiduciary relationship in certain conditions. It is sometimes believed that the advisory function leads to the assumption that all advisors are fiduciaries of their clients[43] but this may be incorrect and it is not clear what the position is in relation to putative clients (the employees) in the AE situation. Edelman warns of the danger of relying on status for implication of terms because the same status can describe many different types of relationship[44] and Miller warns that 'Many of the tasks undertaken pursuant to these relationships may not be trust-like or attract a fiduciary obligation.'[45] For example, a financial advisor undertakes to provide advice and will be considered a fiduciary but a tied advisor may not be where he provides only information and not advice. Edelman refers to Australian case law on this point. In one case, financial advisors were recognised as being within the class of recognised fiduciaries but it was emphasised that this was because the financial advisor had voluntarily assumed the established fiduciary obligations.[46]

The nature of undertakings, here the provision of advice, taken with the status forms evidence of the extent of the fiduciary obligations. In addition to the giving of advice, it is suggested that there must be an element of discretion being exercised to establish that the advisor is a fiduciary. A financial firm may owe fiduciary duties where the firm moves beyond a 'mere salesman'.[47] Another example is the situation where a bank advises a customer on financial affairs and an expectation of advice is created with the customer relying on this.[48] It is clear from my empirical study that there are misunderstandings about the role of product providers and advisors and whether information or advice is provided. Consequently, both employers and employees may be able to demonstrate that the provider of information was relied on and trusted as an advisor and undertook the fiduciary responsibility of advisor rather than merely acting as a salesman, especially where there is a discretionary element.

b. Status: Employer as Fiduciary

It might be assumed that in agreeing a contract of employment, the parties have determined the basis of their relationship and that there is consequently no room for 'equity to supervise abuses of discretionary power'.[49] The obligations arising from the contract of employment and what this means for AE are discussed below.[50] Despite this, a presumption that the employment relationship can give

[43] Miller, 'The Fiduciary Relationship', (n 13) 83.
[44] Edelman, 'The Role of Status in the Law of Obligations', (n 27) 37.
[45] Miller, 'The Fiduciary Relationship', (n 13) 83, quoting *Hodgkinson v Simms* [1994] 3 SCR 377.
[46] *Wingecarribee Shire Council v Lehman Bros Australia Ltd (in liq)* [2012] FCA 1028 [733], per Rares J.
[47] *Bathurst Regional Council v Local Government Financial Services Pty Ltd (No 5)* [2012] FCA 1200 [2324].
[48] *Commonwealth Bank of Australia v Smith* [1991] FCA 375; (1991) 42 FCR 390, 391.
[49] Murray, 'Conceptualizing the Employer', (n 15) 337–366, 346.
[50] Part IV, below.

rise to fiduciary duties has been established by case law over the past 60 years.[51] Brodie is critical of the development stating that:

> The fact that, from time to time, the employee may owe some fiduciary obligations may lead to the erroneous assumption that the employment relationship is fiduciary in nature. The emergence of the implied obligation of mutual trust and confidence, and in particular the manner in which it is expressed, may also serve to confuse.[52]

Brodie considers the question of disclosure as an example. An employee is not obliged to disclose his own misconduct but a fiduciary would be. This may categorise some relationships as fiduciary where the circumstances of the contractual obligations and role oblige senior employees to disclose their own misconduct. There are increasing examples of senior managers being found to owe fiduciary obligations where they can exercise discretion and affect the employer's economic interests.[53] It could be a logical extension to say that the employer may also owe such obligations to the employee in some circumstances. However, the operation of the employment law relationship where the parties do not subjugate their own interests to the other may prevent such a finding.[54] Exploring the distinction between fiduciary duties and the implied obligation of mutual trust and confidence, Brodie suggests that the courts must 'determine how the implied obligations of mutual trust and confidence and fidelity should be read together' and suggests that older cases dealing with fidelity 'may have been based on the erroneous view that the employment contract is fiduciary in nature'.[55]

However, the law appears to be shifting away from finding the entire employment law relationship to be fiduciary.[56] In the *Fishel* case, an embryologist who was employed by the University undertook a number of private engagements abroad. When he left to set up his own private clinic the University alleged breach of the employment contract and breach of fiduciary duties. In respect of his own work there was found to be no conflict of interest with the University, but in so far as he had deployed colleagues from the University a conflict did arise. His financial gain from using colleagues for this work was at the expense of the University and was found to be in breach of his fiduciary obligations. The implied contractual obligation of fidelity was used as 'a hook on which to hang the breach'.[57] The most important component is the relationship of trust and confidence and the duty of

[51] *Reading v Attorney General* [1951] UKHL 1; 1951 AC 507; *Stoelwinder v Southern Health* [2001] FCA 115, [39]; *Hospital Products Ltd v United States Surgical Corporation* [1984] HCA 64, 156 CLR 41.

[52] D Brodie, 'The Employment Relationship and Fiduciary Obligations' (2012) 16 *Edinburgh Law Review* 198, 200.

[53] *Anderson Smyth and Kelly Customs Brokers v World Wide Customs Brokers* [1996] 7 WWR 736; *Collidge v Freeport* [2007] EWHC 1216 (QB); [2007] 5 WLUK 673.

[54] See part IV(A)(i), below.

[55] Brodie, 'The Employment Relationship and Fiduciary Obligations', (n 52) 208.

[56] *University of Nottingham v Fishel* [2000] EWHC 221 (QB), IRLR 471; *Samsung Semiconductor Europe v Docherty* [2011] CSOH 32, [2011] SLT 806.

[57] Murray, 'Conceptualizing the Employer', (n 15) 344.

loyalty is key.[58] However this case clearly sets out that mere employment does not create fiduciary obligations but the duties exist where they arise from particular contractual obligations and within the constraints of the contractual relationship.[59] This case supports the argument that, whilst the employment relationship itself is not entirely fiduciary in nature, it may give rise to fiduciary obligations where these are undertaken as part of the contractual obligations. A fiduciary may not be a fiduciary for all purposes. This would allow a finding that the employer is a fiduciary in respect of choosing the AE scheme but not in other respects.[60]

Much of the consideration of the point has related to the extent to which the obligation is owed by employees to the employer, but in our case the question is whether the employer might owe a fiduciary duty to its employees. The courts have more recently recognised the asymmetry in information and power in the employment relationship which Brodie opines 'makes it highly improbable that the employment relationship will move into the world of fiduciary relations'.[61] He contends that the required vulnerability in a fiduciary relationship cannot really be attributed to the employer but asks whether recognition of the employee's vulnerability might result in the employer owing fiduciary obligations to the employee. The mutuality in the relationship, however, means the employer is entitled to have regard to its own interests rather than simply considering those of the employee. Sims also identifies the mutuality in the employment relationship as differing from the fiduciary relationship[62] it is distinct and 'The implied term of trust and confidence is not some watered-down version of a fiduciary obligation.'[63]

It may be that the facts disclose fiduciary obligations within the employment relationship on an ad hoc basis and the courts have been willing to construe this in some instances.[64] In relation to the question of financial control and the relationship, many aspects can be controlled by the employment contract itself. However, the control of contributions deducted from salary for AE is often not mentioned in contractual terms. It may be that the holding of assets in this way further characterises this part of the relationship as agency with its own specific fiduciary obligations.[65] It seems unlikely that the whole employment relationship will be classed as fiduciary in nature but there may be particular aspects or undertakings which are fiduciary in nature.

v. *Contractual Undertakings*

Rather than considering status as the key factor in determining whether fiduciary duties arise in a situation, the alternative approach is to consider the nature and

[58] V Sims, 'Is Employment a Fiduciary Relationship?' (2001) 30 *Industrial Law Journal* 101, 102.
[59] *University of Nottingham v Fishel*, (n 56).
[60] *Beach Petroleum v Kennedy*, (n 34) 188.
[61] Brodie, 'The Employment Relationship and Fiduciary Obligations', (n 52) 209.
[62] Sims, 'Is Employment a Fiduciary Relationship?', (n 58) 103.
[63] ibid.
[64] *Credit Lyonnais Bank Nederland NV v Burch* [1996] EWCA Civ 1292; [1997] 1 All ER 144.
[65] See part III, below.

extent of undertakings. The question really is whether the relationship between the parties has a role in defining the fiduciary duties or whether it is dependent on the nature of the voluntary undertaking. Much of the case law seems to establish the relationship first and then find that the duties follow. For example, in the solicitor and client relationship the position of trust in which the solicitor is held may result in the finding of a general duty where the solicitor is found to have undertaken responsibility for certain matters in a fiduciary capacity.[66] Fiduciary undertakings to one party may also preclude a finding of fiduciary duties being owed to another, as in the case of a company director. The nature of the relationship of three natural persons who sat on the board of an LLP and whether this made them agents of a holding company when they also owed fiduciary duties to the LLP was recently considered.[67] Fiduciary obligations were found to arise where a person assumes responsibility for the management of another's property or affairs but this does not depend on contract. However, the contract will provide the 'contextual framework in which the question [which fiduciary obligations apply in the context] arises'.[68] The contractual relationship in this way moulds the fiduciary obligations,[69] in that the 'Fiduciary duties are obligations imposed by law as a reaction to particular circumstances of responsibility assumed by one person in respect of the conduct of the affairs of the other.'[70] In other words, fiduciary duties are like implied terms construed in return for other voluntary undertakings. It is not the relationship that causes the fiduciary obligations to apply but the obligations cause the relationship to be fiduciary. Finn described this saying that a person 'is not subject to fiduciary obligations because he is a fiduciary; it is because he is subject to them that he is a fiduciary'.[71] Edelman argues that a fiduciary's duty is not derived from status although 'status may play an important part of the background material by informing the duties which are undertaken by particular persons'.[72] It is the undertaking which is manifested in the conduct, words and circumstances of the fiduciary which can identify the obligations.[73] If the undertaking incorporates a pledge that it will be performed in a particular way, perhaps in the best interests of one party, then this might indicate that a fiduciary duty arises.[74]

A person can assume some form of responsibility without a contract but it will be more difficult to prove.[75] A detailed contractual agreement setting out terms which demonstrate that there is no fiduciary intent may also dispel the suggestion of extra obligations.[76] Contract does not fully provide for all situations where

[66] Edelman, 'When do fiduciary duties arise?', (n 31) 311.
[67] *F & C Alternative Investments (Holdings) Ltd v Barthelemy (No 2)*, (n 29).
[68] ibid, 650.
[69] *Hilton v Barker Booth & Eastwood* [2005] UKHL 8; [2005] 1 WLR 567.
[70] *F & C Alternative Investments (Holdings) Ltd v Barthelemy (No 2)*, (n 29) 652.
[71] P Finn, *Fiduciary Obligations* (Federation Press, 1977) 2.
[72] Edelman, 'The Role of Status in the Law of Obligations', (n 27) 21.
[73] ibid, 24.
[74] ibid, 25.
[75] Birks, 'The Content of Fiduciary Obligation', (n 9) 20.
[76] *F & C Alternative Investments (Holdings) Ltd v Barthelemy (No 2)*, (n 29).

undertakings have legal effect and the key is whether there has been a voluntary assumption of responsibility for some matter.[77] Conaglen argues that the fiduciary duties, where they arise, are like supporting duties, 'in the sense that they protect non-fiduciary duties, but they are not secondary duties'.[78] Fiduciary duties are likened to 'legal polyfilla'[79] which can be moulded to fill gaps but are not the whole structure. In other words, fiduciary obligations are there to ensure proper performance of contractual obligations. Case law has favoured the contract as the foundation for the relationship:

> Where a fiduciary relationship arises, it must accommodate itself to the terms of any contract between the parties. The courts will not superimpose a fiduciary relationship upon a contract so as to alter the operation which it was intended to have.[80]

In this Australian case, the majority of the court found that fiduciary duties did not apply but the dissenting judgement of Mason J has subsequently been widely cited with approval.[81] The dissenting judgement applies 'an attenuated fiduciary duty to the contract in order to intensify the duties of due performance and curb the contractor's powers of efficient breach.'[82] The implication of fiduciary duties into contract must be justified by the surrounding circumstances and should not be imposed on the parties where the surrounding circumstances do not support this.

a. Contractual Undertakings: Loyalty

A key undertaking of the fiduciary is loyalty. A fiduciary is someone who has undertaken to act for, or on behalf of, another in a particular matter in circumstances which give rise to a relationship of trust and confidence. The distinguishing obligation of a fiduciary is the obligation of 'single-minded loyalty of his fiduciary'.[83] From this duty of loyalty follows the duties to act in good faith, not profit from the trust, not expose himself to conflict of interest and not act in such circumstances without the informed consent of the principal.[84] Getzler questions how the undertaking leads to the fiduciary liability, asking whether consent is required for each duty or implied by law.[85] He contends that in fiduciary law the highly protective default position protects the vulnerable creating a 'penalty default' and

[77] Edelman, 'When do fiduciary duties arise?', (n 31) 309.

[78] M Conaglen, 'The Nature and Function of Fiduciary Loyalty' (2005) 121 *Law Quarterly Review* 452, 471.

[79] The Law Commission, *Fiduciary Duties of Investment Intermediaries*, (n 3) 6.

[80] *Hospital Products Ltd v United States Surgical Corporation*, (n 51).

[81] *Kelly v Cooper* [1993] AC 205, 215; *Rosetti Marketing Ltd v Diamond Sofa Company Ltd* [2012] EWCA Civ 1021, [2013] 1 All ER (Comm) 308; *Hilton v Barker Booth & Eastwood.*

[82] J Getzler, 'Ascribing Fiduciary Obligations' in AS Gold and PB Miller (eds), *Philosophical Foundations of Fiduciary Law* (Oxford University Press, 2014) 47.

[83] *Bristol and West Building Society v Mothew* [1996] EWCA Civ 533, [1998] Ch 1, 18.

[84] AS Gold, 'The Loyalties of Fiduciary Law' in AS Gold and PB Miller (eds), *Philosophical Foundations of Fiduciary Law* (Oxford University Press, 2014).

[85] Getzler, 'Ascribing Fiduciary Obligations', (n 82) 48.

that any departures should be on the basis of well informed consent.[86] Birks has also commented that loyalty as a concept is less than useful.[87] There must also be an element of specification in a fiduciary exercise of power. A duty 'cannot be a legal duty unless it specifies sufficiently narrowly the conduct that it requires' which leads Smith to argue that loyalty is not a specific enough term and that it is the particular way that the fiduciary exercises judgement which encapsulates the duty.[88]

Smith's argument is persuasive and, when applied to the AE situation, it is possible to find that the employer owes a duty to the employee because of the exercise of judgement and discretion when choosing a pension to invest the employees' contributions in. It is the position of power, held by the employer, which may limit the effect of contractual exclusions. The fiduciary duties are imposed because of the social and economic power wielded by employers.[89] A key element of this is the deduction of employee contributions from salary which the employer is then entrusted to invest on behalf of the employee. In holding the employees' assets and using discretion and judgement to invest them it is difficult to imagine that the employer does not owe a duty of some kind but whether this is fiduciary in nature is unclear because of competing employer interests. If the undertakings were agreed, without the imposition of AE, it would seem to be a voluntary fiduciary undertaking but the fact that the undertakings are imposed by the AE legislation rather than voluntarily assumed may impact on such a finding. The position is arguable and the courts may find fiduciary duties can exist in this situation but the lack of certainty of the legal position here is unsatisfactory. Rather than just set out the basic AE requirements a standard of care in exercising judgement to comply with AE would be an improvement.

B. The Consequences of Fiduciary Obligations

Whether it is the status or the undertaking which establishes the fiduciary obligation, the key element is whether one party has a reasonable expectation that the other will act in his best interests in some respect.[90] It is important then to consider which duties might be considered to be fiduciary in nature: leading to the conclusion that the relationship is fiduciary. They are often described in terms of loyalty and arise where there is a voluntary undertaking to act in the interests of the other party:

> It is partly because the fiduciary's exercise of power or discretion can adversely affect the interests of the person to whom the duty is owed and because the latter is at the mercy

[86] ibid, 61.
[87] Birks, 'The Content of Fiduciary Obligation', (n 9) 12.
[88] Smith, 'Can We Be Obliged to Be Selfless?', (n 21) 151.
[89] S Freeman, 'Women at Work: The Broken Promise of Flexicurity' (2004) 33 *Industrial Law Journal* 299, 301.
[90] Edelman, 'The Role of Status in the Law of Obligations', (n 27) 25.

of the former that the fiduciary comes under a duty to exercise his power or discretion in the interests of the person to whom it is owed.[91]

Edelman describes the coalescence of academic and judicial thinking into a 'test based upon the 'reasonable' or 'legitimate expectations of a principal' as part of the process of identifying the nature of fiduciary duties which have been voluntarily undertaken.[92] In general terms the obligations include:

- avoiding conflicts of interest;
- not making a profit at the principal's expense (without their express consent);
- a duty to act in the best interests of the beneficiaries; and
- performing obligations or undertakings in good faith.

The duty to act in the best interests of the beneficiaries is considered above in consideration of the role of loyalty in establishing whether the relationship is fiduciary in nature. The difficulty with such broad terms is that they can be vague and it can be unclear from contractual or other evidence of the undertakings as to what is expected by the parties. It might be that these are construed as the 'proper purposes for which the trustee had agreed to act',[93] emphasising that the obligations come from voluntary undertakings rather than the status of the individuals.[94] The performance of obligations in good faith can be difficult to define and 'the precise content of the obligation will vary depending on the particular circumstances'.[95] There can be recovery for breach of a fiduciary duty in a situation in which there is no loss caused by breach of contract. If a fiduciary obligation is owed then this would allow disgorgement of profits made by the fiduciary to remove any benefit gained from a fiduciary who has acted in conflict of interest.[96] The beneficiary may also rescind a resultant transaction where the fiduciary is found to have breached its obligations.

Whilst it is possible that the employer or its advisors may owe fiduciary like duties to the employees, in respect of choice of AE scheme and provision of information, this does not make them fiduciaries in law. Loyalty precludes self-interest and so should be restricted in its use only where it is genuinely applicable. The restriction on self-interest is one factor which is likely to preclude a fiduciary finding in the employment relationship and also between the employee and providers of AE information or guidance. Many of the indicators of a fiduciary relationship are in evidence in the AE situation but it is uncertain whether the courts would find that employers owe a general fiduciary obligation to employees in complying with AE. Providers or advisors may also owe fiduciary obligations if they have

[91] *Hospital Products Ltd v United States Surgical Corporation*, (n 51) 97.
[92] Edelman, 'When do fiduciary duties arise?', (n 31) 8.
[93] D Nicholls, 'Trustees and Their Broader Community: Where Duty, Morality and Ethics Converge' (1995) 9(3) *Trust Law International* 71, 74.
[94] Edelman, 'When do fiduciary duties arise?', (n 31) 10.
[95] *F & C Alternative Investments (Holdings) Ltd v Barthelemy (No 2)*, (n 29) [655].
[96] Conaglen, 'The Nature and Function of Fiduciary Loyalty', (n 78) 463.

taken on the role of advisor to the employee as well as to the employer, but my research indicates that they are unlikely to do this.

III. Duties Owed by the Employer as an Agent

Even if there is no general fiduciary relationship between the employer and employees, it might be argued that in taking charge of arranging the pension contract, choosing provider, deducting contributions from the employee's salary and making decisions about when to change providers or schemes in future, the employer acts as an agent of the employee. If so, the employer may owe fiduciary duties under agency even if these are not apparent from the general contractual terms or the relationship generally. The power of the agent (employer) in this instance, is to enter into and act under a legally valid contract on behalf of the principal (employee).[97]

This will not occur in all instances of AE because, where employers use a trust-based scheme for AE, the employer does not contract with a provider on behalf of the employee but facilitates admission to a trust based scheme with its own trustees and administrators. The scheme trustees will then owe fiduciary duties to scheme members. Fiduciary duties of trustees extend to careful consideration of investing the funds and appropriateness of defaults.[98] This also means that employers of trust based DC schemes must commit to the costs required to allow the scheme trustees to execute their duties but the fiduciary duties remain with the trustees. This contrasts with the US where plan administrators have fiduciary duties to select prudent investment options meaning that the plan sponsor retains responsibility for the investment options available to employees under the plan.[99] In many cases, the US employer has responsibility for choosing the range of investment options for the 401k plan. Employers might delegate this fiduciary duty to an investment firm but these firms are then in conflict as they have commercial considerations, are employed by the plan sponsor and may not always provide advice in the best interests of the beneficiaries.[100] These concerns led to a direction that the Securities and Exchange Commission undertake a study into whether there were clear duties for advisors and brokers.[101] In the resulting study, it was noted that 'many retail investors do not understand and are confused by the roles played by investment advisors and broker-dealers'.[102] Consequently it is

[97] Miller, 'The Fiduciary Relationship', (n 13) 79.

[98] Pensions Act 1995, ss 33–36; Occupational Pension Schemes (Investment) Regulations 2005 (SI 2005/3378); Pensions Act 2008, s 17(2).

[99] Secunda, 'The Behavioural Economic Case', (n 8) 505, 518–519.

[100] ibid.

[101] Dodd Frank Wall Street Reform and Consumer Protection Act (2010), r 913(g).

[102] SEC, 'Study on Investment Advisers and Broker-Dealers as Required by Section 913 of the Dodd-Frank Wall Street Reform and Consumer Protection Act' (2011), 128. www.sec.gov/news/studies/2011/913studyfinal.pdf.

recommended that there should be a 'uniform fiduciary standard of conduct for broker-dealers and investment advisors when providing personalized investment advice about securities to retail customers'.[103] Similar provisions for advisors exist in Australia[104] so that the client's interests are always key but this is not prescriptive in terms of, for example, how many funds should be reviewed before recommending investments.[105] Those providers permitted to offer the MySuper products act as trustees and product providers in Australia may have to 'juggle their fiduciary obligations under trust law and their role as product providers in a competitive market'.[106] Research demonstrates that the fiduciary obligations to members are paramount.[107] However, the strict default options for MySuper, discussed in previous chapters, mean that the employer does not have the same opportunity to affect the investment options as in the US.

A complication in the case of a UK employer contracting with a provider using a personal pension, is that the employer contracts on behalf of the employee to take out a personal pension contract but will also contract with the provider separately in relation to the administration. It may also be argued by the employer that the product provider or financial advisor acts as its agent in providing information and assistance to employees on its behalf, although standard contractual terms with the provider may exclude agency obligations in this context. Agents act subject to the instructions of their principals and limitations are generally specified by agreement.

The contract of employment is unlikely to specify the basis on which the employer contracts with the provider to enrol the employees into personal pension contracts under AE. This does not mean that the agency relationship does not exist as agency may arise without a formal contract. Facts and circumstances may be averred to prove the existence of the agency relationship.[108] In Scotland, this need not be a written agreement and the party alleging agency must show who the parties are, where and when the contract was entered and the terms and form of the contract.[109] In England, there is no requirement for a contract to establish agency and so the facts must establish that one party consented to the exercise of authority to act.[110]

[103] ibid, vi.

[104] Introduced from 2012. The Australian Government, Cooper Super System Review: final report (2010) 158 https://treasury.gov.au/sites/default/files/2019-03/R2009-001_Final_Report_Part_1_Consolidated.pdf.

[105] H Bateman, 'The Future of Financial Advice and MySuper' (2012) 3 *The Finsia Journal of Applied Finance* 50.

[106] Butt et al 'Design of MySuper default funds: influences and outcomes' (2017) 57 *Accounting and Finance* 47–85, 48.

[107] ibid.

[108] L Macgregor, 'Defining Agency and Its Scope (I)' in H DiMatteo and M Hogg (eds), *Transatlantic Perspectives on Commercial Contract Law* (Oxford University Press, 2015) 4.

[109] *Rodewald v Taylor* [2011] CSOH 5, [2011] 1 WLUK 238 [33]; L Macgregor, *The Law of Agency in Scotland* (Scottish Universities Law Institute: W Green/Thomson Reuters, 2013) 35.

[110] PG Watts and FMB Reynolds, *Bowstead and Reynolds on Agency* 19th edn (Sweet and Maxwell, 2010), 1-001.

A. The Agency Relationship

The law of agency 'refers to a relationship, usually created by contract, in terms of which the principal instructs the agent to act on his behalf in order to produce legally binding effects for the principal'.[111] This relationship is fiduciary in that the agent owes loyalty to the principal. The generic terms in the contract of employment and lack of contractual instruction by the principal (employee) is not fatal to a finding of agency as the employer is responsible for implementing AE under statute and contracting on behalf of the employee in the context of the employment law contract. There is no requirement that the agency contract is in writing and even where there are instructions, these are often incomplete leaving the agent to decide what to do.[112] Non-consensual agency could be established where the power ceded to the agent is sufficient to establish the relationship. The creation involves 'the grant of legal powers to the so-called agent, and the creation of correlative liabilities in the principal'.[113] It can be argued that the employee cedes power to the employer to contract with pension providers on his behalf and that the employer has control of the employee's assets (deductions from salary as contributions). This ceding of power is evidence of an agency relationship.

The employee may be said to have granted authority to the employer to contract with any pension provider it chooses although, with AE, the employee is simply advised of AE and he has no right to opt-out until after the contract is concluded. The employee has no say in the choice of provider and the employer's unfettered power may go against a finding of agency.[114] However, if we consider other examples of agency, such as the lawyer acting as agent for the client, many decisions will be made without the client's express consent and the client may lack knowledge to properly supervise the actions of the agent. DeMott describes control in an agency relationship as 'prescribing on an ongoing basis what the agent shall or shall not do'.[115] The principal's inferior expertise means that he exercises control by selecting a particular agent and scoping objectives. In a similar way to the lawyer described by DeMott, the employer is not completely controlled by the principal's wishes and must also follow other rules and requirements. For the lawyer, the agency relationship does not justify breaches of conduct or crimes and as such agents are still subject to legal limits of what may be undertaken on behalf of the principal. In our scenario, the employee cannot ask the employer not to auto-enrol him as this is required externally by

[111] Macgregor, *The Law of Agency in Scotland*, (n 109) 13.

[112] DA DeMott, 'The Fiduciary Character of Agency' in AS Gold and PB Miller (eds), *Philosophical Foundations of Fiduciary Law* (Oxford University Press, 2014) 323.

[113] WN Hohfield, 'Some Fundamental Legal Conceptions as Applied in Judicial Reasoning' (1913) 23 *Yale Law Journal* 16, 46.

[114] DA DeMott, 'Defining Agency and Its Scope (I)' in H DiMatteo and M Hogg (eds), *Transatlantic Perspectives on Commercial Contract Law* (Oxford University Press, 2015).

[115] DA DeMott, 'The Lawyer as Agent' (1999) 67 *Fordham Law Review* 301, 303.

operation of the AE legislation. It may also be difficult to establish how the parties characterise the AE situation given the complexities of a multi-faceted employment law relationship.

i. Implied Agency

Agency can be implied from the facts, and proof depends on both facts and law. Silence of the employee may imply consent to the agency if it is clear that there was intention to be bound. However, tacit agency may be difficult to distinguish from cases where the agent acts without authority.[116] It seems impossible that the employer could be considered a general agent for the employee in all matters but it might be implied in respect of the specific purpose of choosing a pension scheme for AE. Implication was considered recently in the context of whether the party who had been served notice of a break clause had authority, as an agent, to receive the notice.[117] Lord Hodge found that 'In the absence of express authority creating a general agency, there must be clear evidence to support the inference of such agency.'[118]

An agency relationship was recently found to exist between a credit broker and its consumer client.[119] The client had been sent a guide which she did not read and was also advised on the telephone that Norton only offered information and not advice. Considering whether a contract of agency existed, Tomlinson LJ identified that the key question was whether Norton was 'acting in a capacity which involved the repose of trust and confidence' and that 'one critical factor is the nature of the borrowers'.[120] Tomlinson LJ found that a person could appear reasonably competent at dealing with straightforward financial transactions but not be considered financially sophisticated and could have a legitimate expectation that the other party will consider his best interests.[121]

This may be important for employees who have not read the pensions information given to them but instead rely on the relationship with the employer to ensure the best decisions are made. In the *McWilliam* case, the information given to the couple was found to be insufficient to adequately alert them to the commission payments and consequently they did not give informed consent. Employees could claim that there is an implied agency relationship within the employer/employee relationship in the specific role of the employer selecting a pension scheme to use to implement AE. This may also increase the requirements of communications to employees to contain more specific information and warnings.

[116] Macgregor, *The Law of Agency in Scotland*, (n 109) 37.
[117] *Batt Cables Plc v Spencer Business Parks Ltd* [2010] CSOH 81, (2010) SLT 860.
[118] ibid, [36].
[119] *McWilliam v Norton Finance* [2015] EWCA Civ 186, [2015] 1 All ER (Comm) 1026.
[120] ibid, [40]–[41].
[121] ibid, [42].

B. Consequences of Agency

An agent has implied authority to perform those actions required to execute the agency agreement.[122] AE is unlikely to create contractual terms of agency. As such, all the terms are likely to be implied and so it would be almost impossible to determine the difference between actual and apparent authority. Actual authority exists where there is consensual agreement between two parties that one will act as agent. Implied actual authority may be implied to ensure that such acts as are necessary for performance of the agency obligations are included within actual authority.[123] Apparent authority occurs where a third party believes that an agent has authority to act and relies on this. This in effect binds the principal to the third party even where they did not consent, the principal is personally barred from claiming lack of authority and denying the contract.[124] In effect apparent authority provides a backstop to actual authority when proving actual authority would be difficult for a third party.[125]

If the employer acts as an agent for the employee in relation to AE does this mean that particular care standards would need to be adhered to in choosing the provider, scheme and making decisions about changes in future? Agents owe fiduciary obligations to their principal and must avoid conflicts of interest as discussed generally above.[126] Agents also owe separate non-fiduciary duties to act with reasonable care in the performance of their agency duties.[127] For non-gratuitous agency, such as this, the agent must 'act with that diligence and discretion which a man of prudence uses in his affairs'.[128] The employer does not act here as a professional agent but must still act with reasonable care in performance of duties. Consequently, it could be argued that employers, acting as agents, must demonstrate that they acted with care in making choices about pension providers, selecting pension plans and benefits and administering the arrangement. The difficulty with the employer/employee relationship is the expectation that the employer has legitimate interests in considering its business needs as well as the needs of the employee and this may prevent a finding that the employer acts as an agent in relation to AE. The employer may decide not to spend money on advice and pick any provider or scheme that comes to hand without any thought. If the employer were making a similar decision for itself more care might be exercised. Failure to exercise the same care when choosing an AE plan could then be a breach of the agent's standard of care toward the principal as implied in the agency contract. The cost of obtaining advice on the continuing compliance with AE might also prevent

[122] *JM & JH Robertson v Beatson, McLeod & Company Ltd* [1908] SC 921.
[123] ibid, 84, 87.
[124] ibid, 265.
[125] DeMott, 'The Fiduciary Character of Agency', (n 112) 331.
[126] Macgregor, 'Defining Agency and Its Scope (I)', (n 108).
[127] Macgregor, *The Law of Agency in Scotland*, (n 109) 106.
[128] J Erskine, *An Institute of the Law of Scotland III.3.37* (1695–1768).

an employer changing scheme or provider even if the existing scheme offers poor value compared to other products. In an agency relationship, the fiduciary duties and non-fiduciary duties of care might assist the employee in claiming for loss arising from poor decisions by the employer as his agent.

As discussed under general fiduciary obligations above, some case law suggests that fiduciary obligations are constrained by the contractual agreement.[129] The facts and circumstances of the agency relationship can also limit the scope of obligations owed. In Scotland, agents have long been recognised as acting for single transactions or as special agents and this will restrict fiduciary and non-fiduciary obligations.[130] 'Where there is … a limited, as opposed to a general agency, any duties of care imposed on the agent must be related to and limited by the extent of the agency.'[131]

In this case, the relationship was contractual but not fiduciary.[132] In the case of the employer acting to contract with a provider for the employee, the fact that the employer also holds the employees' assets (deductions from salary as contributions) may be significant and make a finding that the employer is a fiduciary more likely. The deductions remain the employee's money but are dealt with by the employer (possibly as agent). Where the money is deducted and paid into a trust-based scheme the funds are entirely separate from both the employer's and employee's funds. However, where a personal pension contract is used, the funds are paid over to the product provider and are held as assets in a policy in the name of the employee. The deductions and payment process is regulated by the AE legislation and require timeous payment and accounting to the employee but it is the employer who is responsible for ensuring calculations are correct and making the deductions from pay and transfers.

Agents are also obliged to impart knowledge to the principal so information given to the employer by the provider should be passed on.[133] In AE, the product provider is often contracted by the employer to provide the employees with information and support in relation to AE and it is not clear what role the provider takes on as they are party to contracts with both the employer and the employee. Most providers will offer strict standard terms excluding any liability as an agent or otherwise.

An agent also has non-fiduciary obligations which may be just as significant as the fiduciary duties namely: the duty to follow instructions; to exercise skill and care; duty not to delegate and duty to account. For AE, the employee cannot give instructions to the employer as the employer is required to implement AE under statutory obligations. A failure to meet the skill and care obligation may result in a claim in delict or under the contractual terms of agency but does not have

[129] *Hospital Products Ltd v United States Surgical Corporation*, (n 51).
[130] *Sao Paolo Alpargatas SA v Standard Chartered Bank* [1985] SLT 433.
[131] ibid, 436.
[132] ibid, 438.
[133] DeMott, 'The Lawyer as Agent', (n 115) 307.

the sanctions of disgorgement or forfeiture of profit available under the fiduciary obligations.[134] An agent may act for multiple principals in some circumstances and we might say that the employer acts in this way by enrolling all its employees into pensions. The balancing of interests here may lead to a more generic product which may not be in the best interests of all the employees and may breach conflict of interest requirements. However, it seems that the interests of the employees are generally aligned and this is not the same as the agent acting for a competitor and the difficulties of identifying the particular duty depend on the case.[135]

The law of agency might be used in an ad hoc way if there are sufficient policy reasons to do so.[136] Sitkoff also describes courts imposing fiduciary duties in ad hoc relationships to deal with the agency problem (failure to contractually anticipate all the obligations and opportunism in asymmetrical relationships) using concepts such as influence, trust and confidence and superiority to justify the inference and finding of fiduciary obligations.[137] Many indicators of agency are present in AE with the employer enjoying superiority in the relationship, the employee reposing trust in the employer and the employer being ceded power to manage the employees' money and select a pension provider and plan. However, the difficulty in identifying the terms of the agreement and the fact that the undertakings arise from statutory obligations may go against a finding that the employer acts as an agent in this regard. It might be difficult to demonstrate that the employer has chosen to undertake its duties but this is not fatal to any claim. Having considered the agency relationship it seems that the facts surrounding the AE relationship may look like a case of agency giving rise to fiduciary and non-fiduciary obligations owed by the employer to its employees. However, although it might be argued successfully in the courts, it is not sufficiently clear to say with certainty that a legal remedy exists under this head and, consequently, statutory clarification would improve the regime.

IV. Duties Arising from the Contract of Employment

Even if there is no finding of general fiduciary or agency obligations, the contract of employment may create obligations in the form of implementing AE. The nature of the relationship, factual circumstances and explicit and implied contractual terms are all relevant. I believe that this is the strongest basis for a claim for loss arising from the AE situation. Employees derive benefits for occupational pension schemes from the contract of employment and so its terms are crucial to

[134] Macgregor, *The Law of Agency in Scotland*, (n 109) 160.
[135] ibid, 70.
[136] Macgregor, 'Defining Agency and Its Scope (I)', (n 108).
[137] RH Stikoff, 'An Economic Theory of Fiduciary Law' in AS Gold and PB Miller (eds), *Philosophical Foundations of Fiduciary Law* (Oxford University Press, 2014) 200.

considering the extent of any obligations.[138] However, employment contracts often say little about pensions and may refer to member booklets and other externally provided information. For AE, this would also include information given as part of the statutory AE information requirements. The contract of employment is the control mechanism in the relationship and may in some circumstances justify a finding of fiduciary obligations to correct asymmetries of power.[139] Courts have been willing to use fiduciary obligations to correct imbalances and abuse of power although, as discussed above,[140] the relationship as a whole is unlikely to be fiduciary in nature.[141]

It has been argued that employers may be obliged to monitor or reconsider the pension as part of the mutual trust and confidence obligation but this is unlikely to require monitoring the suitability of investments in contract-based schemes.[142] Contracts of employment operate on trust and this has long been interpreted as including an implied obligation by the employee to prevent conflicts of personal interest with those of the employer.[143] A number of questions arise here. The first is whether the contract of employment contains fiduciary obligations on the employer to execute its obligations under AE in a particular way to ensure that the employees' interests are paramount. *Imperial* would suggest that this is unlikely.[144] However, even without a general fiduciary obligation, there may be express or implied contractual obligations such as a duty to consider the employees' economic interests and whether sufficient information has been given to employees to ensure that they can make their own decisions.

An employee owes a duty of loyalty to his employer but this does not necessarily equate to a fiduciary obligation.[145] Where a fiduciary relationship is found to exist, the existence of a conflict of interest will give rise to a duty to account.[146] However, the contract of employment does not place the same duty of loyalty on the employer and there is authority that the implied term of mutual trust and confidence does not perform this function.[147] Murray argues that a fact based approach might lead to findings of fiduciary obligations in some cases.[148] 'The right to act self-interestedly in the performance of the contract is not inconsistent with more limited fiduciary duties.'[149] The House of Lords determined in the *Scally* case that junior doctors' contracts of employment contained an implied term that they would be advised of pension changes which they could not be expected to

[138] *Mettoy Pension Trustees Ltd v Evans* [1990] 1 WLR 1587.
[139] Sims, 'Is Employment a Fiduciary Relationship?', (n 58) 106.
[140] Part A.
[141] *Autoclenz Ltd v Belcher* [2011] UKSC 41, [2011] 4 All R 745.
[142] The Law Commission, *Fiduciary Duties of Investment Intermediaries*, (n 3) 156.
[143] *Pearce v Foster (No 2)* (1886) 17 QBD 536 CA.
[144] *Imperial Group Pension Trust v Imperial Tobacco* [1991] 1 WLR 589.
[145] *University of Nottingham v Fishel*, (n 56).
[146] *Samsung Semiconductor Europe Ltd v Docherty*, [32].
[147] Murray, 'Conceptualizing the Employer', (n 15) 347.
[148] ibid, 351.
[149] ibid, 348.

know about – in this case the fact that they could buy added years to top up their pensions.[150] However, the ratio on this point was very precise and great care was taken to prevent the widening of any obligations. In *Scally*, the contract was not negotiated directly by the employee, it contained a valuable right dependent on employee action and the employee could not reasonably be expected to be aware of the term.[151] These were cited as the reasons that made it necessary to imply a term into all the individual contracts of employment requiring 'the employer to take reasonable steps to bring the term of the contract in question to the employee's attention, so that he may be in a position to enjoy its benefit'.[152] In other words, the employees had to know of the term in order to give effect to the contractual provisions. This recognises the different bargaining positions of the parties. The narrow application of *Scally* has been followed in a recent Pensions Ombudsman case.[153]

A. Implied Terms

Where there is no explicit undertaking in contract, the courts have also implied terms into voluntary undertakings on the basis that this would be what the reasonable person would assume the document would mean. As described by Lord Hoffman:

> The question of implication arises when the instrument does not expressly provide for what is to happen when some event occurs … In some cases, however, the reasonable addressee would understand the instrument to mean something else … The instrument may not have expressly said so, but this is what it must mean … But the implication of the term is not an addition to the instrument. It only spells out what the instrument means.[154]

Lord Neuberger recently considered the *Belize* case, finding that *Belize* did not dilute the requirements which have to be satisfied in order for a term to be implied, despite views to the contrary.[155] Some of Lord Hoffmann's observations in the *Belize* case, were said to be interpreted wrongly in law causing confusion.[156] Lord Neuberger stresses that the question of whether a term is to be implied must be judged at the date the contract is made and only where the term is so obvious as to go without saying or be necessary for business efficiency.[157] In an employment

[150] *Scally v Southern Health and Social Services Board* [1992] 1 AC 294.
[151] ibid, 307.
[152] ibid.
[153] Pensions Ombudsman case (April 2013) (PO-680) Major R Farrimond.
[154] *AG of Belize v Belize Telecom Ltd* [2009] UKPC 10; [2009] 1 WLR 1988 [18], as approved in *PDPF GP Ltd v Santander UK Plc* [2015] CSOH 410, (2015) Hous LR 45.
[155] *Marks and Spencer plc v BNP Paribas Securities Services Trust Co (Jersey) Ltd* [2015] UKSC 72; [2016] AC 742 [24].
[156] ibid, [26].
[157] ibid, [23].

context, the courts may imply terms which 'can sometimes leap over their basic principle' in contract to protect the worker.[158] Implied terms may be read into the undertaking whereby the employer exercises discretion, such as the discretion to choose a pension provider or whether to change provider, or this might instead justify statutory change to correct the 'inadequacy of the ordinary private law'.[159]

Under the contract of employment, there is a reciprocal duty of good faith which extends to powers exercised by the employer in relation to the pension scheme.[160] Good faith is a distinct and differing obligation and is not the same as a fiduciary duty. The duty to act in good faith will not usually require one party to place another party's interests above its own interests. This is different from a fiduciary duty where one party must place the other party's interests above its own and the intention or motivation in a course of action is irrelevant.[161] The *Imperial* case considered whether there were constraints on the exercise of discretionary power and it was argued that the company was under a fiduciary or other duty to consider the interests of members and not just the company's interests when considering whether to consent to the increases.[162] The company was found to have a clear interest in the operation of the scheme, as it would bear excess costs, and so a fiduciary obligation could not be implied as that would require the employer to consider only the members' interests.[163] However, an implied obligation of good faith may be read into the contract to apply to 'the exercise of his [the employer's] rights and powers under a pension scheme as they do to the other rights and powers of the employer'.[164] So whilst the employer has the right to consider its own financial interests, the implied obligation of good faith ensures that decisions must not be undertaken in a way which undermines trust and confidence.[165] If the employer is considered to be an agent of the employee, the duties are so comprehensive that an additional duty to act in good faith is unnecessary.[166] However, if there is no agency then it is necessary to consider the extent of any good faith obligations arising under the contract of employment and, in this situation, the motivation for action is important. The discretion to choose provider, change provider and set contribution levels might all come under this umbrella of employer discretion to be exercised in good faith.

[158] P Davies and M Freedland, 'Employees, Workers, and the Autonomy of Labour Law' in H Collins, P Davies and R Rideout (eds), *Legal Regulation of the Employment Relation* (Kluwer Law International Ltd, 2000) 276.

[159] H Collins, 'Justifications and Techniques of Legal Regulation of the Employment Relation' in H Collins, P Davies and R Rideout (eds), *Legal Regulation of the Employment Relation* (Kluwer Law International Ltd, 2000) 276.

[160] *Imperial Group Pension Trust v Imperial Tobacco*, (n 144).

[161] Macgregor, *The Law of Agency in Scotland*, (n 109) 124.

[162] *Imperial Group Pension Trust v Imperial Tobacco*, (n 144) 594.

[163] ibid, 597.

[164] ibid.

[165] ibid, 599.

[166] Macgregor, *The Law of Agency in Scotland*, (n 109) 124.

i. Implied Terms: Mutual Trust and Confidence

The Pensions Ombudsman found that an employer was contractually obliged to advise an employee that an enhanced pension would have been available if retirement had been delayed. The Pensions Ombudsman relied on trust and confidence duties and on the *Scally* case, finding that insufficient information had been provided.[167] On appeal, Hart J distinguished the facts of the case from the *Scally* case and overturned the Ombudsman's findings. A careful reading of the booklet would have alerted the member to the consequences of retiring at the different dates.[168] The onus was on the employee to ensure information was considered. If the relationship was categorised as fiduciary then a positive obligation by the employer to disclose any negative consequences from the proposed action would exist. The employment relationship is unlikely to be an entirely fiduciary relationship. There is a close connection between fiduciary obligations and the implied term of trust and confidence but, in employment law, trust and confidence has a different and distinct meaning. Namely, that the parties do not conduct themselves in a way which is likely to destroy the relationship of trust and confidence between them.[169] However, Hart J rejected the University's argument that an inadvertent omission could never amount to a breach of the implied duty of trust and confidence finding 'it may … have a positive as opposed to merely negative content' whilst recognising that this would be an extension of existing law.[170] Hart J was cautious of extending the implied term to create a positive obligation to warn and considered that this does not sit well with other default obligations or *Scally*.[171] It was also noted that the employee did not ask for advice.[172] So, in cases where the employee has asked for advice and information is given in return it may be more difficult to determine what the implied obligation requires. The trust and confidence in the employment relationship can be undermined in many ways:

> The conduct must, of course, impinge on the relationship in the sense that, looked at objectively, it is likely to destroy or seriously damage the degree of trust and confidence the employee is reasonably entitled to have in his employer.[173]

The purpose of the implied term is to facilitate the proper functioning of the contract and protect the employment relationship. Brodie finds that the obligation of mutual trust recognises that the employment relationship is distinct from commercial relations and operates to prevent exploitation of workers,[174] or

[167] *University of Nottingham v Eyett* [1999] 2 All ER 437, [1999] ICR 721.
[168] ibid, 724.
[169] Sims, 'Is Employment a Fiduciary Relationship?', (n 58) 103.
[170] *University of Nottingham v Eyett* [1999] 2 All ER 437, [1999] ICR 721, 728.
[171] ibid.
[172] ibid.
[173] *Malik v Bank of Credit and Commerce International* SA [1998] AC 20, 35.
[174] D Brodie, 'Mutual Trust and the Values of the Employment Contract' (2001) 30 *Industrial Law Journal* 84, 85.

to prevent abuse of power.[175] It is particularly important to guard against such abuse in the exercise of discretionary powers by the employer given the power imbalance,[176] as was discussed in the *Imperial* case above. Lord Steyn considers the employer's motives to be irrelevant,[177] agreeing with and referring to Douglas Brodie's work: 'In assessing … breach … what is significant is the impact of the employer's behaviour on the employee rather than what the employer intended.'[178]

The duty of trust and confidence has been used by the courts to compel employers 'to conduct themselves in a proactive manner by imposing a standard of care'.[179] Other implied duties, such as the duty to take reasonable care for the employee's welfare, have a narrower application than the duty of trust and confidence.[180] *Scally* is authority for the principle that the employer is under no duty to exercise reasonable care in respect of the economic well-being of employees, but contrasts with the *Visa* case from which it appears that a similar factual situation might result in a successful claim under breach of trust and confidence.[181] In this case the breach of the implied duty of trust and confidence occurred when the employer failed to advise the employee about a post that she thought would suit her. Cabrelli notes:

> It provides support for the emergence of an overarching and distinct concept of trust and confidence since it suggests that an employee can be successful if they raise a claim for recovery of economic loss for a failure of the employer to inform based on a repudiatory breach of the duty of trust and confidence.[182]

The question here is whether a lack of care in the selection of provider or fund could allow recovery for economic loss based on a breach of the trust and confidence obligation. Recovery for such loss under the contract of employment is more likely than under agency or a general fiduciary duty argument. The law may be willing to supply omissions in the employment contract to an extent not seen in other areas of contracts and so the courts may imply this or it might require to be codified in the AE legislation.[183] However, the implied obligation of mutual trust and confidence may be constrained by specific contractual provisions or statute. Where this concerns a discretionary power exercised by the employer this may also be subject to the implied duty to take reasonable care.[184]

[175] ibid, 90.
[176] ibid, 93.
[177] *Malik v Bank of Credit and Commerce International* SA [1998] AC 20, 47.
[178] D Brodie, 'The Heart of the Matter: Mutual Trust and Confidence' (1996) 25 *Industrial Law Journal* 121, 121.
[179] D Cabrelli, 'The Implied Duty of Mutual Trust and Confidence: An Emerging Overarching Principle' (2005) 34 *Industrial Law Journal* 284, 285.
[180] ibid, 284.
[181] *Visa International Service Association v Paul* [2004] IRLR 42.
[182] Cabrelli, 'The Implied Duty of Mutual Trust and Confidence', (n 179) 289.
[183] B Watt, 'Regulating the Employment Relationship: From Rights to Relations' in H Collins, P Davies and R Rideout (eds), *Legal Regulation of the Employment Relation* (Kluwer Law International Ltd, 2000) 342.
[184] Cabrelli, 'The Implied Duty of Mutual Trust and Confidence', (n 179) 298.

The court in *Johnson* held that the growth of the use of the implied obligation should be restricted to operate within legislative policy.[185] Brodie calls for consideration of this dual regulation,[186] and highlights the reluctance of courts to provide a remedy in tort where one has been laid down by statute, often specified as the Employment Tribunal.[187] Brodie finds that there is tension between this restraint and the *Scally* case in which it was held that the failure to provide information gave rise to a breach of contract. However, part of the *Scally* claim failed on the basis that statute provided for a remedy of failing to provide written particulars. If statutory intention was to prevent a remedy in tort could a contractual one exist?[188] For AE, enforcement is largely reserved to the Pensions Regulator but the legislation does not deal with form or method of implementation, other than technical failings. One can conclude that form of implementation is unspecified by Parliament. The implied term may also be restricted where the contract contains specific terms, giving one party the right to exercise a particular power in a way that they choose, although even this might be restricted by the implied term as in the *Imperial* case discussed above. It is also possible that even negligent acts will not constitute a breach of the implied term if it does not seriously undermine trust and confidence, although they may constitute a breach of the implied term to exercise reasonable care.[189] It is not clear whether poor decisions relating to choice of provider, fund or switching could ever undermine trust and confidence to the extent required to establish breach although it might be easier to establish a breach of the exercise of reasonable care.

ii. Implied Terms: Good Faith

Good faith has increasingly been implied into commercial contracts including the implication to act honestly, adhere to accepted standards of commercial behaviour and without arbitrary or irrational exercise of contractual discretion.[190] This may require performance of the employer duties under AE to be of a particular standard but it 'does not require a party to act in the interests of the other party or to subordinate its own legitimate interests to the interests of the other party'.[191] The question of implying a term of good faith into commercial contracts has also been considered by the courts.[192] English law has traditionally rejected a general duty

[185] *Johnson v Unisys* Ltd [2001] UKHL 13, [2003] 1 AC 518.
[186] D Brodie, 'Mutual Trust and Confidence: Catalysts, Constraints and Commonality' (2007) 37 *Industrial Law Journal* 329.
[187] Employment Tribunals Act 1996.
[188] Brodie, 'Mutual Trust and Confidence', (n 186) 330.
[189] *Hagen v ICI Chemicals and Polymers Ltd* [2002] IRLR 31.
[190] D Ohrenstein, 'In Good Faith?' (2015) 7664 *New Law Journal* 19, 19.
[191] *F & C Alternative Investments (Holdings) Ltd v Barthelemy (No 2)*, (n 29) [147].
[192] *Yam Seng Pte Ltd v International Trade Corporation* Ltd [2013] EWHC 111, [2013] 1 All ER (Comm) 1321.

to perform contracts in good faith,[193] but there was limited Scottish authority for the implication of such a term,[194] and increasing influence of Europe to include this.[195] Leggat J considered whether the term might be implied more widely to commercial contracts where the facts indicate that this is the parties' intention.[196] This consideration of implied terms has been subsequently approved although it is unclear to what extent the case provides general principles for commercial contracts and it will depend on the factual context.[197] Recent cases have attempted to interpret the ratio of *Yam Seng Ltd* in very narrow terms,[198] and so there are discrepancies about the direction of the law.[199] In particular, a court should not impose its view of what is fair where the documentation is extensive and detailed.

The expansion of the implied term has continued in Scotland,[200] where the Inner House 'applied its conception of a fair interpretation of the lease provisions'.[201] This decision applied a contextual approach to construction which considered what a reasonable person would have understood the parties to mean.[202] Fairness to both parties was implicit in the common law in the view of the Inner House, a point which may not reflect commercial reality.[203] However, the authority of the *Grove* case has subsequently been questioned by an Inner House case in which Lady Smith was critical of attempts to read too much into the *Grove* case finding that 'there is no general rule that a commercial contract requires to be fair'.[204] However, where the contract in question is a relational one, such as a contract of employment, then the argument in favour of a general implied term requiring good faith is stronger.[205] It may require the employer to objectively justify any exercise of discretion.[206] A recent case considers the employer's exercise of discretion in the context of the employment contract which is 'of a different character from an ordinary commercial contract.[207] Any decision making function entrusted to

[193] AL Bogg, 'Good Faith in the Contract of Employment: A Case of The English Reserve' (2011) 32 *Comparative Labour Law and Policy Journal* 729, 729.

[194] *Smith v Bank of Scotland* [1997] SC (HL) 111.

[195] *Yam Seng Pte Ltd v International Trade Corporation Ltd* [124]–[130].

[196] ibid, [142].

[197] *D&G Cars Ltd v Essex Police Authority* [2015] EWHC 226 (QB), [2015] 2 WLUK 452; *Emirates Trading Agency LLC v Prime Mineral Exports Private Ltd* [2014] EWHC 2104 (Comm), [2015] 1 WLR 1145; *British Groundschool Ltd v Intelligent Data Capture Ltd* [2014] EWHC 2145 (Ch), [2014] 7 WLUK 58.

[198] *Greenclose Ltd v National Westminster Bank plc* [2014] EWHC 1156 (Ch), [2014] 2 Lloyd's Rep 169; *Myers v Kestrel Acquisitions Ltd* [2015] EWHC 916 (Ch), [2015] 3 WLUK 926.

[199] E Sheppard, 'Good Faith in the Aftermath of Yam Seng' (2015) 7 *Butterworths Journal of International Banking and Financial Law* 407, 409.

[200] *Grove Investments Ltd v Cape Building Products Ltd* [2014] CSIH 43, (2014) Hous LR 35.

[201] L Macgregor, 'Crossing the Line between Business Common Sense and Perceived Fairness in Contractual Interpretation' (2015) 19 *Edinburgh Law Review* 378, 378.

[202] *Grove Investments Ltd v Cape Building Products Ltd* [9].

[203] Macgregor, 'Crossing the Line', (n 201) 378.

[204] *@SIPP Pension Trustees v Insight Travel Services Ltd* [2015] CSIH 91, 2016 SC 243, [44].

[205] *Johnson v Unisys Ltd*, (n 185).

[206] *Clark v Nomura International plc* [2000] IRLR 76 (QB).

[207] *Braganza v BP Shipping Ltd and Another* [2015] UKSC 17, [2015] 1 WLR 1661.

the employer has to be exercised in accordance with the implied obligation of trust and confidence.'[208]

The employer is expected to know what the law is and how to deal with decisions made under the contract of employment.[209] The court is not entitled to substitute its own view of what a reasonable decision is but instead considers the rationality of the decision made and whether the process is flawed by failure to consider relevant facts or consideration of irrelevant ones.[210] On this basis, the employer choosing a scheme for AE must exercise the decision in a way that demonstrates that the process is reasonable and is in keeping with the obligation of trust and confidence. The bystander might ask whether the employer has a duty under the contract of employment to take care in choosing the provider. The parties may agree as they had assumed this was the case. However, the parties may not intend a special level of care to be taken and the employer might argue that only the minimum required to comply with the AE legislation would be included in the contract. Whilst the employer has a right to consider its own interests in making these decisions, the factors such as trust, asymmetries of power and information, reliance and expectation will all be evidence of the expectations of the employee as a party to the contract. The increasing significance of good faith in contractual performance of employment contracts may require the employer to demonstrate that discretionary powers were exercised rationally.[211]

iii. Implied Terms: Duty to Advise

The Employment Rights Act 1996[212] requires basic pensions' information to be contained in the contract of employment. This is often fulfilled by a simple statement that the employer will comply with its duties under the Pensions Act 2008 and a reference to a booklet or handbook for further pensions' information. Contractual changes were mentioned in my empirical study in relation to changed providers, contributions etc but it became clear that even where changes were contractually agreed that does not mean that employees understood the changes. Changes effected by reference to booklets or by letter add to misunderstandings and can make it difficult to prove what has been contractually agreed. Under AE there are specific information requirements requiring employers to give workers certain key information.[213] The employer retains responsibility for providing this information, even if a pension provider performs this information function[214] and

[208] ibid, [32].
[209] ibid, [36].
[210] ibid, [52]–[54].
[211] Bogg, 'Good Faith in the Contract of Employment: A Case of The English Reserve', (n 193) 756.
[212] ERA 1996, ss 1 & 5.
[213] Occupational and Personal Pension Schemes (Automatic Enrolment) Regulations, SI 2010/772.
[214] Pensions Regulator Detailed Guidance for Employers, Information to workers: The new duties: www.thepensionsregulator.gov.uk/-/media/thepensionsregulator/files/import/pdf/detailed-guidance-10.ashx p6.

this could create some tensions. Contractual exclusions in the standard employer/provider contract may exclude the pension provider's liability for loss arising from its failures in this regard leaving the employer responsible to the Regulator and potentially in respect of civil claims by employees. Technical failures to comply with the AE legislation will be enforced by the Pensions Regulator,[215] but in requiring the employer to provide information to employees this could place the employer in the position of being seen to offer advice depending on the nature of information given. This would explain the fear and reluctance of employers to discuss pension benefits beyond the basic information given. If the employer tries to provide a better quality scheme which allows the employee access to its own financial advisor this might be construed as giving advice which could leave it open to claims in tort/delict. This tension between information and advice is evident in the reported data.

Claims might arise on the basis of poor information about choices, contributions or in respect of the employer's decisions relating to the provider itself. It seems unlikely that a contractual claim in respect of failure to provide the statutory required information would be successful as that would fall within the remit of the Pensions Regulator under AE. However, knowledge of others is not an objective test and, if a positive finding of fiduciary duties is made, the employer would have to consider regularly whether the form and content of information given was enough for the principal to make decisions. The Deputy Pensions Ombudsman considered the accuracy of information and whether requests were for advice or information.[216] The Deputy Ombudsman found that the member was seeking information rather than advice but that it was inadequate to refer the member to an intranet site without some guidance. As the member relied on inaccurate information, she was to be reinstated in the scheme. This determination does not sit entirely comfortably with *Scally* as the member had the information she needed but it indicates the importance of the balance between providing adequate information and providing advice.

The Court of Appeal decision in *Outram* concerned the question of whether there was a duty to avoid causing economic loss.[217] In particular, the question was asked, if there is such a duty, whether 'It will result in liability for an omission (failure to advise) in circumstances where it is not alleged that the company was asked or expressly or impliedly assumed any contractual responsibility to give such advice.'[218] The Court of Appeal found that there was no general duty on an employer or trustees of a pension scheme to provide information or advice to employees to prevent economic loss emphasising the specialist nature of advice.[219] It was also important that the company had not assumed any responsibility to

[215] See part B below.
[216] Pensions Ombudsman (November 2014) (PO-3750) Mrs Oona Perret.
[217] *Outram v Academy Plastics Ltd* [2001] ICR 367.
[218] ibid, 372.
[219] ibid, 372–73.

provide advice and liability in tort under a duty of care could only succeed where there was an express or implied contractual duty to provide advice. Following *Scally*, any claim in tort is bound to fail if there is no contractual obligation to advise.[220]

My empirical research demonstrates that employers are cautious about providing information that might be construed as advice which can result in more generic information being provided. Employees also seemed unsure about whether advice or information was provided. The question of information versus advice was considered recently, where the pursuers argued that bank employees had given advice in relation to an interest swap agreement.[221] The contractual basis of the agreement made it clear that the bank was not providing advice and correspondence advised the individuals to seek their own professional financial advice. Lord Hodge considered the duty of care test and summarised it as the assumption of responsibility test coupled with reliance, reasonable foreseeability of loss and reasonableness of imposition of responsibility based on the relationship.[222] In ascertaining that there was no an advisory relationship Lord Hodge said that 'It is not sufficient to set up a duty of care to assert the existence of an advisory relationship. There is a clear distinction between giving advice and assuming legal responsibility for that advice.'[223] It was quite clear in this case that the contractual terms agreed did not set up an advisor/client relationship and even if the clients treated it as advisory and relied on it this reliance was not reasonable in the face of the contractual agreement.[224] The fact that the parties had signed the agreement meant they were bound by its terms even if they had not read them. This may prevent the product provider from any liability arising from provision of information to employees as the documentation usually excludes this.

The employment contract is likely to be silent on the issue and it will be a matter of fact to determine if the information given by an employer makes it clear that the relationship is not advisory or whether it might be reasonable for employees to rely on the information as advice. It is also unlikely that the employee will sign anything to complete AE unless consent for salary sacrifice or some other change is required before AE. The lack of consent by the employee is required under the AE legislation, discussed in Chapter 2, along with the lack of voluntariness of the employer's undertaking and could go against a finding of agency or fiduciary duties. Lack of specification of the standards to be followed by the employer in implementing AE may also to be fatal to any claim based the existence of agreement between the parties.

[220] ibid, 373.
[221] *Grant Estates Ltd v Royal Bank of Scotland plc* [2012] CSOH 133, (2012) GWD 29-588.
[222] ibid, [69].
[223] ibid.
[224] ibid, [76].

iv. Implied Terms: Contractual Duty to Avoid Economic Loss

Economic loss was considered in the *Lennon* case[225] where it was established that advice was sought and given with assurances and reliance on the advice resulted in loss. Mr Lennon could not sue for breach of contract as he was a member of the police force and had no contract of employment. Instead he sued in tort in respect of economic loss arising from a breach of duty of care arising from an assumption of responsibility for handling the transfer. Reference was made to the *Spring Guardian* case in which Lord Goff held that the duty of care was not limited to provision of information and advice,[226] but would also include special knowledge and a failure to exercise due care and skill in 'drawing on that source of information for the purpose of communicating it to another'.[227] In a similar way, the personnel officer had assumed responsibility for giving advice to Mr Lennon in relation to the benefit which he had asked her about. Although she was not a professional advisor, she had special knowledge and led Mr Lennon to believe that he could rely on her which was sufficient to attract the duty to give advice.[228] The duty of care arises from an express assumption of liability for a particular matter, which was relied upon.[229]

The implied term to prevent economic loss is unlikely to be inferred on the basis that it is too significant an extension of the existing law and secondly that it would 'impose an unfair and unreasonable burden on employers'.[230] This public policy constraint of unreasonable burden on employers may also prevent a finding that employers are obliged to do anything other than the AE minimum. Where the employer assumes responsibility for the giving of financial advice then it is under a duty to take reasonable care in the giving of that advice. However, it is quite different to imply that the employer is obliged to provide such advice or to generally safeguard the employee's well-being. With the simplification of schemes to reduce costs, advice may not be available in future. Employees may ask more questions of the employer but these will go unanswered as employers and HR representatives are now very wary of answering questions which might be construed as advice, as demonstrated by the research data. This means that whilst there may be a remedy for poor advice, employers may choose not to respond to questions and instead refer employees to the product provider. The product provider may also disclaim any responsibility to answer questions or advise (particularly at the pre-contract stage) and this leaves the employee with an information gap. The AE regime was intended to be simple and it was considered unnecessary to include provision for financial advice but it is clear that in failing to obtain advice some individuals will

[225] *The Commissioner of Police of the Metropolis v Lennon* [2004] EWCA Civ 130, 1 WLR 2594.
[226] *Spring v Guardian Assurance* [1995] 2 AC 296.
[227] ibid, 318 G-H.
[228] *The Commissioner of Police of the Metropolis v Lennon* [28].
[229] ibid, [34].
[230] *Crossley v Faithful & Gould Holdings Ltd* [2004] EWCA Civ 293, [2004] 4 All ER 447 [43].

suffer as a consequence of the regime. Employees would have to understand this and then pay for advice and this acts as a barrier to understanding and engagement and can also be described as a further cost of the regime.

B. Auto-Enrolment Compliance and the Contract of Employment

The Pensions Act 2008 sets out the requirements for compliance with AE, as discussed in Chapter 2. In respect of failure to comply with any of the employer duty provisions there is no right of action for a breach of statutory duty.[231] Exclusive jurisdiction on these matters is reserved to the Pensions Regulator. However, the act does not affect 'any right of action arising apart from these provisions' which are then defined as those arising in sections 2 to 11 of the Act. These are the basic technical requirements relating to implementation of AE. This means that rights of action outlined in the rest of this chapter are not reserved to the Pensions Regulator, being beyond the scope of the sections 2 to 11 exclusive jurisdiction. The Pensions Regulator is responsible for ensuring compliance with AE duties through a combination of 'education, enablement and enforcement'.[232] In the two-year period between commencement of AE and 2014, the Pensions Regulator reported it had closed 917 cases.[233] Between April 2018–March 2019 the Regulator reported use of formal powers 128,807 times with the rise attributed to the transition from enforcing against medium employers to the higher-volume small and micro employers.[234] This is a comparatively small number of cases when compared to the scale of AE with more than ten million workers enrolled to date.[235] This could either indicate the success of the regime or the lack of understanding of individuals who suffer negative consequences. It could also be the case that negative consequences will not be identified until individuals reach retirement and so reports may increase as AE members start to retire.

Whilst it is important that the Pensions Regulator has a good record of the methods employed to ensure compliance with AE, this focus stresses technical compliance whilst the practical and sometimes negative consequences arising from discretionary aspects of AE such as form of information, choice of provider and fund remain. It appears that many of the negative consequences identified in my

[231] Pensions Act 2008, s 34(2).
[232] The Pensions Regulator, 'Automatic Enrolment Commentary and Analysis: April 2014–March 2015' (July 2015) 8.
[233] The Pensions Regulator, 'Automatic Enrolment: Compliance and Enforcement, Quarterly Bulletin 1 April–30 June 2014' (June 2014) 2.
[234] The Pensions Regulator Automatic enrolment Commentary and analysis: April 2018–March 2019, 33 & 37: www.thepensionsregulator.gov.uk/-/media/thepensionsregulator/files/import/pdf/automatic-enrolment-commentary-analysis-2019.ashx.
[235] ibid, 3.

research are not covered by the legislation to date and, consequently are not within the remit of the Pensions Regulator for enforcement. If an employer is careless and chooses a poor provider, there will be no remedy unless this is accompanied by a technical failure such as failure to provide information or pay contributions on time. If employees misunderstand the information they are given then the legislation provides no remedy where they have been given the requisite information, even if it is in a form which acts as a barrier to the employee. Indeed, previous research by the Pensions Regulator itself supports my concern that employers may choose a poorer pension for their employees without even seeking advice.[236] There is no compulsion on employers to demonstrate that they have considered the scheme quality and this may leave employees in a difficult situation and possibly suffering negative consequences in years to come when they draw benefits. Lack of advice can also lead to technical breaches, such as reliance on others to complete the enrolment process and misunderstanding the role of product providers.

The question remains whether an employer could meet the basic statutory requirements in terms of compliance and scheme quality and nevertheless be open to a claim. This might be under obligations owed as fiduciaries, agents or under the implied contractual obligation to take care or breach of mutual trust and confidence. This might arise because of the lack of care taken in choosing a scheme, the decision making process when having to change scheme to meet new quality standards or in choosing a provider. It seems that, whilst enforcement of the basic implementation of AE is reserved to the Pensions Regulator, questions which relate more generally to the contract of employment or relationships may still be considered under the private law. In considering whether the mutual trust obligation is breached by an employer when being careless in choosing a scheme or provider or failing to change from a poorly performing scheme to save money in advice fees, it is important to remember that the employer has a legitimate business interest in implementing AE in a cost-effective way for its business. The competing interests which exist between the employer and the employee may prevent any basis of claim being established, even where the employee suffers loss.

The fact that the statutory minimum scheme governance requirements were only introduced after the main AE requirements indicate that the employer's main obligations are simply to enrol employees and ensure contributions are paid. The information requirements may put employers in a difficult position if they do not get the correct balance between giving enough information to allow employees to be informed and giving it in a way that allows employees to feel they are in receipt of advice from the employer or its representative IFA. Brodie talks of the importance of fair procedure in relation to such matters as pay reviews and this may also apply to decisions made in relation to AE. Even if the results could have been better for employees if alternate decisions were made, if the employer can demonstrate a fair

[236] The Pensions Regulator, 'Automatic Enrolment: Compliance and Enforcement, Quarterly Bulletin 1 April–30 June 2014' 4.

process for the decisions made then it will be less likely to breach the obligation.[237] As a minimum, I would argue that employers should be able to demonstrate that a fair process has been taken to make discretionary decisions under AE.

V. Duties Owed to the Employee by the Pension Provider or Advisors

The Law Commission found that the position in relation to contract-based pensions was more complicated than simply saying that the provider holds funds on behalf of the investor to produce returns. Whilst providers may influence the interests of members in the way they invest funds and incur costs and charges, this in itself is insufficient to confer a fiduciary obligation owed by the provider. The question here is whether the contractual terms support the member's legitimate expectation that the provider will act as a fiduciary in their relationship or whether other non-fiduciary obligations arise, such as a duty of care resulting from provision of professional services.[238]

A. Provision of Advice

There are difficulties in applying this contractual model in AE as it is the employer who agrees the contract with the provider rather than the employee. If the provider owes fiduciary duties to the employee member this would simplify matters but this may depend on whether advice is given. The giving of advice may lead to a finding that there is a fiduciary relationship but that is not inevitable.[239] Often the provider is not involved in the advisory process at all and an independent advisor is employed to find a scheme for the employer. The advisor will be contracted to provide advice to the employer on a suitable scheme which complies with AE within particular parameters of cost or quality as directed by the employer. In this situation, the advisor may owe duties to the employer which are contractual and fiduciary but is unlikely to owe these to the employees unless the provider has engaged in providing direct advice to them.

B. Misunderstandings and Mis-statements

My empirical research demonstrates that employees may be unsure about the role of the advisor. If the advice in question came from a professional advisor, then

[237] Brodie, 'Mutual Trust and Confidence', (n 186) 341.
[238] The Law Commission, *Fiduciary Duties of Investment Intermediaries*, (n 3) 159.
[239] ibid, 187.

a duty of care under the law of delict may exist. The classic test from the case of *Hunter v Hanley* requires the pursuer to demonstrate that there is an industry practice, that this has not been applied in this case and that the course taken is one which no professional of ordinary skill would have taken.[240] The importance of the FSA Conduct of Investment Business Handbook (COBS) here is that it could demonstrate the industry practice and any failures to follow the handbook might therefore constitute a failure to adhere to this and result in a finding of negligence in the law of delict.[241]

Setting aside consideration of fiduciary duties discussed above,[242] for a claim in delict, the employee would have to demonstrate that the advisor owed him a duty which was breached. This would be difficult as the employee would need to demonstrate that the advisor had assumed responsibility for the employee without any contractual undertakings or special relationship.[243] Consideration of negligent misstatements in the absence of a contract or fiduciary relationship was famously considered by the House of Lords in the *Hedley Byrne* case.[244] 'In the absence of any contractual or fiduciary duty, what circumstances give rise to a special relationship between the plaintiff and the defendant sufficient to justify the imposition of the duty of care in the making of statements?'[245] The key is the assumption of responsibility which indicates the special relationship. In AE, where information is given it will usually include a disclaimer to the effect that the advisor is only offering information. This would go against any suggestion that the advisor assumed responsibility, although the disclaimer may be not be enforceable. Firms must not seek to exclude or restrict duties which would otherwise arise and an exclusion may also be deemed to be an unfair contract term.[246] Even if responsibility is proved then the employee would still need to demonstrate that the breach of duty caused the loss alleged. Again, the consequence is that the employees' questions are likely to remain unanswered as providers and advisors are cautious not to undertake responsibility for providing advice, as demonstrated by my empirical findings.

C. Third Party Liability

It may also be the case that, where the claimant is someone other than the party being given direct advice, the middle party may be responsible for negligent advice. For example, the employer may be liable if it passes on advice to the employee that

[240] *Hunter v Hanley* 1955 SC 200.
[241] *Loosemore v Financial Concepts* [2001] Lloyd's Rep PN 235.
[242] Part IV.
[243] *Hines v Sturge LLP* [2010] CSIH 86, (2011) SLT 2, 21.
[244] *Hedley Byrne & Co Ltd v Heller & Partners Ltd* [1964] AC 465.
[245] *White v Jones* [1995] 2 AC 207.
[246] Consumer Rights Act 2015.

it has received from its own advisor. This was discussed by the Law Commission in the context of investment chains and whether it might be possible to owe duties beyond the immediate client. The Law Commission found that the courts were reluctant to impose such duties and would approach fiduciary duties in the same way.[247] In respect of information given directly to employees by advisors or product providers, then these professionals are governed by the FCA rules.[248] In our example this means that the FCA regulations would provide strong evidence of the practice expected of advisors and providers in this situation. The FCA rules on fairness, conflicts and suitability would all be relevant considerations and, where the advisor or provider is found to have breached these, would give rise to a claim in contract or delict.[249]

D. Reliance on Financial Regulation

When dealing with retail clients all information given is to be fair, clear and not misleading and should feature a prominent indication of risks associated with the investment.[250] As part of this advice process the advisor must have adequate information from the customer to demonstrate the suitability of the product. Whilst insurance and personal pensions are not included within the scope of the Markets in Financial Instruments Directive 2004/39/EC (MiFID) I or II the FCA included such products within the regime.[251] Therefore, the majority of the COBS rules which incorporate MiFID I and II will apply in the UK to pensions and insurance products. It is unclear at times what role advisors and product providers play in implementing AE and whether negatively affected employees have any right of action. For example, for failure to advise in the pre-contract period or in relation to member choices. The MiFID regime, with its intention of ensuring a high level of investor protection, could be invoked directly by investors without having to rely on domestic private causes of action.[252] MiFID II was expected to contain civil liability provisions to be part of the enforcement of good practice, but these were not included.[253] The introduction of a directly enforceable right under MiFID II might have brought greater discipline to the financial market.[254]

[247] The Law Commission, *Fiduciary Duties of Investment Intermediaries*, (n 3) 204.
[248] ibid, 199.
[249] ibid, 201.
[250] MiFID I, art 19(2) and MiFID II, art 24(3).
[251] Financial Conduct Authority Developing Our Approach to Implementing MiFID II, 10: www.fca.org.uk/publication/discussion/dp15-03.pdf.
[252] OO Cheredbychenko, 'The Regulation of Retail Investment Services in the EU: Towards the Improvement of Investor Rights' (2010) 33 *Journal of Consumer Policy* 403, 409.
[253] D Busch, 'Why MIFID Matters to Private Law – The Example of MIFID's Impact on an Asset Manager's Civil Liability' (2012) 7 *Capital Markets Law Journal* 386, 387.
[254] N Maloney, 'Liability of Asset Managers: A Comment' (2012) 7 *Capital Markets Law Journal* 414, 415.

However, the UK explicitly provides a remedy for breaches suffered by private persons under section 138D of the Financial Services and Markets Act (FSMA) 2000. A private person (usually an individual) can sue an intermediary which has caused him loss through breach of the FCA rules.[255] The loss must be proved to be reasonably foreseeable and not too remote. The private person definition would prevent an employer raising a claim and it would have to rely on contractual or delictual/tortious liability.[256] Even in the situation where an employee might have provided advice, the contractual provisions excluding such advice were decisive[257] except where the action was raised by the FSA (now FCA) for failures to meet its rules. The FCA principles, such as fairness and suitability are excluded from the scope of such direct actions and the Law Commission considered whether these should be included and also whether to allow non-private individuals to be able to sue under this provision.[258] The Law Commission had some sympathy for the extension but indicated that this was a matter for Parliament to legislate further on if it felt that this would further implement the Kay Review findings. The role of COBS has recently been considered in relation to asset managers and expectations of competence when considering the common law duty of skill and care in the law of delict.[259] COBS will form strong evidence of required standards and that private law duties of agency and delict will be breached where the asset manager fails to comply with COBS prior to conclusion of a contract.[260] The analogy with the AE scenario is that the pension provider or advisor may owe obligations under COBS to the employees in the period prior to conclusion of the contract effecting the personal pension. However, Busch warns against the legal uncertainties caused by courts imposing differing duties of care which are stricter than required under the MiFID regime.[261] Further statutory clarification on the extent of duties arising out of AE, similar to that of company directors under the Companies Act 2006, would be justified on the basis of legal certainty.

VI. Conclusion

This chapter considered whether private law provides an adequate remedy for those who suffer loss as a consequence of the AE regime. Potential unintended consequences and loss have been described throughout the work and, before considering statutory change, it is important to explore whether this is necessary. Contractual changes relating to pensions and other benefits may be accompanied

[255] Financial Services and Markets Act 2000, s 138D.
[256] *Grant Estates Ltd v Royal Bank of Scotland plc*, (n 221) [62].
[257] ibid.
[258] The Law Commission, *Fiduciary Duties of Investment Intermediaries*, (n 3) 209.
[259] Cabrelli, 'The Liability of Asset Managers in Scots Law', (n 24): http://ssrn.com/abstract=1859453.
[260] ibid, 17–32.
[261] Busch, 'Why MIFID Matters to Private Law', (n 253).

by complex information and this chapter has considered possible private law remedies in respect of loss or detriment arising from the provision of information and advice and the exercise of employer discretion under AE. If employers are found to owe particular standards of care when exercising discretionary decisions under AE, this might improve both the default positions and the level of engagement of employees. The asymmetric information and power in the AE relationship may result in a finding that the employer acts as a fiduciary or agent in respect of the AE decisions it makes for the employee.

This chapter has considered whether the employer acts as a fiduciary in respect of AE. My empirical research demonstrates that employees trust their employers and cede the power of decisions and assets to their employer without much thought. The discretion exercised by employers adds weight to the possibility that these factual circumstances create fiduciary or agency duties in respect of the execution of AE duties. If pension providers and advisors engage with employees during this process, they may also owe duties to the employees. Vulnerability, exercise of discretion, management of affairs by one party, status of the parties and contractual provisions may all indicate the existence of a fiduciary obligation. It can be said that the employee is vulnerable and cedes power over pension contributions to the employer to manage using discretion. This could support the argument that the employer exercises discretionary powers under AE as a fiduciary. Although the whole employer/employee relationship is unlikely to be categorised as fiduciary in nature some aspects may be. The employment law contract is likely to be silent on the issue of AE but terms may be implied which allow duties to be inferred. A key duty of the fiduciary is loyalty and, whilst this may not affect the entire employment relationship, as the employer is entitled to consider its own interests, loyalty might be owed in respect of choosing a pension provider and scheme. If the employer is considered to act as a fiduciary in this respect then the obligation to avoid conflicts of interest, act in the best interests of the beneficiaries and perform duties in good faith would all attach to the process of the employer implementing its AE obligations. The employee could expect that AE decisions will be made with care and that employees' interests will be placed above the employers' interests.

Even if there are no general fiduciary duties, the employer may act as an agent for the employee in arranging his AE pension. In choosing provider, form of benefits, contract and deducting contributions from pay the employer exercises discretion and control over employees' assets. This might allow a finding of agency if an action is brought before the courts. In that case, the employer would have to demonstrate that care was taken in exercising discretionary decisions, such as choice of provider, default funds and plan structure. The employer would have to demonstrate that it had performed the fiduciary and non-fiduciary obligations of an agent in its implementation of AE.

As an alternative basis of claim, the contract of employment may require the employer to fulfil its AE duties to a particular standard. The implied duties of mutual trust and confidence and good faith may impose a standard of care in respect of AE compliance. Although there is no duty to advise employees, the parties must act in good faith towards each other in order to maintain the mutual trust and confidence which exists in the relationship. This will require employers to demonstrate that the process used for selection of provider, scheme and subsequent reviews is objectively reasonable. There is no obligation on the employer to provide advice to employees but where this is proffered then this may prove actionable in delict where there is a failure in the duty of care in providing that advice.

Employees may also have a direct right of action against the pension provider or professional advisors if it can be established that they failed to comply with the FCA handbook in some way in their dealings with the employee.

Whilst it may be possible to argue that these duties are present and create obligations, it is not clear how the courts would respond. The costs involved in bringing such claims may also be prohibitive, compared to losses, unless a group action is raised. A group claim may be raised at some point in the future which will clarify the position but, until then, legal certainty requires statutory clarification. Codification of the AE obligations in a similar way to the codification of directors' fiduciary duties under the Companies Act 2006 would assist and bring clarity. This could be done by further statutory amendment to the AE legislation which outlines the extent of duties and processes in the implementation of AE, making it clear to employees that they have this additional protection. Employers would have to demonstrate that the employees' interests were properly considered and show the process used when exercising discretion. This would have the benefit of bringing these implementation decisions within the scope of the Pensions Regulator remit and would make it more cost-effective for those suffering losses. The role of advice is still difficult to deal with as it was not deemed necessary in the original legislation. The reality is that there are gaps in the process leaving employees with unanswered questions, misunderstandings and, in some cases, causing detriment or loss to the individual. Without further legislation, the advice needs are unlikely to be undertaken voluntarily by employers or product providers for fear of increasing potential liability and costs but Parliament would have to change position on the need for advice in AE.

Where a policy produces negative effects then there should be a means of redress, either by the courts, as outlined here, or by extension of the AE regulations by Pensions Regulator guidance or further statutory codification. This chapter has demonstrated that some of the detrimental external effects of AE have no clear remedy under the AE legislation or under private law remedies and this should be corrected.

7

Conclusion

I. Why Do We Have Auto-Enrolment?

A. The Ageing Population

We have AE because, for many reasons, private pension saving in the UK has been in decline. There has also been a shift from defined pension benefit or DB structures to defined contribution (DC) pensions which has moved responsibility and risk from the employer to the individual pension saver. The state pension system was never designed to provide full income replacement and is not linked to salary so it now provides a small income which is inadequate for many. The ageing nature of the UK population also means that there are fewer workers paying tax and NICs to support a growing number of pensioners who are living longer.[1] With this combination of increasing costs of welfare and a reduction in private pension saving it was decided that a new approach to funding retirement was needed. In addition to reform of the state pension, mandatory private pension saving was introduced into the workplace.

B. Combat Behavioural Traits

Whilst there may be a benefit to the state and future generations from an increase in private pension saving, the parliamentary intention was to increase private saving to help individuals fulfil their retirement aspirations and to combat inertia and myopia. Policy makers concluded that individuals do not always behave rationally and that it was justifiable to interfere with choice to help individuals save more for their own good. Part of the justification for this policy intervention was to convince individuals that the AE pension provides good value so that they are convinced not to opt-out of the scheme.

It was decided to implement a policy of AE requiring all employers to assess their workforce and enrol eligible employees into a qualifying pension scheme

[1] R Cracknell, 'The Ageing Population: Key Issues for the New Government 2010' (*parliament.uk*, House of Commons Library Research) www.parliament.uk/business/publications/research/key-issues-for-the-new-parliament/value-for-money-in-public-services/the-ageing-population.

chosen by the employer. The intention was to ensure that most workers, even lower paid workers, had access to a pension to which their employer would contribute. Behavioural economics was relied on to support the argument that legal intervention was necessary to help workers to save. This relied on evidence that, despite there being many private pensions available in the workplace, workers failed to self-enrol in significant numbers. It was accepted that these behavioural biases would need the default saving position to be set by regulations to require saving into the pension at a minimum level, without requiring employees to consent or make any decisions. However, as this represents a significant reduction in personal choice and, recognising that some individuals might have good reasons for choosing not to save into a pension, it was agreed that the individual should have the right to opt-out of this automatic saving. Workers were to be educated on financial matters and protected from employer pressures in order to minimise the level of workers choosing to opt-out. The regime was intended to operate without the need for individual specific financial advice instead relying on free generic advice to ensure individuals understand their options.

II. Choice Architecture and Justification

A. Intervention not Persuasion

The legislation implementing AE has not always worked well alongside existing legislation governing employee benefits and many statutory adjustments have been made since the implementing Pensions Acts of 2007 and 2008. A wide category of workers aged between 16 and 75 were envisaged as beneficiaries of AE but eligibility also depends on pay. This has been criticised as the minimum pay criteria has resulted in the exclusion of some of the lowest paid workers. For example, part-time workers with multiple employers may not benefit. AE is also very complicated and administratively demanding for employers who are responsible for its implementation. The employer has been allocated a wide discretion in the selection of the pension scheme which has been criticised because this creates significant variations in benefits offered under AE and consequently the experience of workers.

Several options for policy intervention might have been chosen but the AE policy of soft paternalism was chosen. The actual design of the legislation and individual schemes is described as choice architecture which reflects the fact that a range of limited choices will be available, and the individual will make choices within that range. For AE this means that the individual will be enrolled into a default scheme at a default savings rate with a default investment fund. The employer will use its discretion in relation to the scheme benefit design and provider and within this the employee can make some choices. Individuals may choose to leave the scheme, stay in the scheme, increase contributions or change the investment fund and all of these choices are at the heart of the legitimacy of the regime.

All of these policy decisions were made on the basis that there was a legal justification for intervening in personal choice for the good of the individual and it has been demonstrated that AE is a form of legal paternalism. As such, it should be assessed with regard to the safety mechanisms of the right to opt-out and acceptance of the intervention by those affected by it because they believe it is for their benefit. In implementing AE, the state has effectively determined that the interests of the individual are best served by being a member of his employer's pension scheme. This is justified on the basis that the individual may choose to leave the scheme or may agree with the intervention and stay in the scheme. It is this operation of choice which is key in the regime and my assessment of it. If this choice is to be effective then the individual needs to understand that they have a choice. The policy should also consider how this choice is affected by the inertia and myopia which served as justification for the intervention in the first place. The apparent retention of choice allows the regime to be classified as soft paternalism. The data in Chapter 5 allowed comparison of the benefits of intervention against potential negative consequences or unintended effects and used this to evaluate the regime.[2] In comparing the reality with the aspiration this considers whether the benefits outweigh the costs and does this validate the policy? A further consideration is how the policy deals with those who suffer costs.

Table 1 Costs and Benefits of AE

Costs	Benefits
Administrative compliance costs for pension providers and employers eg new software, payroll systems	More people saving privately for retirement
Opportunity cost of the loss of value of contributions which employers and employees might have invested elsewhere	Increased investment by increasing pension funds, supports economic growth
Disengagement by some workers leads to misunderstandings and disappointment	Increased business for the financial services industry
Some workers would pay higher contributions under self-enrolment which would be more valuable to them in the long term	Less reliance on the welfare state
Some workers benefit at the expense of others	Relieves burden on future generations of taxpayers
Not all intended recipients will benefit eg part-time workers below the earnings trigger	Low opt-out rates
Costs of establishing claims, recovering loss for those who suffer negative consequences eg litigation	

(continued)

[2] Table 1 below.

Table 1 *(Continued)*

Costs	Benefits
Difficulties in the employer/employee relationship	
Costs of changing existing pensions and contractual agreements to vary past pension arrangements	
Loss of freedom to contract	
Business changes eg recruitment company changed to exclude short-term agency workers	
Revisions to the legislation require further changes to schemes or further advice costs	

The government research focus has been on the benefits of the regime as evidenced by low opt-out rates. My focus has been to consider whether low opt-out rates support a finding that the regime is a success or instead indicate that the key safety measure, active choice, is not working. This is not about free choice having an intrinsic value in itself but about the difficulties of replacing choice with default positions and the interplay between this policy and the behavioural biases which support it. If the policy intervention was for the benefit of the individual, then to be measured as a success, there either needs to be a demonstration that individuals do benefit or that they have subsequently elected to use their free choice to accept the policy intervention. This may all seem academic as surely it is always beneficial that everyone is defaulted into saving in a pension scheme when they were not saving before? However, there will be instances where the default position does not benefit everyone. The extent to which this might happen, the circumstances and whether this affects the justification of the regime have all been considered. The extent to which negative or unforeseen consequences are permissible for the regime still to be considered a success has also been considered and where there is evidence that an individual has not benefitted from the intervention, the operation of choice becomes crucial to assessing the legitimacy of the regime. If neither personal benefit nor choice are demonstrated then the regime appears to fail in legitimacy and paternalistic motivation and, at the very least, must provide a remedy for the party suffering external losses. For this reason, it is crucial that further improvements are made to make sure individuals properly engage in relation to their pension to ensure that, even if there is the potential that they do not benefit from intervention, they make personal active choices which verify the policy.

B. Behavioural Economics

The work of behavioural economics was relied on in support of the introduction of the AE policy. Reference to behavioural bias, procrastination and inertia are all evidence of the use of the work in creating the AE policy. Whilst this is a relatively new policy influence in the UK, the work has been highly influential in policy in the US for many years and more recently in Australia and New Zealand, as discussed throughout this book. This work challenges the accepted notion of the rational person, particularly when dealing with complex and long-term financial products such as pension policies. The work identifies a number of behavioural traits which are said to be predictable and it is then used to support policy intervention which is designed to counter the bias.

Inertia is said to operate to keep individuals in the default or status quo position and this was said to be the problem with self-enrolment in workplace pensions. It operated with procrastination, whereby individuals know what they should do but lack the willpower or resolve to do it, to delay or prevent individuals joining their workplace pensions. However, the bias which may have operated to prevent self-enrolment in the past may also work against the individual exercising any choices under AE. It may in fact result in the individual being worse off than if there had been no policy intervention. Chapter 4 describes evidence that although individuals may procrastinate, they will eventually take action and save for retirement and may do so at a much higher level than they do in the situation where they are automatically enrolled at a low default contribution level. The employee knows that they have a pension under AE and may disengage with any other pension decisions for a long time. The importance of default positions cannot be underestimated, and, for AE in the UK, the minimum contributions have been set at a low level to ensure minimum opt-outs. This means that the level of contributions is unsuitable for many and there is currently no break point in AE to increase contributions, unless the individual proactively decides to do this. Therefore, whilst AE may increase the number of individuals saving in a workplace pension this may be at the expense of some paying lower contributions than they would have otherwise paid.

In scheme and fund selection too, it seems that there are significant differences between fund performance and many individuals stick with default selections until retirement when other funds may be more beneficial in the long term. It has been suggested that some employers use these behavioural biases in their plan designs to ensure that the lowest level of employer contributions is paid and that this means that some proactive members of the workforce benefit at the expense of those subject to inertia and procrastination. Such negative consequences challenge the legitimacy of the regime.

Improvements could be made to default positions to encourage more active engagement which would increase legitimacy and to confirm that the regime reflects the will of the individual. Behavioural economics identifies the importance of framing and disclosure in decision making and is critical of the financial services industry's traditional method of disclosure as evidence of fair dealing. The way that information is received is very important and influences how much of it people engage with and understand and this consequently affects decisions. The AE regime requires key information to be given to employees about their pension but employers must also ensure that they are not guilty of inducing opt-outs or seen to be providing financial advice and so employers have been cautious to ensure that they meet the AE information disclosure requirements without going beyond that. This can cause tension in the employer/employee relationship and leave employees with unanswered questions or large volumes of paper that they do not read, removing some of the ability or willingness to choose. My empirical study suggests that this can lead to employees relying on employers or colleagues and disengaging from the workplace pension entirely.

The form of AE chosen has been designed to follow the policy of increasing the volume of people saving privately for a pension but this has resulted in defaults at the lowest common denominator which can be unhelpful for some. In setting the contribution levels very low the legislation has achieved a low opt-out rate but this may be at the expense of the operation of choice. There is little to encourage active decision making and no built-in points for verification or affirmation by individuals that they agree to stay in at the default position. This may result in under-saving for many who would have saved more if they had joined later, on a voluntary basis. This is a clear cost of the regime. Employer discretion to design the plan and select providers may also result in detriment for some as there is evidence that some designs will result in lower employer contributions and cross subsidisation of the workforce. Again, this cost does not have a clear remedy. There is also little recognition of the potential for conflicts of interest within the stakeholder group, with employers having legitimate business interests competing with the employees' interests in being enrolled into the best value scheme available.

A further policy concern is that in setting the earnings trigger at £10,000 for AE, a large number of workers are excluded from the regime which was intended to ensure that even the lowest paid workers had access to a workplace pension into which their employer made contributions. This figure was calculated on the basis of affordability and costs on the assumption that to include workers below this would increase the level of opt-outs. It seems implicit in this that the operation of choice as justification for the intervention is questionable and the policy has been compromised to keep opt-out rates low. It also means that those part-time workers with multiple contracts below the trigger will be excluded from AE unless they can demonstrate that they all form part of one larger contract with a particular employer. There has to be a balance between the policy intention and the legitimate business interests of employers and this is perhaps the reason for this compromise of the policy. It is the employer who is responsible for administering the operation of the scheme and so would have to bear the costs of administering the enrolment and opt-outs of these lower paid workers. However, this may result in a skewing of effects for those with and without pensions and may have more of an impact on women than men as women tend to undertake more part-time roles.

III. Has Legislative and Practical Implementation Reflected the Policy Intention?

The reality of implementation was considered through the lens of the data presented in Chapter 5. This explored default positions established by AE, the role of information and advice on understanding and action and whether any negative or unintended consequences are apparent. Much of the research focus to date has been on low opt-out rates and what influences employees to opt-out; whereas my research considers what is going on when employees stay in or make no choices. The alternative justification that the individual perceives benefit from the regime is also explored with some individuals complaining that they lost out on cash alternatives, which they would have preferred.

A. Defaults

The empirical study demonstrates that defaults exert a strong influence on individuals who often remain with the default contribution and fund even if they are unsure what that is. Matching of contributions by employers seemed a particularly strong influence with many reporting that they paid enough to get the matching amount but did not know what this was as a percentage of salary or a monthly amount. This would appear to indicate that inertia influences workers to stay with whatever default they are given and so the selection of defaults is extremely important. It may also be an example of anchoring whereby individuals see matching as the benchmark with which to compare their own position. If the employer sets matching at just above the minimum contribution level for AE, for example at four per cent, then the employee may be inclined to pay the matching amount which means they would have a total contribution of eight per cent. This is the minimum required for AE, and unlikely to be adequate for a reasonable pension, but the employee might not realise this. Employees placed trust in their employers to choose a good scheme and were willing to accept a change of provider on this basis. Changes were often dealt with by a change to the staff benefits handbook rather than by requiring agreed contractual changes and this can also lead to a lack of transparency and consequential disengagement with the pension. Employees often do not pay attention to the communications they receive about changes and also perceive the pension as being within the control of the employer only.

B. Employer Discretion

Whilst the pension must meet the certain minimum quality criteria, the employer has significant discretion in scheme design and provider. The increased demand for compliant schemes has placed some strain on the market with some employers reporting poor service delivered by some pension providers. This is a difficulty with creating a policy which relies on products created in the free market because private providers will only supply products which are profitable. Some have withdrawn from the AE market and others are being more selective in the employees for whom they will provide pensions. Employers can always use NEST but it is a more basic product and may lead to a two-tier pension offering for the workforce.

The private pensions market has discretion to provide or amend existing schemes to be AE compliant in accordance with profitability. Given the past record of the financial services industry it seems that there is potential for the industry to exploit this position and there is some evidence that providers have been unwilling to amend existing schemes to become AE compliant which has resulted in new schemes needing to be created. Employees felt that it would be better if they could choose their own pension provider rather than relying on the employer but employers are likely to be able to negotiate a better deal on costs where they are buying in bulk. The difficulties of reliance on the private pension industry may have been prevented if the AE policy had been operated on the basis of a state-run scheme or a very controlled industry offering such as the operation of the KiwiSaver or MySuper funds in New Zealand and Australia. The NEST scheme was established as a fall-back position to allow employers access to a compliant scheme but it may not be suitable for all employees forcing employers to use private sector schemes.

The reforms restricting charges, costs and improving governance of AE schemes and default funds have gone some way to levelling out the significant differences between schemes which impacts on the individual consequences of the policy. The new governance standards also bring group personal pension schemes, which are used in large numbers to comply with AE, into line with existing governance standards for occupational trust-based schemes. However, these reforms do not equalise schemes or create uniform rules like we have seen in other jurisdictions, so there is still scope for employers' discretion to impact on the consequences for its workers.

C. Communication and Active Choice

The data also showed that individuals see pension decisions as having to be made once only and they do not tend to revisit them. This might be because of difficulties in assessing probability or projection bias, which prevent individuals from appreciating that they will not always feel the same as they do now, as discussed in Chapter 4. These factors can act as barriers to active decision making by the employee. Sometimes the actual process of communication adds to the misunderstanding and creates a barrier to decision making. For example, employees do not read e-mail attachments or are put off reading large volumes of information. Respondents mentioned difficulties communicating with illiterate or foreign workers and it seems that for these workers it will be very difficult to encourage engagement and active decision making. For those workers, the default position is likely to be even more powerful and so there should be adequate protections to ensure that the default position does not have unintended or negative consequences. Improvements to governance and quality are therefore welcomed but do not negate the fact that default positions are replacing choice, which goes to the heart of the justification of this policy intervention.

Whilst certain minimum information is required to be provided under AE, the employer may delegate information duties to pension providers to ensure that they do not fall foul of the restrictions on inducement to opt-out provisions of the AE legislation. Some respondents reported difficulties in finding the information they wanted, including how to opt-out. One respondent was surprised to find out, during our conversation, that he could opt-out at all so whatever information he was given did not sufficiently alert him to his choice. I would suggest that this questions the success and justification of the regime. If individuals are not aware of the right to opt-out or have difficulties finding out how to do this, it is not surprising that opt-out rates are low. It is also possible that employees will simply miss the opt-out window, which is only four weeks, and will remain in the pension for a while but will stop payments when they engage with the information and make a decision. The way the regime was set up means the employees will only receive a refund of contributions if they opt-out and so if they stop paying, they will be left with a small pension pot which they must remember to deal with.

Whilst opt-out rates are low, this does not equate to people choosing to stay. It is unclear whether the policy intervention was just to increase numbers or if it was truly intended to improve the position of workers whilst maintaining choice. It seems clear that the low opt-out rate would indicate success if it was the former but if the intention is the latter this is more difficult to evaluate. Whilst many benefit from the policy there are also costs to the regime including administration costs and employer costs. In addition to this some workers are excluded when the policy intention was to include the poorest workers. Others suffer costs of misunderstanding where they rely on or misunderstand information as advice which leads to poor decisions or over-reliance on defaults. These individuals may never return to these decisions and continue paying contributions which are too low until they come to draw benefits at retirement. Only at that stage will many realise that they have been operating under a false sense of security or mistake. This cannot have been the policy intention but the focus on achieving low opt-outs has sacrificed the element of active choice which was instrumental to the original justification for the policy.

Advice is sometimes paid for by the employer and will sometimes include information sessions for workers, but the role of the advisor in these circumstances can be unclear. Advisors often see their role as providing information but not advice and are not really trying to get employees to engage with the information. This goes back to the original policy intention which was to introduce AE without the need for specific advice to be provided but ensure people understand the benefits of staying in. The respondents I spoke to did not use the generic advice service available but preferred to seek advice from colleagues or family. Advice has been considered again recently by the government, in relation to the new pension flexibilities, but it has been decided that financial advice is needed at the point of retirement only and there has been no change to the policy on the need for advice during the accumulation phase. The introduction of upfront fees, designed to improve clarity and scheme value, may have the negative consequence of pushing professional advice about pensions beyond the affordability of individuals and some employers.

IV. Are There Unforeseen or Unintended Consequences and How Do These Affect Justification for Legal Intervention?

A. Barriers and Misunderstandings

The data illustrates that pensions are often misunderstood or only understood in very basic terms. Perceived complications or barriers such as time, money or legal barriers all operated to prevent individuals engaging with their workplace pensions. Information itself was also perceived as a barrier in some respects which cannot have been the intention behind the policy. Parliament intended that information would create better financial literacy and understanding of pension benefits but in reality, it can be off-putting and led to over-reliance on default positions. Many individuals did not make active choices in relation to their pension and had no plans to revisit this position. Trust of employers, providers or the state was added to this to put off any idea that individuals should engage with the given information and make active choices. The lack of engagement leads to a lack of understanding and a failure to grasp the value of the benefits realistically to be expected from the default savings position. This may result in negative consequences for some employees who might have made different choices under an active choice model or one which required a revisiting of defaults periodically.

B. Reliance on Defaults

Default positions were identified at the outset, in the behavioural economics literature, as being sticky and needing careful consideration and the empirical evidence supports this. To this extent, many of the consequences of AE must have been foreseen and anticipated to be an acceptable cost of the policy. There were concerns that the minimum contributions set should not act as an anchor or result in employers reducing existing benefits. The employer default contributions starting at one per cent of a band of salary and moving up to three per cent minimum set a low anchor point and it might be necessary to increase all of the minimum contribution levels at some point in the future to ensure that the increased volume of savers is not at the expense of lower total contributions. However, it may be more acceptable to find ways of increasing employee contributions so that the policy is effective in increasing the amount of saving rather than just the number of savers. Some research indicates it would be better to have higher default contributions and opt-out rates to ensure better outcomes for those who choose to stay in. The 'Save More Tomorrow' plan discussed in Chapters 3 and 4 would be an improvement on the current default position as it operates as an agreement with the employee that they will increase their saving at some point in the future, usually when they have their salary increased. Another option might be to have graduated increases with age or salary built into the default structure. The employee could still opt-out of the increase and stay with the basic default plan but it might increase engagement.

There is clearly a difficulty where workers replace their own decisions with trust in others and over-reliance on defaults. Having a conversation with HR or others to affirm what decisions have already been made might also increase awareness of current arrangements and promote active thinking and decision making. This would have the benefit of forcing individuals to acknowledge what decisions they have made or what default positions they have accepted and formally agree that they wish to continue with them. This would be more like active choice but with the default position acting as a safety net. The difficulty might be with employers being involved in the process if they are deemed to be influencing opt-out decisions in any way and so Pension Regulator guidance would be needed on the form of such an affirmation.

The increased volume of pension saving and numbers of workers saving has also increased the number of schemes in existence and the likelihood of some being forgotten when employees change employers. The consequences appear to be unforeseen with a regulatory change which proposed that small pots of less than £10,000 are transferred by default into a scheme with the new employer being brought in and then not brought into force. This leaves the problem of forgotten small pots for those who do not return to work or do so at a salary below the AE earnings trigger. Women often have a broken work pattern and are more likely to work part-time and so may be prejudiced by this policy leaving more women susceptible to leaving small pensions and forgetting about them. People do forget about pensions and it is not always easy to find them years later when the paperwork is missing. An improvement would be to require employers to remind employees about the pension and encourage action before leaving employment and also obliging the pension provider to send further information with options or chase up activity with a phone call.

Where individuals also stay with the default investment fund within the AE scheme this might also be detrimental. In defined benefit schemes, for example, a strategy of equities and high risk is usually employed in respect of younger members with the fund being adjusted slowly to de-risk as the individuals near retirement so these funds use the longevity of the investment to take advantage of higher returns on riskier investments over the longer term. With AE, the default fund is low risk and many employees will not consider changing from this default which is sometimes perceived as being recommended to them. Restrictions on costs and charges on this default fund are beneficial to those who stay in the default but also increase the stickiness of this default for those who might otherwise have been more active. The cost of advice is prohibitive and most employees I spoke to did not seek professional advice so a side effect of the regime is likely to be that lower risk investments will be the normal position for all, at the expense of investment performance and possibly lower accumulation of the fund.

C. Advice

The role of professional advice in workplace pensions is not clear. The Money Advice Service does not provide advice on the selection of choices within a workplace pension and would refer the individual to an IFA so this circular situation is likely to result in inactivity. Whilst the policy envisaged that AE would not need advice as it would be simple, it seems that issues such as transfers, contribution defaults and fund selection all pose difficulties for individuals who would actually benefit from further advice. An improvement would be for advice to be included as a requirement somewhere in the regime. This could be as an expansion of the services provided by the Money Advice Service or as an additional cost to the employer. Reforms should also consider payment of advice costs for small employers to improve discretionary decisions. The alternative is to move away from potentially damaging default positions and require active choice or affirmation of defaults at break points, as I have suggested.

Some employers did provide their employees with access to advisors or pension representatives. However, the nature of such meetings was unclear to employees who were unsure whether they could rely on the advice. This confusion was also experienced by employers. For example, Chapter 5 reported data from an HR manager who discussed how much they had benefitted from the advice of an individual at the product provider but when I spoke to the individual at the product provider, they stated that they did not advise the employer but merely assisted with information and administration. The introduction of AE at the same time as the changes requiring financial advice fees to be paid for in advance rather than by commission may have resulted in a reluctance to seek professional financial advice by individuals and employers at a point when they might previously have taken such advice.

A further difficulty lies in the provision of information which might be perceived as advice and relied on as such by individuals or employers. Standard form contracts and information sent to employees by pension providers contain statements to the effect that the provider is not providing advice. Those advisors I spoke to about briefing sessions at the workplace also mentioned that they were not providing advice. Employees may, however, misunderstand what they are being told and rely on this information as advice. Improved communication generally is needed to try and promote more engagement but it seems that there is at least the possibility of losses resulting from misunderstandings. Employers were also unclear about where responsibilities lie where they had engaged advisors and so further consideration should be given to requiring financial and other advisors to be much clearer on the extent of services and responsibilities under AE.

D. Detriment and Responsibility

The confusion over responsibility for advice and information and even in the discretionary actions of the employer in choosing schemes and providers generally, has potential for detriment and the law may have to evolve to recognise the special relationship within which AE operates. Employers are often in a position of trust in relation to employees and use discretion when implementing AE. Consideration was given to whether employers must go beyond the basic AE implementation required under the legislation to demonstrate that actions have been undertaken in good faith and having proper regard to the interests of the employee. The costs for advice and having to change schemes to meet new criteria might lead employers to be less concerned about quality than price. If the employer acted as a fiduciary or an agent of the employee, in implementing its AE duties, this would be a failure in the employer's duties. This is discussed in detail in Chapter 6 which considers situations in which the law might recognise the employer as acting in these special capacities. It is unclear whether there is a legal remedy for those employees suffering detriment as a consequence of poor exercise of discretionary decisions. The employer may be required to demonstrate that decisions relating to choosing a provider and structure for AE pensions were made in good faith. It seems that a claim for loss based on implied terms in the contract of employment is most likely to succeed, but this is not certain. It is also possible that employees could bring claims against the employer's advisors where employees rely on advice to their detriment. Whilst a private law remedy may already exist, for those suffering detriment, this is not certain. Further statutory rectification should be considered to clarify the extent of employers' obligations in exercising discretionary decisions in relation to AE. In particular, the role of information and advice should be considered along with a particular process or standard to be followed by the employer to demonstrate that care has been taken in the exercise of discretionary decisions which impact on the employee. Smaller employers may be more at risk of failures when exercising discretionary decisions and the position might be improved by the government contributing to advice costs for these employers.

E. Social Costs and Remedies

Whilst the AE regime may increase the volume of savers it must be recognised that this means that vast sums of additional funds are now being invested in the free market of the financial services industry with varying consequences, benefits and costs. There are unforeseen costs in addition to the planned benefits of the policy, as identified throughout this book.

Default positions are difficult for employees to move away from and so additional measures are needed to promote more employee engagement. If the justification for the intervention was to provide a benefit whilst preserving free choice then the law must at least attempt to support both aims or the policy becomes more like hard paternalism. The interference with the employer/employee relationship can cause difficulties and misunderstandings and it is important that these are recognised, particularly where the parties' interests are not always aligned. It is not always clear where the additional burdens should lie but, having taken the policy decision to intervene, it is inevitable that this will lead to the imposition of further obligations and responsibilities and the law will continue to evolve to do this. It has been argued that the AE regime is incomplete and fails to ensure the freedom of choice and employee engagement that was envisaged when the policy was introduced. This must question the justification and validity of the policy. A number of changes which might improve the position and prevent losses have been suggested. For example, the AE regime could be improved by requiring confirmation of default positions at set points or by including increases to contributions after a number of years. Responsibilities for administering these additional checks would have to be allocated by statute and clarify whether that would be to require employers or providers to facilitate these checks. It has also been suggested that improvements need to be made to communications generally if there is a genuine aspiration to engage workers with pensions and further consideration is required to be given to the lack of required advice within the regime. This could be advice for individuals and also smaller employers.

In a situation where a policy results in negative consequences for some then it would be expected that a remedy would be available to compensate for this. However, individuals who perceive a detriment have no clear legal remedy available to them at present and this should be clarified. If detriment is perceived to have been caused as a result of poor exercise of discretionary decisions by the employer or where the individual has relied on information as advice then the legal remedy might be available under fiduciary, agency, contract or tort/delict law or there may be no remedy at all. This may be the next big pensions scandal, or not, but the fact remains that the legal position is unclear which is unacceptable. Further statutory codification would allow employers, employees and professional advisors to be clear about roles, responsibilities and rights when implementing AE using private pension policies. The tripartite relationship is currently complex and leads to misunderstandings and disengagement. As matters stand there is a real danger that information will be perceived as advice and relied upon to the detriment of one of the parties. The unchecked employer discretion under AE should also be clarified as the regime should recognise the special relationship of trust and confidence that exists within the employer/employee relationship. The information asymmetry and the lack of balance of power between the parties are also not acknowledged sufficiently by the regime and the exercise of discretion should not be without limits. Statutory rectification of the regime is therefore required.

Having started on the slippery slope of intervention, unintended consequences and negative effects appear like potholes and, inevitably, further statutory intervention is now required to smooth the journey.

Bibliography

Books

Arksey, H & Knight, P, 1999. Why Interviews? In: *Interviewing for Social Scientists: an introductory resource with examples.* (Sage) 32–42.
Buckley, FH, 2009 *Fair Governance, Paternalism and Perfectionism* (Oxford University Press Inc).
Cabrelli, D, 2012. The Liability of Asset Managers in Scots Law. In: DB and DD (eds), *The Liability of Asset Managers.* (Oxford University Press) 507–533.
Clark, G L & Knox-Hayes, J, 2012 The New Paternalism. In: GL Clark, K Strauss & J Knox-Hayes, (eds) *Saving For Retirement* (Oxford University Press) 136–152.
Collins, H, 2000. Justifications and techniques of legal regulation of the employment relation. In: H Collins, P Davies & R Rideout, (eds) *Legal Regulation of the Employment Relation* (Kluwer Law International Ltd) 3–27.
Davies, P & Freedland, M, 2000. Employees, Workers, and the autonomy of labour law. In: H Collins, P Davies & R Rideout, (eds) *Legal Regulation of the Employment Relation* (Kluwer Law International Ltd) 267–286.
DeMott, DA, 2014. The Fiduciary Character of Agency. In: ASG &. PB Miller, (eds) *Philosophical Foundations of Fiduciary Law* (Oxford University Press) 321–338.
Devlin, P, 1969. *The Enforcement of Morals* (Oxford University Press).
Dworkin, G, 1975. 'Paternalism' in J Feinberg and H Gross (eds), *Philosophy of Law* (Dickenson Publishing Company) 174.
Edelman, J, 2014. The Role of Status in the Law of Obligations. In: ASG. & PB Miller, (eds) *Philosophical Foundations of Fiduciary Law* (Oxford University Press) 21–38.
Erskine, J, 1695–1768. *An Institute of the Law of Scotland III.*
Finn, P, 1977. *Fiduciary Obligations* (Law Book Co, NSW Bar Association).
Flick, U, 2009. *An Introduction to Qualitative Research* 4th edn (Sage).
Getzler, J, 2014. Ascribing Fiduciary Obligations. In: ASG & PB Miller, (eds) *Philosophical Foundations of Fiduciary Law* (Oxford University Press) 39–62.
Glaser, B & Strauss, A, 2000. *The Discovery of Grounded Theory: Strategies for Qualitative Research* (Taylor and Francis).
Gold, AS, 2014. The Loyalties of Fiduciary Law. In: ASG &. PB Miller, (eds) *Philosophical foundations of fiduciary Law* (Oxford University Press) 176–194.
Gold, AS & Miller, PB, 2014. *Philosophical Foundations of Fiduciary Law* 1st edn (Oxford University Press).
Halliday, S & Schmidt, P, 2009. *Conducting Law and Society Research, Reflections on Methods and Practices* (Cambridge University Press).
Larrick, RP, 2004. Debiasing. In: DJK and N Harvey, (eds) *Blackwell Handbook of Judgment and Decision Making* (Blackwell) 316–337.
Kvale, S, 1996. *Interviews: An Introduction to Qualitative Research Interviewing* (Sage).
Lewins, A & Silver, C, 2007. Data and their preparation for CAQDAS packages. In: A Lewins, (ed) *Using software in qualitative research* (Sage) 16–31.
Macgregor, L, 2013. *The Law of Agency in Scotland* (Scottish Universities Law Institute, W Green/ Thomson Reuters).
Macgregor, L, 2016 'Defining Agency and Its Scope (I)' in DiMatteo (ed), *Transatlantic Perspectives on Commercial Contract Law* (Oxford University Press).

Mason, J, 2002. Qualitative Interviewing. In J Mason (ed) *Qualitative researching* (Sage) 62–83.
Miles, MB & Huberman, AM, 1994. *Making Good Sense. In: Qualitative Data Analysis: An expanded sourcebook* (Sage) 245–287.
Mill, JS, 1969 (republished 2011). *On liberty* (White Crane Publishing).
Mill, JS, 1969. *On Liberty* (Currin Shields).
Miller, PB, 2014. The Fiduciary Relationship. In: ASG & PB Miller, (eds) *Philosophical Foundations of Fiduciary Law* (Oxford University Press) 63–90.
Mill, JS, 1975. On the Connection between Justice and Utility. In: J Feinberg & H Gross, (eds) *Philosophy of Law* (Dickenson Publishing Company Inc) 259–270.
Mitchell, O S & Utkus, S P, 2004. Lessons from Behavioural Finance for Retirement Plan Design. In: OS Mitchell & SP Utkus, (eds) *Pension Design and Structure: New Lessons From Behavioural Finance* (Oxford University Press) 3–41.
Murray, J, 2015. Conceptualizing the Employer as Fiduciary: Mission Impossible? In: CCA D & JP Alan Bogg, (eds) *The Autonomy of Labour Law* (Hart Publishing) 337–366.
Ogus, AI, 2004. *Regulation: Legal Form and Economic Theory* (Hart Publishing).
Ogus, A & Van Boom, WH, 2011. *Juxtaposing Autonomy and Paternalism in Private Law* (Hart Publishing).
Pemberton, H, Thane, P & Whiteside, N, 2006. *Britain's Pensions Crisis: History and Policy* (Oxford University Press).
Rawls, J, 1975. Justice as Fairness. In: J Feinberg & H Gross, (eds) *Philosophy of Law* (Dickenson Publishing Company Inc) 276–290.
Richards, L, 2009. Coding. In: *Handling Qualitative Data: A Practical Guide* (Sage) 92–113.
Ritchie, J & Spencer, L, 1994. Qualitative Data Analysis for Applied Policy Research. In: A B and RG Burgess, (eds) *Analyzing Qualitative Data* (Routledge) 173–194.
Ritchie, J, Spencer, L & O'Connor, W, 2003. Carrying Out Qualitative Analysis. In: JR and J Lewis, (eds) *Qualitative research practice: a guide for social science students and researchers* (Sage) 219–262.
Robson, C, 1993. *Real World Research, A Resource for Social Scientists and Practitioner-Researchers* (Blackwell Publishers Ltd).
Rubin, H & Rubin, I, 2005. Structuring the Interview In: Rubin and Rubin (eds) *Qualitative interviewing the art of hearing data* (Sage) 129–151.
Silverman, D, 2005. *Doing Qualitative Research* 2nd edn (Sage).
Sitkoff, RH, 2014. An Economic Theory of Fiduciary Law. In: ASG & PB Miller, (eds) *Philosophical Foundations of Fiduciary Law* (Oxford University Press) 197–208.
Smith, LD, 2014. Can We Be Obliged to Be Selfless? In: A SG & PB Miller, (eds) *Philosophical Foundations of Fiduciary Law* (Oxford University Press) 141–158.
Sunstein, CR, 2014. *Why Nudge?* (Yale University Press).
Sunstein, CR, 2015. *Choosing not to choose, Understanding the Value of Choice* (Oxford University Press).
Thaler, RH & Sunstein, CR, 2008. *Nudge: Improving Decisions about Health Wealth and Happiness* (Yale University Press).
Thaler, RH, 2015. *Misbehaving: The Making of Behavioural Economics* (Allen Lane, Penguin Books).
Watt, B, 2000. Regulating the employment relationship: From rights to relations. In: H Collins, P Davies & R Rideout, (eds) *Legal Regulation of the Employment Relation* (Kluwer Law International Ltd) 335–346.
Watts, PG & Reynolds, FM, 2010. *Bowstead & Reynolds on Agency* 19th edn (Sweet & Maxwell).

Journal Articles

Agudo, L F & Garcia, M A, 2010. 'The Reform of Some European public pension systems: Spain, Italy and Sweden: A Breakthrough?' 15 *Pensions*, 297–304.

Andrews, D, 2012. 'Why Sweden's Notional DC Pension System Needs a Correction Calculation', 5 *Rotman International Journal of Pension Management*, 40–47.

Arlen, J, 1998. 'Comment: The Future of Behavioural Economic Analysis of Law' 52 *Vanderbilt Law Review*, 1765–1788.

Aronson, J, 1994. 'A Pragmatic View of Thematic Analysis' 2 *The Qualitative Report*, 1–3.

Attride-Stirling, J, 2001. 'Thematic networks: an analytic tool for qualitative research' 1 *Qualitative Research*, 385–405.

Bateman, H, 2012. 'The Future of Financial Advice and MySuper' 3 *The Finsia Journal of Applied Finance*, 50.

Benartzi, S & Thaler, RH, 2007. 'Heuristics and Biases in Retirement Savings Behaviour' 21 *Journal of Economic Perspectives*, 81–104.

Birks, P, 2000. 'The Content of Fiduciary Obligation' 34(1) *Israeli Law Review*, 3–38.

Bodie, Z, 1990. 'Pensions as Retirement Income Insurance' 28 *Journal of Economic Literature*, 28–49.

Bogg, AL, 2010–2011. 'Good Faith in the Contract of Employment: A Case of The English Reserve' 32 *Comparative Labour Law and Policy Journal*, 729–772.

Bollen, R, 2007. 'A case Study of Bounded Rationality in the Market for Superannuation Products' 4 *Macquarie Journal of Business Law*, 49–70.

Borsch-Supan, A, 2005. 'From Traditional DB to Notional DC Systems: The Pension Reform Process in Sweden, Italy and Germany' 3 *Journal of the European Economic Association*, 458–465.

Brodie, D, 1996. 'The Heart of the Matter: Mutual Trust and Confidence' 25 *Industrial Law Journal*, 121–136.

Brodie, D, 2001. 'Mutual Trust and the Values of the Employment Contract' 30 *Industrial Law Journal*, 84–100.

Brodie, D, 2008. 'Mutual Trust and Confidence: Catalysts, Constraints and Commonality' 37 *Industrial Law Journal*, 329–346.

Brodie, D, 2012. 'The Employment Relationship and Fiduciary Obligations' 16 *The Edinburgh Law Review*, 198–209.

Bubb, R & Pildes, RH, 2014. 'How Behavioural Economics Trims its Sails and Why' 127 *Harvard Law Review*, 1593–1678.

Bulmer, M, 1979. 'Concepts in the Analysis of Qualitative Data' 27 *Sociological Review*, 651–677.

Burrows, P, 1993. 'Patronising Paternalism' 45 *Oxford Economic Papers*, 542–572.

Burrows, P, 1995. 'Analyzing Legal Paternalism' 15 *International Review of Law and Economics*, 489–508.

Busch, D, 2012. 'Why MIFID matters to private law – the example of MIFID's impact on an asset manager's civil liability' 7 *Capital Markets Law Journal*, 386–413.

Butt et al, 2017. 'Design of MySuper default funds: influences and outcomes' 57 *Accounting and Finance* 47.

Cabrelli, D, 2005. 'The Implied Duty of Mutual Trust and Confidence: An Emerging Overarching Principle' 34 *Industrial Law Journal*, 284–307.

Camerer, C et al, 2003. 'Regulations for Conservatives' 151 *University of Pennsylvania Law Review*, 1211–1254.

Carroll, GD et al, 2009. 'Optimal Defaults and Active Decisions' *The Quarterly Journal of Economics*, 1639–1674.

Cheredbychenko, OO, 2010. 'The Regulation of Retail Investment Services in the EU: Towards the Improvement of Investor Rights' 33 *Journal of Consumer Policy*, 403–424.

Coates IV, JC, 2015. 'Cost Benefit Analysis of Financial Regulation: Case Studies and Implications' 124 *The Yale Law Journal*, 882–1011.

Cole, DH, 2012–2013. 'Law, Politics, and Cost-Benefit Analysis' 64 *Alabama Law Review*, 55–89.

Conaglen, M, 2005. 'The nature and function of fiduciary loyalty' 121 *Law Quarterly Review*, 452–480.

Cronqvist, H & Thaler, RH, 2004. 'Design Choices in Privitized Social-Security Systems: Learning From the Swedish Experience' 94 *American Economic Review*, 424–428.

Crossan et al, 2011. 'Financial Literacy and Retirement Planning in New Zealand' *Journal of Pension Economics & Finance*, 619.

DeMott, D, 1988. 'Beyond Metaphor: An analysis of fiduciary obligation' *Duke Law Journal*, 879–924.

DeMott, DA, 1998–1999. 'The Lawyer as Agent' 67 *Fordham Law Review*, 301–326.

Desai, AC, 2011. 'Libertarian Paternalism, Externalities, and the spirit of liberty: How Thaler and Sunstein are Nudging Us toward an Overlapping Consensus' 36 *Law & Social Inquiry*, 263–295.

Dworkin, G, 1982. 'Is More Choice Better than Less?' 7 *Midwest Studies in Philosophy*, 47–61.

Dworkin, R, 1966. 'Lord Devlin and the Enforcement of Morals' 75 *The Yale Law Journal*, 986–1005.

Dynan, KE, Skinner, J & Zeldes, SP, 2004. 'Do the Rich Save More?' 112 *Journal of Political Economy*, 397–444.

Edelman, J, 2010. 'When do fiduciary duties arise?' 126 *Law Quarterly Review*, 302–327.

Feinberg, J, 1971. 'Legal Paternalism' 1 *Canadian Journal of Philosophy*, 105–124.

Feldman, MS, 1995. 'Strategies for Interpreting Qualitative Data' 33 *Qualitative Research Methods*, 64.

Finn, P, 1989. 'Contract and the Fiduciary Principle' 12 *University of New South Wales Journal*, 76–97.

Freeman, S, 2004. 'Women at Work: The Broken Promise of Flexicurity' 33 *Industrial Law Journal*, 299.

Gibson et al, 2011. 'The Distributional Impact of KiwiSaver Incentives' *Social Policy Journal of New Zealand*, 111.

Glaeser, EL, 2006. 'Paternalism and Psychology' 73 *University of Chicago Law Review*, 133–156.

Halfpenny, P, 1979. 'The Analysis of Qualitative Data' 27 *Sociological Review*, 799–827.

Hammersley, M, 2010. 'Reproducing or constructing? Some questions about transcription in social research' 10 *Qualitative Research*, 553–569.

Hohfield, WN, 1913. 'Some Fundamental Legal Conceptions as Applied in Judicial Reasoning' 23 *Yale Law Journal*, 16–59.

Hospers J, 1980. 'Libertarianism and Legal Paternalism' 4 *The Journal of Libertarian Studies*, 255.

Husak, DN, 1981. 'Paternalism and Autonomy' 10 *Philosophy and Public Affairs*, 27–46.

Jefferson, T, 2012. 'Private Retirement Savings In Australia: Current Policy Initiatives and Gender Equality Implications' 38 *Australian Bulletin of Labour*, 234–250.

Jolls, C, 1988. 'Behavioural Economics Analysis of Redistributive Legal Rules'. *Vanderbilt Law Review*, 1653.

Kennedy, D, 1982. 'Distributive and Paternalistic Motives in Contract and Tort Law, with special reference to compulsory terms and unequal bargaining power' *Maryland Law Review*, 563–658.

Knapp, WS, 1981. 'On the Validity of Accounts about Everyday Life' 29 *Sociological Review*, 543–562.

Krauss, S & Peredaryenko, M, 2013. 'Calibrating the Human Instrument: Understanding the Interviewing Experience of Novice Qualitative Researchers' 18 *The Qualitative Report*, 1–17.

Kronman, AT, 1983. 'Paternalism and the Law of Contracts' 92 *The Yale Law Journal*, 763–798.

Lapdat, JC & Lindsey, A, 1999. 'Transcription in Research and Practice: From Standardization of Technique to Interpretive Positionings' 5 *Qualitative Inquiry*, 64–86.

Law et al, 2017, 'KiwiSaver: an evaluation of a new retirement savings scheme' 51 *New Zealand Economic Papers*, 262.

MacDonald et al, 2012. 'KiwiSaver and Retirement Adequacy' 6(4) *Australasian Accounting, Business and Finance Journal* 61.

Macgregor, L, 2013. '"100 per cent, Body and Soul": The Ability of an Agent to Act for a Competitor of his Principal' 17 *Edinburgh Law Review*, 71–78.

Macgregor, L, 2015. 'Crossing the Line between Business Common Sense and Perceived Fairness in Contractual Interpretation' 19 *Edinburgh Law Review*, 378–383.

Madrian, BC & Shea, DF, 2001. 'The Power of Suggestion: Inertia in 401(k) Participation and Savings Behaviour' 116 *The Quarterly Journal of Economics*, 1149–1187.

Maqueen, KM, Neidig, JL & McLellan, E, 2003. 'Beyond the Qualitative Interview: Data Preparation and Transcription' 15 *Field Methods*, 63–84.

McBarnet, D, 1991. 'Whiter than white collar crime: tax, fraud insurance and the management of stigma' 42 *The British Journal of Sociology*, 323–344.

Milikene, S, Gaizauskaite, I. & Valaviciene, N, 2013. 'Qualitative Interviewing: Field-Work Realities' 12 *Social Work*, 50.
Miller, PB, 2011. 'A Theory of Fiduciary Liability' 56 *McGill Law Journal*, 235.
Moloney, N, 2012. 'Liability of Asset Managers: A comment' 7 *Capital Markets Law Journal*, 414–422.
Muir, D, 2011. 'Building Value in the Australian Defined Contribution system: A Values Perspective' *Comparative Labor Law and Policy Journal* 9.
Nicholls, L, 1995. 'Trustees and Their Broader Community: Where Duty, Morality and Ethics Converge' 9 *Trust Law International*, 71–77.
Nind, M, Wiles, R, Bengry-Howell, A & Crow, G, 2012. 'Methodological innovation and research ethics: forces in tension or forces in harmony?' 13 *Qualitative Research*, 650–667.
O'Connell, Institute of Policy Studies, 2009. 'KiwiSaver: A Model Scheme' 36 *Social Policy Journal of New Zealand* 130.
Ogus, A, 2010. 'The Paradoxes of Legal Paternalism and how to resolve them' 30 *Legal Studies*, 61–73.
Ohrenstein, D, 2015. 'In Good Faith?' 7 *New Law Journal*, 19–20.
Peggs, K, 2000. 'Which pension: women, risk and pension choice' *The Sociological Review*, 349–364.
Rizzo, MJ & Whitman, DG, 2009. 'Little Brother is Watching You: New Paternalism on the Slippery Slopes' 51 *Arizona Law Review*, 685–739.
Roulston, K, 2001. 'Data Analysis and "theorising as ideology"' 1 *Qualitative Research*, 279–302.
Roulston, K, 2010. Considering Quality in Qualitative Interviewing' 10 *Qualitative Research*, 201.
Sadiq, K, 2012. 'Prescriptions for reform of Australia's superannuation tax concessions' 27 *Australian Tax Forum*, 371–385.
Salt, H, 2010. 'Checks and balances in member protection' 15(4) *Pensions: An International Journal*, 249–258.
Schiellerup, P, 2008. 'Stop making sense: the trials and tribulations of qualitative data analysis' 40 *Area*, 163–171.
Secunda, 2016. 'The Behavioural Economic Case for Paternalistic Workplace Retirement Plans' 91 *Indiana Law Journal* 505.
Sheppard, E, 2015. 'Good faith in the aftermath of Yam Seng' *Butterworths Journal of International Banking and Financial Law*, 407–409.
Sims, V, 2001. 'Is Employment a Fiduciary Relationship?' 30 *Industrial Law Journal*, 101–110.
Strauss, K, 2008. 'Re-engaging with rationality in economic geography: behavioural approaches and the importance of context in decision making' 8 *Journal of Economic Geography*, 137–156.
Sunstein, C, 2011. 'Empirically Informed Regulation' 78 *The University of Chicago Law Review*, 1349–1429.
Sunstein, CR & Thaler, RH, 2003. 'Libertarian Paternalism is not an Oxymoron' 70 *The University of Chicago Law Review*, 1159–1202.
Thaler, RH & Benartzi, S, 2004. 'Save More Tomorrow: Using Behavioural Economics to Increase Employee Saving' 112 *Journal of Political Economy*, 164–187.
Thaler, RH & Sunstein, CR, 2003. 'Libertarian Paternalism' *American Economic Review*, 175–179.
Tracy, SJ, 2010. 'Qualitative Quality: Eight "Big-Tent" Criteria for Excellent Qualitative Research' 16 *Qualitative Inquiry*, 838–851.
Valdes, EG, 1990. 'On Justifying Legal Paternalism' 3 *Ratio Juris*, 173–184.

Reports and Papers

Australian Government, Cooper. 2010 'Super system review: final report.'
Department for Work and Pensions, 2006. 'Personal Accounts: A New Way to Save'. (White Paper, Cm 6975, 2006).
Department for Work and Pensions, 2006. 'Security in Retirement: Towards a New Pension System.'

Department for Work and Pensions, Collard & Moore, 2010. Research Report No 663 'Review of International Pension Reform.'
Department for Work and Pensions, July 2011. 'Communications, Automatic enrolment- information for workers qualitative research.'
Department for Work and Pensions, Long-term Impact and Evaluation team, July 2011. 'Workplace Pension Reforms Evaluation Strategy', Research Report No 764.
Department for Work and Pensions, August 2013. 'Automatic enrolment opt out rates: findings from research with large employers.'
Department for Work and Pensions, 2013. 'Automatic Enrolment evaluation report 2013.
Department for Work and Pensions, November 2014 'Automatic Enrolment Evaluation Report', Research Report No 887.
Department Work and Pensions, March 2014, 'Better Workplace Pensions: Further Measures for Savers' (Cm 8840, March 2014).
Department for Work and Pensions, October 2014. 'Official Statistics on workplace pension participation and saving trends of eligible employees.'
Department for Work and Pensions, January 2015. 'Automatic enrolment: Qualitative research with employers staging in 2014.'
Department for Work and Pensions, 17 September 2015. 'Workplace Pensions Update of Analysis on Automatic enrolment.'
Department for Work and Pension and Financial Conduct Authority, 2015 'Transaction Costs Disclosure: Improving Transparency in Workplace Pensions, Call for Evidence' Discussion Paper 15/2.
Department for Work and Pensions, 'Workplace Pensions Update of analysis on Auto Enrolment 2016.'
Department for Work and Pensions, March 2016. 'Employer's Pension Provision survey 2015.'
Department for Work and Pensions Automatic Enrolment Review 2017: Maintaining the Momentum Cm 9546.
Department for Work and Pensions Automatic Enrolment Review 2017: Analytical Report December 2017.
Department for Work and Pensions, 2019. 'Investment Innovation and Future Consolidation: A Consultation on the Consideration of Illiquid Assets and the Development of Scale in Occupational Defined Contribution schemes.'
De Meza, D, Irlenbusch, B & Reyniers, D, for Financial Services Authority 2008. 'Financial Capability: A Behavioural Economic Perspective' (London School of Economics).
Erta, K, Hunt, S, Iscenko, Z & Brambley, W April 2013. 'Applying behavioural economics at the Financial Conduct Authority' April 2013 Occasional Paper No 1.
Financial Conduct Authority, 2014 'Thematic Review of Annuities' (TR14/2).
Financial Conduct Authority, 2014 'Retirement Income Market Study: Final Report – Confirmed Findings and Remedies' (MS14/3.3).
Financial Conduct Authority, 2015. 'Developing our approach to implementing MiFID II conduct of business and organisational requirements.'
Financial Conduct Authority, 2016 'Thematic Review of annuity sales practices.'
Financial Services Authority & Personal Investment Authority, March 1998. 'Pension Transfers and opt outs review, phase 2.'
Financial Services Authority, 2007. Retail Distribution Review DP07/1.
Government Actuary, 1975. 'Occupational Pension Schemes: Fifth Survey' (HMSO).
Hansard, 2008 Report House of Commons Oral Answers.
Hansard, 25 November 2014. Hansard: Report Stage, House of Commons.
House of Commons Library, 'Research Paper 07/94: Pensions Bill' (19 December 2007).
House of Commons Work and Pensions Committee, 2012. 'Automatic Enrolment in workplace pensions and the National Employment Savings Trust', Eighth Report of Session 2010–2012.
Inter-departmental Committee on Social Insurance and Allied Services, Social and Allied Services (Cmd 6404-6405, 1942).

Johnson, P, Yeandle, D. & Boulding, A, 2010. 'Making Automatic Enrolment Work, A review for the Department for Work and Pensions.'
Kay, J, July 2012. 'The Kay Review of UK Equity Markets and Long-Term Decision Making: Final Report.'
The Law Commission, June 2014. 'Fiduciary Duties of Investment Intermediaries, Law Com No 350.
New Zealand Treasury Working Paper 11/04, Law et al, 'KiwiSaver: An initial Evaluation of the Impact on Retirement Saving.'
New Zealand Treasury Working Paper 14/22, Law & Scobie, 'KiwiSaver and the Accumulation of Net Wealth.'
Office of Fair Trading, 2013 (revised February 2014). 'Defined contribution workplace pension market study.'
Pension Law Review Committee, 1993. 'The Report of the Pension Law Review Committee' (The Goode Report), Cm 2342-1.
The Pensions Commission, 2004. 'Pensions: Challenges and Choices, The First Report of the Pensions Commission.'
The Pensions Commission, 2005. 'A New Pension Settlement for the Twenty-First Century.'
The Pensions Regulator, April–June 2015. 'Automatic enrolment Compliance and Enforcement.'
The Pensions Regulator, December 2014. 'Automatic Enrolment Compliance and enforcement quarterly bulletin.'
The Pensions Regulator, January–March 2015. 'Automatic enrolment Compliance and Enforcement Quarterly Bulletin.'
The Pensions Regulator, July 2015. 'Automatic Enrolment Commentary and Analysis: April 2014–March 2015.'
The Pensions Regulator, July–September 2015. 'Automatic Enrolment Compliance and Enforcement Quarterly Bulletin.'
The Pensions Regulator, June 2014. 'Automatic enrolment Compliance and enforcement, Quarterly bulletin.'
Thoresen, O, 2008. 'Thoresen Review of Generic Financial Advice: Final Report' (HMSO, March 2008).
Wheatley, M, 2014. 'Making Competition King – the Rise of Behavioural Economics at the FCA' (*Financial Conduct Authority*, 25 March 2014) www.fca.org.uk/news/making-competition-king.
Work and Pensions Command paper, March 2014. 'Better Workplace Pensions: Further measures for savers' Cm 8840.

Online Sources

Avgouleas, E 2008 'Cognitive Biases and Investor Protection Regulation: An Evolutionary Approach' *Social Science Research Network.*
Baker, S and Edwards, R, 2012. 'How Many Qualitative Interviews is Enough? Expert Voices and Early Career Reflections on Sampling and Cases in Qualitative Research' 9 *National Centre for Research Methods Review Paper.*
Banerjee, S, November 2014. *The Gap between Expected and Actual Retirement: Evidence from Longitudnal Data*, Washington DC: Employee Benefit Research Institute (SSRN (November 2014).
Beshears, J, Choi, JJ, Laibson, D & Madrian, BC, 2006. 'The Importance of Default Options for Retirement Savings Outcomes: Evidence from the United States.' *National Bureau of Economic Research Working Paper* No 12009.
Beshears, J, Choi, JJ, Laibson, D & Madrian, BC, 2010. 'The Limitations of Defaults.' *National Bureau of Economic Research Working Paper.*
Bubb, R, et al 2015. 'A Behavioural Contract Theory Perspective on Retirment Savings.' *Social Science Research Network.*

Bullard, M., 2013. 'The Social Costs of Choice, Free Market Ideology and the Empirical Consequences of the 401(K) Plan Large Menu Defence'. *Social Science Research Network.*

Burman et al 2004. 'Distributional Effects of Defined Contribution Plans and Individual Retirement Accounts'. *The Urban-Brookings Tax Policy Center.*

Cabrelli d, 2011 'The Liability of Asset Managers in Scots Law.' *Social Science Research Network.*

Caven, V, 2012. 'Agony Aunt, hostage, intruder or friend' 8 *Intangible Capital.*

Choi, JJ, Laibson, D, Madrian, BC & Metrick, A, 2004. 'Saving For Retirement on the Path of Least Resistance.' *National Bureau of Economic Research.*

Crawford School of Public Policy, Heng et al, 2015. 'Retirement Policy: a review of the role, characteristics, and contribution of the Australian superannuation system.' *Asian Pacific Economic Literature.*

Fleishman-Mayer, LA et al, 2013. 'Designing Better Pension Benefits Statements'. *RAND Center for the Study of Aging and the NICHD funded RAND Population Research Center.*

INDEX

Note: Alphabetical arrangement is word-by-word, where a group of letters followed by a space is filed before the same group of letters followed by a letter, eg 'tax reliefs' will appear before 'taxation'. In determining alphabetical arrangement, initial articles and prepositions are ignored.

401(k) plans, US, 47, 87, 153

abuse:
 of power, employment relationships prevention, 164
 protection by paternalism inferred into private law, 43
acceptance:
 lack of opt-outs reason, Auto-Enrolment, 80
accessibility, lack of, 116
account, duty to account, *see* **duty to account**
action:
 in context, art of valuing moral effects of, 54–55
 empirical research findings, 97, 98–102
 engagement and, connection between, 101
 individuals, without engagement by, 99
 instinctive, 98
active choice, 186–88
active decision-making barriers, 186
active engagement:
 not encouraged by Auto-Enrolment, 67–68
administration costs, 58, 187
administrative costs, 58
administrators' fiduciary duties of selection of prudent investment options:
 401k plan, US, 153
advice:
 accessing savings, at point of, 37
 Auto-Enrolment, *see* Auto-Enrolment
 debts, 21
 employees unsure where to go for, 127
 employers, *see* employers
 financial planning, 119
 financial, *see* financial advice
 generic, 20, 21
 inadequate, 139
 information:
  and, tension between, Auto-Enrolment, 168
  construed as, employees, 169
  perceived as, 139
  versus, 127
 not durable, 107
 professional, 121
 provision:
  duties owed to employees by pension providers or advisors, 173
  to general public, 21
 schemes without, 139
 specifically requested by pension members, charges for, 31
 trustees, provided to, quality consideration, 34
 unforeseen or unintended consequences, 190
advise, duty to, implied terms, 167–69
advisors:
 claims in delict, 174
 COBS, obligations under, 176
 duties owed to employees by, 173
  advice provision, 173
  information, fair, clear, and not misleading, 175
  financial regulation, reliance on, 175–76
  Law Commission on, 173
  misunderstandings and mis-statements, 173–74
  risks indications, 175
  third party liability, 174–75
 duty of care under law of delict, 174
 to employees, 152–53
 employees unsure of role of, 173–74
 employers, *see* employers
 fiduciary duties to employees, 140
 fiduciary obligations, 152–53
 information given directly to employees, 175
 large commission, motivated by, 9
 over-reliance on, 125
 product providers, 145–46
AE, *see* **Auto-Enrolment**
affordability, 99, 106

age:
discrimination, 12
employees, 22
gender and, impact conclusion, 137
retirement, *see* retirement
ageing population, 10–12, 22, 179–80
agency:
duties, private law, 176
workers, 22, 100, 112
agents, 153–54
agency relationship, 155–56
care and skill obligations, 158–59
consequences of agency, 157–59
employers as agents of employees, 191
employers' duties as to employees, 140
fiduciary duties, 153–59
fiduciary obligations, 157–58
knowledge impartation to principals, 158
law of agency, 159
non-fiduciary duties, 157–58
personal pension contracts, 158
Scotland, 154, 158
skill and care obligations, 158–59
agreements, contractual, 158
anchor effect, 99, 101
anchors, 107
annuities, 37
anomalies:
cognitive shortcuts, creation by, 65–66
assets, 143, 144
assumptions:
inaction and, links between, 108
asymmetries:
effects, 118
information, *see* information
paternalism, 76
power, *see* power
in understanding, 118–19
Attride-Stirling, J, 96, 97
Australia:
Auto-Enrolment in pensions, 14, 15, 183
choice-based system, 27
Cooper Review, 27, 70
corporate funds sector choice-based system, 27
default funds, 27, 87
employer contributions, 24–25
Financial Literacy:
financial matters, education and understanding of, 78
financial service industry, 78
industry sector choice-based system, 27
lump sums, taking savings as, 36
MySuper, 27, 35, 186
default funds, 70
product providers' fiduciary obligations, 154
trustees, 154
private pension plan, 15
public sector choice-based system, 27
retail sector choice-based system, 27
self-selection of investments, 27
superannuation, 7, 15, 24–25, 27
compulsory employer contributions, comparison with, 77
members, 70
policy review, 65
see also MySuper *above*
Auto-Enrolment (AE):
401(k) plans, USA, 47
active choice:
policy intention, 186–88
active engagement not encouraged, 67–68
administration costs, 58, 187
advice, 187
cost prohibitive, 189–90
information and, tension between, 168
lack within regime, 192
asymmetric information, 62
Australia, 14, 15, 183
behavioural bias and, 84–88
benefits, 181–82
bounded rationality problem ignored, 75
charge cap, 30–33
choice:
architecture, *see* choice architecture
default positions replacing, 186
freedom of, failure to ensure, 192
inertia affecting, 181
myopia affecting, 181
retention, 61
cognitive bias, 74
commission charges, 31–32
communication, 186–88, 192
compliance, 58, 171–73
conflicts of interest, 49, 184
consultation charges, 31–32
contract of employment, particulars, 28
contributions:
deducted from pay, 62
increases, 183
legislation setting very low, 184
low value of, 25
lowest level, 183

matching by employers, 185
rules providing anchor or starting point, 88
costs, 30–33, 59, 181–82, 187
cross-party support, 10
defaults, 74
behavioural biases, 83
beneficial position as, 61
caps on charges and fees, 82
choice architecture, 81–83
difficult for employees to move away from, 191
employers deciding on contributions, 85
funds:
investment, 180, 189
protection of those in, 30
importance, 183
improvements, 183
inertia acting with, 81
initial level important, 82
matching contributions, 83, 85
New Zealand, 82, 83
offset, 85
one-size-fits-all, 83
passive saving, 81
policy intention, 185
procrastination, 81
replacing choice, 186
savings patterns shifts, 81
savings rate, 180
schemes, 180
status quo bias, 81, 83
stickiness, 83, 88, 189
deferred pensioners, 31
detriments:
no clear legal remedy, 192
resulting from introduction of, private law remedies, 139
disclosure:
choice architecture, 88–90
discounts for active scheme members, 31
distributive motives, 60
earnings criteria, 23
efficiency motives, 60
eligible jobholders, 23
employees:
advised in advance, 28
employer relationship and, 136–37
employers' duties to under contract or delict relating to, 140
engagement, failure to ensure, 192
employers:
costs, 187
discretion, 79, 185–86
duties to employees under contract or delict relating to, 140
employee relationship and, 136–37
inducement prohibition, 104
responsibilities for implementation, 5
endowment effect, 80
excluded workers, 180, 184, 187
external effects, 57
fall back, beneficial position as, 61
fiduciary duties implied, 62
financial advice lack, 20
financial education as alternative to, 78
financial services industry compliant schemes, 186
framing:
choice architecture, 88–90
fund selection, 183
governance framework lacking, 29
incomplete regime, 192
increased choice, US, 86–87
indirect costs, 58, 59
individual perception of, 135–36
inertia, 185
enlisted, 50
US, 87–88
working in favour of saving, 80
information, 183
advice and, tension between, 168
asymmetry, 192
content, 67
disclaimer included, 174
disclosure, 88–90
employer-provided, 80
form of, 79
frequency, 67
generic, inadequacy, 67
minimum, 187
opting-out inducement prevention, 67
perceived as advice, 190
product providers, delegation to, 187
requirements, 167
to workers, 27–28
international experiences referenced by Pensions Commission, 14
introduction:
by private companies, US, 82
as UK pension policy change, 4–5, 17–38
uncertainty, 118

investment strategies:
  rules providing anchor or starting point, 88
leaver rates, 127–28
legal paternalism, 74
legislation changes, DWP powers to make, 28
legislation compliance, Pensions Regulator enforcement, 28
legislative reality, 22–28
lessons from abroad, 14–15
lowest paid workers exclusion, 180, 184
marginal costs, 58
master trusts, 35–36, 38
minimum contributions, 2
minimum pay criteria, 180
minimum quality standards, 29
misunderstanding, costs of, 187
negative consequences of, 137–38, 139
new paternalism, 47–48
New Zealand, *see* New Zealand
occupational pension schemes, 26
operation, 5
opportunity cost of meeting contribution obligations, 58
opt-outs, 5, 180
  choice, 62
  choice architecture, 80
  costs of, 58
  employers not to induce, 183
  employers prevention on giving financial advice, 103
  inducement prevention by information provision, 67
  lack of, inertia or acceptance as reason, 80
  leaver rates monitored alongside, 127–28
  low rates, 182, 184, 187
  methods, 103–104
  notices from scheme providers, 103
  procrastination about, 80
  product providers sending information about, 80
  safety mechanisms, 181
  unawareness of, 129, 187
  US, 83, 85
  whether allowed to, 122
parliamentary intent, 17
  consensus solution, 19
  generic advice, 21
  increase saving by default, 17–18
  levelling down, 18–19
  prevent reduction in existing pension benefits or levelling down, 18–19
  private pension saving compatible with state benefits, 21–22
  workforce education, 19–21
personal information, consent to disclosure, 103
personal pension schemes, 26
plan design, employer discretion, 184
policy:
  communication and active choice, 186–88
  considerations, 4–5
  defaults, 185
  employer discretion, 185–86
  valuation based on efficiency, 60
post implementation legislative changes, 28–29
  costs and charges, 30–33
  master trusts, 35–36
  pension benefits, taking, 36–37
  scheme governance, 33–35
  value, 29
power, balance between parties lacking, 192
pre-existing schemes use, 18–19, 26
product providers:
  changes of, 185
  employer discretion, 184
qualifying arrangements, 2
qualifying schemes nominated by employers, 33
reasons for, 179
regulatory intervention of, 1
reversibility, 59–60
road to:
  Pensions Commission, 10–14
  voluntary private pensions rise and fall, 5–10
safeguards:
  insufficient, 60
savings patterns shifts, New Zealand, 81
schemes:
  creation, 77
  governance, 33–35
  selection, 183
seasonal summer workers, 128
self-enrolment, switching from, 79
simplicity, 32
social costs, 1
soft paternalism, 74, 180, 181
stakeholder group asserting own interests over others, example of, 44
status quo bias, addressing, 74
taking pension benefits, 36–37
technical failures to comply, 168

transaction costs, 32–33
transfers done automatically, 118
tripartite relationship complexity, 192
trust-based schemes, 153
unforeseen or negative consequences of, 137–38
United States, *see* United States
value, 29
voluntary, US, 14
vulnerability of employees subject to defaults under, 30
women, 24

autonomy, 42
loss of to make personal financial decisions, 61
personal, 63
versus law, 40

awareness planning, 21

bad decisions, 55

barriers:
active decision-making, 186
to decisions, *see* decisions
economic, 106–107
financial, 106–107
language, 139
legal, inherent, 103–104
time, 105–106
uncertainty107–109
unforeseen or unintended consequences, 188

BDT (Behavioural Decision Theory), 45

behavioural biases, 75, 76, 83, 84–88, 180, 182–83

behavioural contract theory, 82

Behavioural Decision Theory (BDT), 45

behavioural economics, 12, 48, 180, 182–84
Auto-Enrolment as choice architecture, 79–80
Auto-Enrolment and behavioural bias, 84–88
defaults, 81–83
framing and disclosure, 88–90
opting-out, 80
choice architecture:
Auto-Enrolment as, *see* Auto-Enrolment as choice architecture *above*
justification and, 182–84
regulatory intervention and, *see* regulatory intervention and choice architecture *below*
Financial Conduct Authority, 70, 72
Financial Services Authority, 70
framing, 67–68, 78
individual choices based on irrational bias, 49
inertia, 66–67
information tailored and salient, 127
law, influence on, 70–72
legal intervention role, 64–91
policy, influence on, 70–72
presentation, 67–68
probability, difficulties in assessing, 69–70
procrastination, 66–67, 71
regulatory intervention and choice architecture, 72–73
alternatives to soft paternalism/choice architecture, 77–79
choice architects, 74–76
policy of legal paternalism, 73–74
social influences, 68–69

behavioural economists, 44, 45
choice architecture, 48, 49
faulty decisions, intervention to correct, support for, 54
focussing on means rather than ends, 48
influence on regulation, 49
law making influence, 64
policies influence, 64
see also behavioural economics

Behavioural Insights Team, 70

behavioural science, 64

behavioural traits, 183
combatting, 179
financial services products susceptible to, 71
individuals, 47
literature, 64
status quo, favouring, 43–44

behaviours:
predictable, ascertaining, 72
rational, of investors, assumed, 12
see also entries beginning with behavioural

***Belize* case,** 161

beneficiaries:
best interests, fiduciary obligations acting in, 152
trustees and, relationships between, 144

benefits:
Auto-Enrolment, 181–82
awareness planning, 21
external, contracts, 51
handbooks, pension benefits described in, 99, 112
investor confidence, 59
legal paternalism, 58–59

non-market goods, 59
pension, *see* pension benefits
reduction of overall package, 19
state, 21–22
structure:
employers' prerogative, 118
tangible, 22
trust, 59
unequally distributed, KiwiSaver, New Zealand, 84
***Better Workplace Pensions: Further Measures for Savers* (DWP March 2014),** 29
Beveridge, Sir William, 5–6
biases:
behavioural, *see* behavioural biases
cognitive, 65, 74
consumer, newly identified, FCA, 72
industry, policy makers, 76
irrational, 46, 49
predictable, ascertaining, 72
projection, 70
status quo, *see* status quo
Birks, P, 151
bonuses, 23
bounded rationality, 73–74, 75
bounded willpower, individuals, 75
breach of contracts, 53
breach of fiduciary duties, 152
Brodie, Douglas, 147, 148, 163, 164, 172
broker-dealers, US, 154
burden of proof, 58
Burrows, P, 60, 61
Busch, D, 176
business interests, 184

Cabrelli, D, 164
Canada:
state pension, designed to reduce poverty, 11
capitalism, 50
caps on charges and fees, 82
care:
duty of, 144
standards of, employers, 164
care and skill:
agents' obligations, 158–59
career earnings:
mandatory pensions based on part of total, US, 15
case law:
fiduciary duties owed by employers to employees, 150
cash:
access for first home deposits, New Zealand, 36
graduate cash alternative, 114
***caveat emptor* rule,** 142
certainty of contracts, 53
CFEB (Consumer Financial Education Body), 21
changes causing uncertainty, 107
charges:
for advice specifically requested by pension members, 31
caps on, 30–33, 82
commission, employers, 31–32
consultation, employers, 31–32
post implementation legislative changes, 30–33
for services specifically requested by pension members, 31
unknown, 113
see also costs
children:
setting aside contract decisions made by, 54
choice:
active, 186–88
architecture, *see* choice architecture
Auto-Enrolment, *see* Auto-Enrolment
awareness necessary, 129–30
collective concerns, 55
defaults and, 131–33
exercise of, 61, 139
fiduciary duties owed by employers to employees, 151
freedom of, 44, 114–15, 192
increased, Auto-Enrolment, US, 86–87
instrumental value of, 61
intrinsic value in, 61
opting-out of Auto-Enrolment, 62
within paternalism, 49
personal, 181
private, 41
retention, Auto-Enrolment, 61
choice architecture, 72–73
Auto-Enrolment as, 79–80, 180
behavioural bias and, 84–88
defaults, 81–83
disclosure, 88–90
framing, 88–90
opting-out, 80
behavioural economics, 74–79
behavioural economists, 48, 49

employee decision-making shaped by, 83
issues, 77
justification and, 180–84
choice-based system:
industry sector, Australia, 27
clients:
lawyers and, relationships, 144
solicitors and, relationships, 149
closure:
salary related pension schemes, 8
COBS (Conduct of Investment Business Handbook), 175, 176
coding, 96
coercion:
decision-making by individuals free from, 44
cognitive biases, 65, 74
cognitive shortcuts, 65–66
collective choice concerns, 55
collective will of society, 41
combatting behavioural traits, 179
commission:
as barrier to switching, OFT, 31
charges, employers, 31–32
errors of, 66
large, advisors motivated by, 9
communications:
active choice and, 186–88
employers, 125
foreign workers, difficulties, 186
illiterate workers, difficulties, 186
improvements, Auto-Enrolment, 192
policy intention, Auto-Enrolment, 186–88
communities, self-created, 68–69
companies, private, US, 82
Companies Act 2006, 144, 176
company directors' fiduciary duties, 144, 149
competence, utilitarian argument of, 41
compliance costs, 58, 59
compromise:
on personal autonomy, 40
compulsory membership system:
default funds importance in, Australia, 27
compulsory retirement age removal, 2, 12
Conaglen, M, 150
conduct:
of business, FCA minimum standards, 34–35
fiduciary law imposed standards of, 144
Conduct of Investment Business Handbook (COBS), 175, 176
confidence:
empirical research findings, 122
mutual trust and, *see* contracts of employment; mutual trust and confidence
conflicts:
FCA rules, 175
conflicts of interest:
advisors and employers, 120
Auto-Enrolment, 49, 184
avoidance, fiduciary obligations, 152
employers and advisors, 120
employers and financial service industry, 77
fiduciaries, 152
consensus solution:
parliamentary intent, Auto-Enrolment, 19
consent, individuals, *see* **individuals**
consequences:
of fiduciary obligations, 151–53
unforeseen, *see* unforeseen consequences
unintended, *see* unintended consequences
consultation charges, 31–32
consumer biases, FCA, 72
consumer contracts, 54, 69
Consumer Financial Education Body (CFEB), 21
consumer protection legislation, 52
consumers:
regret, 69
contract-based schemes:
default investment strategies, 34
FCA protection, 140
governance, 34
group personal pensions, 34
personal pensions, 34
contracts:
breach of, 53
caveat emptor rule, 142
certainty of, 53
children, setting aside decisions made by, 54
cooling off periods, 54
consumer, 54, 69
disappointment and regret, difference between, 53
disputes, costs of, 61
economic efficiency and distributive justice paternalistic intervention in, 52–53
employment, *see* contracts of employment
extended negotiations costs, 61
external benefits, 51
external costs, 51
financial, 54
freedom to contract, 50, 51

good faith, implied duty of, 53–54
implied terms, 50, 61, 63
information asymmetry, 142
judgement and moral imagination intervention in, 52
legal costs, 61
limitations, 50
mental disabilities, setting aside decisions made by those with, 54
non-paternalistic reasons for nudging parties' intentions, 51–52
paternalism and, 43, 50–55
personal integrity intervention in, 52, 53–54
predictability of, 53
rationality, 53
reflection periods, 54
regret and disappointment, difference between, 53
responsibility without:
fiduciary duties owed by employers to employees, 149
standard terms, 51
transaction costs, 51, 61
uncertainty costs, 61
unconscionability, set aside on grounds of, 50
see also entries beginning with contractual

contracts of employment, 22
asymmetries of power correction, 160
automatic enrolment particulars, 28
changes in, 167
as control mechanism, 160
duties arising from, 159–61
Auto-Enrolment compliance and, 171–73
contractual duty to avoid economic loss, implied terms, 170–71
duty to advise, implied terms, 167–69
good faith implied terms, 165–67
implied terms, 161–73
mutual trust and confidence implied terms, 163–65
employees:
asymmetries of power and information, expectations of, 167
economic interests, express or implied obligations to consider, 160
employers considered to be agents of, 162
personal interests conflicts with employers', prevention, 160
reliance, expectations of, 167
trust, expectations of, 167
employers:
considered to be agents of employees, 162
decision-making under implied obligation of trust and confidence, 166–67
discretion, exercise of, 166
duties to employees, 140
fiduciary obligations, 160
fiduciary relationships, 160
good faith:
implied obligation of, 162
implied term, 165–67
in performance of contracts, 167
reciprocal duty of, 162
mutual trust and confidence:
decision-making under, 166–67
implied term, 163–65
negligent acts, 165
obligation, 160
pension benefits often not described in, 99
pension information in, 28, 103, 112, 167
performance, good faith in, 167
trust, operation on, 160

contractual agreements:
agents' fiduciary obligations constrained by, 158

contractual enrolment, 25–26, 104

contractual limitations, 50

contractual obligations, private law, 140

contractual relationships:
moulding fiduciary obligations, 149

contractual status, employees, 22

contractual undertakings:
fiduciary duties, 148–51, 152

contributions:
affordability, 106
Auto-Enrolment, *see* Auto-Enrolment
deducted from pay, Auto-Enrolment, 62
employees, New Zealand, 25
employers, 12, 24
holidays, employees, New Zealand, 25
low value of, Auto-Enrolment, 25
matching, 12, 83, 85, 101
minimum, 2
rules providing anchor or starting point, Auto-Enrolment, 88
uncertainty about, 108

control mechanism:
contracts of employment as, 160

cooling off periods, 54, 69

Cooper Review, Australia, 27, 70

corporate funds sector, Australia, 27

cost-benefit analysis, 58

costs:
administration, 58, 187
administrative, 58
Auto-Enrolment, 30–33, 181–82, 187, 189–90
compliance, 58, 59
contract disputes, 61
employers' commitments to, trust-based schemes, 153
of establishing schemes, employers, 32
external, contracts, 51
financial advice, 121
financial services products, 71
fixed by employers, 33
freedom, 61
high, barriers overcoming, 13
indirect, 58, 59
legal, contracts, 61
marginal, 58, 59
of misunderstanding, 187
opportunity, 58
of opting-out of Auto-Enrolment, 58
post implementation legislative changes, 30–33
to those who do not benefit, Auto-Enrolment, 59
uncertainty, 61
unknown, 113
see also charges; transaction costs
courts:
fiduciary duties imposed by courts, agency problem 159
fiduciary obligations use, contracts of employment, 160
credibility:
individuals' different levels of, 44
criminal law:
preventing individuals harming others, 40
cross-party support for Auto-Enrolment, 10
cultural differences, EU, 121
currency, uncertainty over, 122
cycle helmets, wearing of, 57, 59

damage, reputational, 9
data protection, 110
DB (defined benefit) schemes, *see* **defined benefit schemes**
DC (defined contribution) schemes, *see* **defined contribution schemes**
debts, 20 21, 106
decision makers:
key influences on, 46
decision-making:
active, no provisions to encourage, 139
disclosures in, 183
employers under implied obligation of trust and confidence:
contracts of employment 166–67
framing in, 183
imperfect, 48
individuals, *see* individuals
informed, 129–30
under mutual trust and confidence, contracts of employment, 166–67
poor, 55
process, 98–99
decisions:
bad, 55
barriers to:
empirical research findings, 97, 102–109
inherent, 103–104
time, 105–106
faulty, 54
financial, personal, 61
future:
experience drawn on, 122
individuals, *see* individuals
informed, making, 129–30
making, *see* decision-making
pensions, 117
proactive, 117
revisiting, putting off, 105
default:
decisions, legislative, 20
increase saving by, 17–18
default funds:
401(k) plans, 47
Australia, 70, 87
importance in compulsory membership system, Australia, 27
protection of those in, 30
default investment funds, 180, 189
default investment strategies, 34
default positions:
individual decision-making, influencing, 20
pension membership as, 13
replacing choice, Auto-Enrolment, 186
default rules, inertia and, 66
default strategy design:
trustees consideration, 34
defaults:
Auto-Enrolment, *see* Auto-Enrolment
reliance on, unforeseen or unintended consequences, 188–90

deferment, 100
deferred pensioners, 31
defined benefit (DB) schemes:
decline, 8
auto-enrolment, 24
decline, 34
defined contribution, conversion to, 36
benefit transfers:
to defined contribution schemes, advice on, 37
to personal pension policies, 9
downward trend, 83
employers moved from providing to defined contribution schemes, 82–83
savings decline, 8
younger members, 189
defined benefits:
state pension, 7
defined contribution (DC) schemes:
costs fixed by employers, 33
defined benefit schemes benefits transferring to, advice on, 37
'Defined Contribution Workplace Pension Market Study' (OFT report 2013), 29
employers' choice of schemes, 29
employers moved from providing defined benefit schemes to, 82–83
final salary pension schemes conversion to, 36
governance, 34
guidance guarantees, 37
investment risks borne by individuals, 19, 33
performance risks borne by individuals, 19
tax benefits accruing to highest-income earners, US, 84
trust-based, *see* master trusts
value for money not to be relied on, 29
'Defined Contribution Workplace Pension Market Study' (OFT report 2013), 29
defined contributions:
notional, Sweden, 6–7
United States, 15
deliberation-promoting nudges, 65
delict, 140, 158, 168, 174, 175, 176, 178, 192
see also tort
DeMott, D, 145, 155
Department for Work and Pensions (DWP):
Better Workplace Pensions: Further Measures for Savers (March 2014), 29
Automatic-Enrolment legislation changes, powers to make, 28
design:
pensions, 139
design and methodology:
empirical research, 94–96
detailed transcripts, 96
detriment:
Auto-Enrolment, no clear legal remedy, 192
resulting from introduction of Auto-Enrolment, private law remedies, 139
unforeseen or unintended consequences, 191
directors, 144, 149
disclaimer:
Auto-Enrolment information included, 174
disclosures:
in decision-making, 183
fiduciaries, 147
financial services industry, 183
information, Auto-Enrolment, 88–90
discounts, 31
discretion:
employers' exercise of, contracts of employment, 166
exercise by one party, 142–43
discretionary powers, employers, 164
discrimination, age, 12
disgorgement, 145
disincentive to saving, 22
disputes:
contracts, costs of, 61
distribution reviews, retail, 107
distributional concerns:
non-paternalistic legal intervention, 55–57
distributive justice, 52–53
distributive motives, 60–61
dominant parties:
fiduciary relationships, 142
down-market:
employers going, 19
drawdown:
occupational pension schemes, 4
duties:
arising from contracts of employment, *see* contracts of employment
of loyalty, 143
duty of care test, 169
duty to account:
contracts of employment, 160
Dworkin, G, 58, 61
DWP, *see* **Department for Work and Pensions**

earnings:
career, US, 15
criteria, Auto-Enrolment, 23
gross, 23
qualifying, workers, 23–24
EasyJet, 32
economic barriers, 106–107
economic efficiency, 52–53
economic interests, employees, 160
economic loss, 168–71
economic power, 151
economic principles, 65
economic theory, 72
economic well-being, 140
economics, behavioural, *see* **behavioural economics**
Edelman, J, 143, 145, 146, 149, 152
education:
employees, 78
provision, 121, 129
understanding and, 121–22
workforces, 19–21
efficiency:
Auto-Enrolment policy valuation based on, 60
economic, 52–53
motives, 60–61
egalitarian impulses, US, 86
egalitarian rights, 55
eligible jobholders, 23
empirical research:
age and gender impact conclusion, 137
Auto-Enrolment:
employee/employer relationship and, conclusion, 136–37
individual perception of, conclusion, 135–36
negative or unforeseen consequences of, conclusion, 137–38
choice and defaults conclusion, 131–33
conclusion, 131–38
design and methodology, 94–96
findings, 96–97
action, 97, 98–102
barriers to decisions, 97, 102–109
confidence, 122
economic barriers, 106–107
education and understanding, 121–22
emotional ownership of pensions, 116–17
employers, 109–12, 122–30
engagement and understanding, 97, 115–30
financial barriers, 106–107
free choice, 114–15
implementation and intervention, 97, 109–15
information provided by employers and providers, 122–30
inherent legal barriers in the regime, 103–104
intervention and implementation, 97, 109–15
mistrust, 130
pension financial planning, 119–21
perceived asymmetries in power and understanding, 118–19
providers, 112–13, 122–30
time barriers, 105–106
trust, 130–31 97
uncertainty barriers, 107–109
understanding and education, 121–22
understanding and engagement, 97, 115–30
gender and age impact conclusion, 137
information conclusion, 134–35
introduction to research, 92–94
methodology and design, 94–96
understanding:
conclusion, 133–34
education and, 121–22
engagement and, 97, 115–30
employees:
active decision-making barriers, 186
advice, 127, 169
advisors, 152–53
fiduciary duties to, 140
information given directly to, FCA rules, governed by, 175
unsure of role of, 173–74
age, 22
automatic enrolment advised in advance, 28
contracts of employment, *see* contracts of employment
contractual enrolment, 25–26
contractual status, 22
contributions, New Zealand, 25
data, management of, 110
decision-making, 83
duties owed to:
by advisors, *see* advisors
fiduciary, *see* fiduciary duties owed by employers to employees
by pension providers, *see* product providers

education, information framing for, 78
employers:
as agents of, 162, 191
duties to, *see* employers
as fiduciaries of, 191
information to, *see* employers
overlapping roles and responsibilities and, 126
relationships, Auto-Enrolment and, 136–37
engagement, failure to ensure, Auto-Enrolment, 192
from EU, 121
inaction, 99
information gap, 170–71
interests:
business interests of employers competing with, 184
lack of trust by, 10
members
pension providers' fiduciary duties to, 173
opting out, 25, 28
product providers:
dealing with on providers' terms, 113
information provision, 131
overlapping roles and responsibilities and, 126
questions unanswered, 170, 174
salary, 22
social moral responsibilities shared with employers, 114
trust in employers, 130–31
understanding, lack of, 127
vulnerability, 30, 142
see also workers
employer-provided information, Auto-Enrolment, 80
employer-related investments, 10
employers:
advice:
caution not to give, 120
from product providers, 125
provision, 123–25
advisors, 152–53
as fiduciaries, 145–46
conflicts of interest, 120
dealing with, issues, 20
as agents of employees, 162, 191
as fiduciaries, 146–48, 191
asymmetrical power, 118
Auto-Enrolment:
defaults contributions, deciding on, 85
discretion in implementation 79
benefit structure prerogative, 118
business interests competing with employees' interests, 184
caution not to give advice, 120
choice of schemes, 29
commission charges, 31–32
communications, 125
consultation charges, 31–32
contracts of employment, *see* contracts of employment
contributions, 24–25
costs:
Auto-Enrolment, 187
of establishing schemes, incurrence of, 32
data protection, 110
decisions:
fair process, 172–73
defined benefit schemes, 82–83
discretion:
pension design, 139
policy intention, 185–86
powers, 164
down-market, going, 19
duties to employees:
as agents, 140
contract relating to AE, under, 140
delict relating to AE, under, 140
economic well-being, implied, 140
employment contracts, under, 140
fiduciary, *see* fiduciary duties owed by employers to employees
financial well-being, implied, 140
mutual trust and confidence, implied, 140
non-fiduciary, 140
empirical research findings, 109–12, 122–30
employees:
data, management, 110
information, 20, 22
overlapping roles and responsibilities and, 126
relationships, Auto-Enrolment and, 136–37
expertise lack, 111
fiduciary obligations on, contracts of employment, 160
financial advice, prevention on giving, 103, 183
financial service industry and, conflicts of interests, 77
group personal pensions, purchasing, 125–26
HR personnel:
information provision, 122–30

inducement:
  prohibition, 104
  to opt out, 111, 117, 123–25, 126
influences:
  individuals' decisions, difficulties with, 75
information from, 122–30
information provision, 27–28, 111, 122–30, 169
intermediaries, 126
mandatory contributions, Australia, 7, 15
matching, 12, 106
maternity pay issues, 111
occupational pension schemes contributions, 6
opt-out, 126
over-caution from fears over responsibility, 125
payroll issues, lack of guidance on, 111
Pensions Regulator information and templates, reliance on, 127
personal pensions, 154
proactiveness, 164
product providers:
  choice prerogative, 118
  communication with, helping shaping, 127
  contracts between and, 125
  delegating responsibility, 131
  guidance and advice, 38
  lack of trust in, 130
  overlapping roles and responsibilities and, 126
  sympathy for, 110–11
professional help with AE compliance, 109–10
qualifying schemes nominated by, 33
reliance on financial services industry, 77
responsibilities, 113, 114, 126
  for Auto-Enrolment implementation, 5
  for choosing investment options, 401k plan, US, 153
salary sacrifice, 111
social moral responsibilities shared with employees, 114
standard of care, 164
unreasonable burden on, public policy constraint, 170

employment contracts, *see* **contracts of employment**
employment law:
  trust and confidence, 163
employment legislation:
  workers definition used in, 22
employment relationships:
  abuse of power prevention, 164
  fiduciary, 163
  mutuality, 148
  not entirely fiduciary, 147–48
Employment Rights Act 1996, 103, 167
endowment effect, 46, 66, 69, 80
ends:
  behavioural economists focussing on means, rather than, 48
engagement:
  action and, connection between, 101
  active not encouraged, 67–68
  no provisions to encourage, 139
  understanding and, 97, 115–30
Equitable Life, 9
equities strategy, 189
equity:
  fiduciary law historical development from, 145
errors of commission, 66
errors of omission, 66
EU, *see* **European Union**
Europe:
  three pillars approach to pension policy, 6
European Union:
  cultural differences, 121
excluded workers, 180, 184, 187
execution only transactions, 143
expertise:
  employers' lack, 111
exploitation under capitalism, 50
extended negotiations costs, 61
external benefits, contracts, 51
external costs, contracts, 51
external effects:
  Auto-Enrolment, 57
  policy makers, 75
external payroll providers, 126
externalities:
  non-paternalistic legal intervention, 55, 57

fair process:
  employers' decisions, 172–73
fairness:
  FCA rules, 175, 176
  function of law, 42
fall back:
  Auto-Enrolment beneficial position as, 61
faulty decisions, 54
FCA, *see* **Financial Conduct Authority**
fees, caps on, 82

Feinberg, J, 43, 44, 51
fiduciaries:
conflicts of interest, 152
disclosure, 147
disgorgement, recovery under, 145
duties:
not derived from status, 149
judgement exercise encapsulating, 151
self-interest, restriction on, 152
trustees and, 141–42, 144
fiduciary agency, 140
fiduciary duties:
breaches, recovery for, 152
implied, Auto-Enrolment, 62
fiduciary duties owed by employers to employees, 140–41
agents, 153–59
company directors, 144, 149
consequences of obligations, 151–53
contractual undertakings, 148–51, 152
discretion, exercise by one party, 142–43
economic power imposing, 151
existence of obligations, 141–51
management of affairs by one party, 143–44
pension choice, 151
relationships, 141, 144–45, 148
social power imposing, 151
status, 141, 144–48
vulnerability, 142, 148
fiduciary employment relationships, 163
fiduciary law:
penalty default, 150–51
historical development from equity, 145
imposed standards of conduct, 144
relationships marked by asymmetries of power, 142
fiduciary obligations:
advisors, 152–53
agents, *see* agents
beneficiaries' best interests, acting in, 152
conflicts of interest avoidance, 152
consequences of, 151–53
contracts of employment, *see* contracts of employment
contractual relationships moulding, 149
good faith, performing in, 152
imposed by law, 149
management of property of others, 149
product providers, 152–53
MySuper, Australia, 154
profits, not making at principals, expense, 152
senior managers, 147
fiduciary relationships:
contracts of employment, *see* contracts of employment
dominant parties, 142
obligations causing, 149
solicitors, 149
subordinate parties, 142
vulnerability, 148
final salary schemes, *see* **defined benefit schemes**
financial advice, 106–107
costs, 121
generic, 21
high quality affordable, access to, 21
lack, Auto-Enrolment, 20
not to be given to employees by employers, 183
not valued highly, 120
for rich, US, 89
upfront payment, 107
financial barriers, 106–107
Financial Conduct Authority (FCA):
advisors' information given directly to employees, 175
behavioural economics, 70, 72
conduct of business minimum standards, 34–35
Conduct of Investment Business Handbook (COBS), 175, 176
conflicts rules, 175
consumer biases newly identified, 72
fairness rules, 175, 176
nudging, 71, 72
pension providers' information given directly to employees, 175
personal pensions, 3
private persons suing intermediaries, 176
protection, contract-based schemes, 140
sale methods of products, concerns with, 72
suitability rules, 175, 176
financial contracts, 54
financial decisions, personal, 61
financial education, 78
financial literacy, 20
Financial Literacy, Australia:
financial matters, improvement in education and understanding of, 78
financial loss:
misunderstandings leading to, 139
financial planning:
advice, 119
benefits, awareness planning, 21

debt payments, 20
future, something for, 119
income protection, 20
investments, 20
pensions, 119–21
protection, 20
for retirement, 106–107
savings, 20
financial regulation:
reliance on, advisors' duties to employees, 175–76
financial services:
industry, 45
AE compliant schemes, 186
difficulties of reliance on, Australia, 78
disclosure, 183
employers and, conflicts of interests, 77
employers' reliance on, 77
reputational damage, 9
vast sums of additional funds being invested in, 191
products, 71
regulation, assumed norms for, 45
Financial Services Act 2010, 21
Financial Services and Markets Act (FSMA) 2000, 176
Financial Services Authority (FSA):
behavioural economics, 70
Conduct of Investment Business Handbook (COBS), 174
generic advice, 21
miss-sold personal pension cases, 9
Retail Distribution Review (RDR), 21
financial well-being:
employers' duties to employees, implied, 140
Finn, P, 142, 143–44, 149
***Fishel* case,** 147
flat rate state pension system, 2
foreign workers:
complication to understanding, 130
cultural differences, 121
difficulties communicating with, 186
foreseeability, degrees of, 42
framing:
Auto-Enrolment as choice architecture, 88–90
behavioural economics, 67–68, 78
in decision-making, 183
information, 76, 78, 105
investments choice and amount, influencing, 67
narrow, 46, 76
freedom:
costs, 61
individual, intervention in, 50
freedom of choice, 44, 114–15, 192
freedom to act, individuals, 40
freedom to contract, 50, 51
frequency:
Auto-Enrolment information provision, 67
FSA, *see* **Financial Services Authority**
FSMA (Financial Services and Markets Act 2000), 176
full rationality, individuals, 73–74
funds:
movement of, 139
security of, 108
selection, Auto-Enrolment, 183
transfers, 101
future decisions:
experience drawn on, 122
future reductions:
pension pots protected against, 106–107

gas industry, offshore, 51, 52
gender:
age and, impact conclusion, 137
general public:
advice and information provision to, 21
generic advice, 20, 21
generic information, 67, 123
Getzler, J, 150–51
Glaser, B, 95
global financial crisis, 8, 122
Goff, Lord, 170
good faith:
contracts of employment, *see* contracts of employment
duty of, 144
fiduciary obligations performing in, 152
implied duty of, contracts, 53–54
implied terms, 165–67
Scotland, 166
good of individuals, 46
Goode Report, 9–10
governance:
contract-based schemes, 34
defined contribution schemes, 34
framework lacking, Auto-Enrolment, 29
gaps, OFT, 34
group personal pension schemes, 186

occupational trust-based pension schemes, 186
schemes, post implementation legislative changes, 33–35
trust-based schemes, 34
trustees, 33–34
GPP (grouped personal pensions), 3
graduate cash alternative, 114
gross earnings, 23
group personal pension schemes:
contract-based schemes, 34
employers purchasing, 125–26
governance, 186
product providers, changing, 118
grouped personal pensions (GPP), 3
***Grove* case,** 166
guaranteed compulsory state pensions, 6
guidance guarantees, 37

habitability:
residential property leases, 52
Hain, Peter, 17
hard paternalism, 48, 49–50, 63, 68, 72, 74–76, 192
harm:
degrees of, 42
done by others, consent to, 43
to others, defining, 41
self-harm, 40, 43
Hart J, 163
***Hedley Byrne case*,** 174
heuristics:
individuals, own systems of, 70
high cost:
barriers overcoming, 13
high quality affordable financial advice, 21
high-risk strategy:
defined benefit scheme younger members, 189
higher rate taxpayers, 108
higher rates of tax, 114
higher taxes, France, 114
highly educated members:
KiwiSaver, New Zealand, 89
Hoffman, Lord, 161
Hospers, J, 43
human resources personnel, *see* **employers; HR personnel**
***Hunter v Hanley*,** 174
Hutton of Furness, Lord, 3
hybrid schemes, 83
identifying individual will, 40
idiots, 66
IFA (Independent Financial Advisors), 125–26
IGC (Independent Governance Committees), 34–35
illiteracy, 130, 186
imagination, moral, 54
imperfect decision-making, 48
***Imperial* case,** 160, 162, 164, 165
implementation:
empirical research findings, 97, 109–15
intervention and, empirical research findings, 97, 109–15
implied agency, 156
implied obligations of good faith, 162
implied terms:
consumer protection legislation, 52
contracts, 50, 61, 63
contractual duty to avoid economic loss, 170–71
duties arising from contracts of employment, 161–73
duty to advise, 167–69
good faith, 165–67
mutual trust and confidence, 163–65
***in loco parentis*, interests,** 42
inaction:
assumptions and, links between, 108
employees, 99
uncertainty and, links between, 108
inadequate advice, 139
inattentive passive workers, 85, 86
incentives:
KiwiSaver, New Zealand, 86
income poverty, US, 15
income protection, 20
indecision:
time as justification for, 105
Independent Financial Advisors (IFA), 125–26
Independent Governance Committees (IGC), 34–35
Independent Public Service Pensions Commission, 3
Independent Retirement Savings Commission, 35
indirect costs, 58, 59
individual freedom, 50
individual perception of Auto-Enrolment, 135–36

individuals:
actions:
without engagement by, 99
impacting negatively on others, 40
behavioural traits, 47
bounded rationality, 73–74, 75
bounded willpower, 75
choices, 41, 60, 77–78
consent:
lack of understanding frustrating, 44
to medical treatment, 44
public interest and, 42
uninformed, 44
decision-making:
default positions influencing, 20
free from coercion, 44
paternalism nudging into more rational decisions, 46
voluntariness, 43
decisions:
employer influences, difficulties with, 75
for own good, difficulties with, 71
state influences, difficulties with, 75
different levels of credibility, 44
economic theory assumptions, 72
freedom to act, 40
full rationality, 73–74
good of, 46
harming others, law preventing, 40
heuristics, own systems of, 70
information, 88–89
interests evaluation, 71
intervening in personal choice for good of, 181
law assisting to do what they should, 45
legal paternalism assisting to do what they should, 45
libertarian view, 41
long term wants and needs, 43
loss aversion, 89
multiple pension pots, 100
norms, own systems of, 70
promotion of own ends, 48
rationality, 65
lacking, 85–86
responsibility retention, 41
self-control, 71
lack of, 73
self-harm, law protecting from, 40
status quo biases, 75
traditional economic principles assumptions about, 65
voluntariness, 43, 44
will of:
actions appearing to be, 44
freedom of choice, 44
identifying, 40
public interest and, 42
inducement, *see* **employers**
industry biases, 76
industry sector:
choice-based system, Australia, 27
inequality under capitalism, 50
inertia, 18, 31, 48, 182, 183
acting with Auto-Enrolment defaults, 81
Auto-Enrolment, 185
US, 87–88
barriers overcoming, 13
behavioural economics, 66–67
choice, affecting, Auto-Enrolment, 181
default rules and, 66
enlisted, Auto-Enrolment, 50
harnessing, legal paternalism, 74
lack of opt-outs reason, Auto-Enrolment, 80
working in favour of saving, Auto-Enrolment, 80
inflation, uncertainty over, 122
influences:
social, 68–69
states, 75
information:
advice:
perceived as, 139
versus, 127
asymmetries, 62, 143
Auto-Enrolment, 192
contracts, 142
expectations of employees, contracts of employment, 167
financial services products, 71
protection by paternalism inferred into private law, 43
Auto-Enrolment, *see* Auto-Enrolment
clear, 175
contracts of employment, 167
empirical research conclusion, 134–35
employers, provided by, 122–30
fair, 175
framing, 76, 78, 105
gap, employees, 170–71
generic, 67, 123
individuals, 88–89
misunderstandings of, 139
New Zealand campaign, 69

not misleading, 175
personal, 103
processing, individuals, 88–89
product providers, provided by, 122–30
provision:
different approaches to, 129
education rather than, 121
employers, 111, 122–30
to general public, 21
HR personnel, 122–30
product providers, 122–30, 167–68, 169
to workers, Auto-Enrolment, 27–28
quality, individuals, 89
salient, behavioural economics, 127
tailored, behavioural economics, 127
informed decisions, making, 129–30
inherent legal barriers, 103–104
instinctive action, 98
instincts, 71
instrumental values of choice, 61
intention, legal intervention, 55–57
interests:
business, 184
conflicts of, *see* conflicts of interest
employees, 184
evaluation, individuals, 71
in loco parentis, 42
public, 42
self-interest, fiduciaries restriction, 152
intermediaries:
employers, 126
private persons suing, FCA, 176
intervention:
empirical research findings, 97, 109–15
implementation and, empirical research findings, 97, 109–15
in individual freedom, 50
not persuasion, 180–82
paternalistic, 50
interviews, semi-structured, 96
intrinsic values, in choice, 61
investments:
advisors:
uniform fiduciary standard of conduct, US, 154
financial planning, 20
framing influencing choice and amount, 67
funds:
choice, 100
default, 180, 189
performance, trustees' consideration, 34
risks borne by individuals, 19, 33
self-selection, Australia, 27
strategies:
default, 34
rules providing anchor or starting point, Auto-Enrolment, 88
investors:
confidence benefits, 59
rational, 46
rational behaviour assumed, 12
irrational biases, 46, 49
irrational myopic workers, 85
irrationality:
in making choices, 54
Italy, 6

job security, uncertainty, 109
jobholders, 22–23
eligible, 23–24
workers eligible defined as, 22–23
***Johnson* case,** 165
joining:
procrastination about, 105–106
judgement:
exercise encapsulating fiduciaries' duties, 151
intervention in contracts, 52
justice, distributive, 52–53
justification, objective, 72

Kay Review, 141, 176
Kennedy, D, 62
KiwiSaver, *see* **New Zealand**
knowledge:
agents' impartation to principals, 158
Kronman, AT, 52–54

***Lakshmi* case,** 54
language barriers, 130
law:
of agency, 159
assisting individuals to do what they should, 45
autonomy versus, 40
behavioural economics influence on, 70–72
fairness function, 42
fiduciary obligations imposed by, 149
predictability function, 42
preventing individuals harming others, 40
private, *see* private law
protecting individuals from self-harm, 40
self-harm, protecting individuals from, 40

Law Commission:
on duties owed to employees by advisors, 173
fiduciary duties in pensions, 141
on pension providers' duties to employees, 173
law making:
behavioural economists influence, 64
lawyers:
clients and, relationships between, 144
leakage:
KiwiSaver, New Zealand, 86
leases, residential property, 52
leavers:
preserved pensions for, 8
rates monitored alongside opting out, Auto-Enrolment, 127–28
legal barriers, inherent, 103–104
legal costs, contracts, 61
legal intervention:
behavioural economics role, 64–91
behaviours predictable, ascertaining, 72
biases predictable, ascertaining, 72
effect, categorisation difficulties, 61
hard paternalism, 72
intention, 55–57
legal paternalism intention of, 55–57
motivation, categorisation difficulties, 61
non-paternalistic, 55–57
nudging, 72
objective justification, 72
paternalistic, 55
policies influencing behaviour, checklist, 72
soft paternalism, 72
legal paternalism, 18, 39–45, 62–63, 181
administrative costs, 58
assisting individuals to do what they should, 45
Auto-Enrolment, 74
autonomy versus law, 40
behavioural economics policy of, 73–74
benefits, 58–59
compliance costs, 58
cost-benefit analysis, 58
hard paternalism prohibition, 74
indirect costs, 58
individual long term wants and needs, assumptions about, 43
inertia harnessing, 74
intention of legal intervention, 55–57
laws protecting individuals from self-harm, 40
libertarian paternalism distinguished, 48
new paternalism distinguished, 48
nudges, 74
paternalistic legislation, 45–48
personal autonomy restrictions, 41
policies, 73–74
proof measurement, 58–62
soft paternalism or nudge distinguished, 48–50
state intervention, 46
state knowing individual citizens' interests best, 41–42
value measurement, 58–62
Leggat J, 166
legislation, legitimacy, 40
legislative changes:
post implementation, *see* Auto-Enrolment
legislative default decisions, 20
legislative reality, Auto-Enrolment, 22–28
legitimacy of legislation, 40
Lehman Brothers collapse, 9
***Lennon* case,** 170
levelling down:
parliamentary intent, Auto-Enrolment, 18–19
LGPS (Local Government Pension Scheme), 3
liability, third party, 174–75
libertarian paternalism, 47, 48, 76, 86
libertarian view, individual responsibility, 41
life cycle theory, 73
lifetime allowances:
caps, pension funds, 104
losing, 126–27
limitations, contracts, 50
limited paternalism, 76
literacy, financial, 20
literature:
behavioural traits, 64
loans, student, 106, 114
Local Government Pension Scheme (LGPS), 3
longevity, 22
loss:
abatement, optimal, 59
aversion to, 46, 66, 69, 89
economic, 168–71
financial, 139
lowest paid workers, 180, 184
loyalty:
duty of, 143, 144
fiduciary duties owed by employers to employees, 150–51, 152
lump sums, 4, 36

management:
of affairs by one party, 143–44
managers, senior, 147
mandatory pensions, US, 15
marginal costs:
Auto-Enrolment, 58
of compliance, 59
Markets in Financial Instruments Directive (MiFID II), 33, 175
master trusts, 35–36, 38
matching, 101, 106
maternity:
leave, pension changes whilst on, 129
pay, 23, 111
Maxwell, Robert, 9–10
***McWilliam* case,** 156
means:
behavioural economists focussing on, 48
testing, 13, 14, 21–22
medical care cost, US, 120
medical treatment:
individual consent to, 44
members:
financial advice for, trustees consideration, 34
membership, *see* **pension membership**
men and women:
state pension equalisation for, 2
mental disabilities:
setting aside contract decisions made by those with, 54
'Messenger' effect, 87
methodology and design:
empirical research, 94–96
MiFID II (Markets in Financial Instruments Directive), 33, 175
Mill, JS, 41
Miller, PB, 146
minimum contributions, 2
minimum pay criteria, 180
minimum quality standards, 29
minimum scheme solvency, 10
minimum wage, 60–61
Mirror Group Newspaper Pension Fund, 9–10
mis-selling pensions, 9, 38
mis-statements:
advisors' and pension providers' duties to employees, 173–74
mistrust, 130
misunderstandings:
advisors' duties to employees, 173–74
costs of, Auto-Enrolment, 187
financial loss, leading to, 139
of information, 139
negative consequences, leading to, 139
pension providers' duties to employees, 173–74
unforeseen and unintended consequences, 188
Money Advice Service, 21, 120, 190
money management, 21
money purchase schemes, *see* **defined contribution schemes**
moral effects of actions in context, 54–55
moral imagination, 52, 54
mortgage debts, 106
movement of funds:
between product providers, 139
multiple pension pots, 100, 128–29, 139
Murray, J, 160
mutual trust and confidence:
contracts of employment, *see* contracts of employment
employers' duties to employees, implied, 140
mutuality:
employment relationships, 148
myopia, 18, 181
myopic workers, 85–86
MySuper, *see* **Australia**

naïve myopic workers, 85–86
NAPF (National Association of Pension Funds), 35
narrow framing, 46, 76
narrow paternalism, 39
National Association of Pension Funds (NAPF), 35
National Employment Savings Trust (NEST), 2, 13, 20, 27
compliant scheme, 77
as fall-back position, 186
government set up, 45
personal pensions, as alternative to, 38
use:
for AE, 185
instead of private pension schemes, 26, 32
National Health Service (NHS), 120
National Insurance Contributions (NIC), 6, 14, 56
National Pension Savings Scheme (NPSS), 14
necessity, degrees of, 42
negative consequences:
of Auto-Enrolment, 137–38
misunderstandings leading to, 139

negligent acts:
mutual trust and confidence, contracts of employment, 165
negotiations costs:
extended, contracts, 61
NEST, *see* **National Employment Savings Trust**
Neuberger, Lord, 161
new paternalism, 47–48
New Zealand:
annuities, 37
auto-enrolment, 14, 183
default, 82, 83
savings patterns shifts, 81
voluntary scheme, 15
cash, access for first home deposits, 36
employee contributions, 25
information campaign, 69
KiwiSaver, 15, 23, 25, 26–27, 38, 70, 81, 82, 186
access, 116
benefits unequally distributed, 84
highly educated members contribute higher levels of salary to, 89
house deposits, use for, 116
incentives applied in unintended way, 86
leakage, 86
tax savings applied in unintended way, 86
lump sums, taking savings as, 36
state pension:
designed to reduce poverty, 11
NHS (National Health Service), 120
NIC (National Insurance Contributions), 6, 14, 56
non-fiduciary duties, agents, 157–58
non-fiduciary employers' duties to employees, 140
non-market goods benefits, 59
non-paternalistic legal intervention, 55–57
non-paternalistic reasons for nudging contract parties' intentions, 51–52
norms:
individuals' own systems of, 70
notional defined contributions, Sweden, 6–7
NPSS (National Pension Savings Scheme), 14
nudges:
deliberation-promoting, 65
Financial Conduct Authority, 71, 72
legal paternalism, 74
paternalism, 46, 48–50, 59, 63, 76
objective justification, 72
objectivity, scientific, 75
obligations:
causing fiduciary relationships, 149
consequences of, 151–53
existence of, 141–51
fiduciary, *see* fiduciary obligations
inherent in relationships, 145
mutual trust and confidence, contracts of employment, 160
occupational pension schemes, 3, 4, 6, 26
see also defined benefit schemes; defined contribution schemes:
occupational savings, decline, 8
occupational trust-based pension schemes, 186
Office of Fair Trading (OFT):
commission as barrier to switching, 31
'Defined Contribution Workplace Pension Market Study' (report 2013), 29
governance gaps, 34
offset defaults, 85
offshore oil and gas industry, 51, 52
OFT, *see* **Office of Fair Trading**
Ogus, AI, 57, 59
oil industry, offshore, 51, 52
omission, errors of, 66
one-size-fits-all:
defaults, Auto-Enrolment, 83
opportunity costs:
of meeting Auto-Enrolment contribution obligations, 58
opt-outs:
Auto-Enrolment, *see* Auto-Enrolment
employers, 126
forms, 126
optimal loss abatement, 59
optimism, unrealistic, 69
opting out, *see* **Auto-Enrolment: opt-outs**
***Outram* case,** 168–69
over-caution:
employers, from fears over responsibility, 125
over-reliance on advisors and product providers, 125
overdraft fees, 68
overtime, 23
own ends:
individuals' promotion of, 48

parliamentary intent:
Auto-Enrolment, *see* Auto-Enrolment
passive saving, 81

paternalism:
asymmetrical, 76
burden of proof, 58
choices within, 49
contracts and, 43, 50–55
hard, *see* hard paternalism
inferred into private law, 43
legal, *see* legal paternalism
libertarian, 47, 48, 76, 86
limited, 76
more extensive, 49
narrow, 39
new, 47–48
nudges, *see* nudges
policies, 47
private law areas, inferred into, 43
risks for state intervention, 42
strict, 42, 43
unacceptably intrusive forms of, 49
paternalistic interventions, 50
paternalistic legal intervention, 55
paternalistic legislation, 45–48
paternalistic reasons for nudging contract parties' intentions, 51–52
pay, maternity, 23, 111
payroll issues:
employers, lack of guidance on, 111
payroll providers:
blamed by product providers, 113
external, 126
opt-out forms, 126
product providers blamed by, 113
PCSPS (Principal Civil Service Pension Scheme), 3
penalty default, 150–51
pension benefits:
in contracts of employment, often not described, 99
described in benefits handbooks, 99, 112
existing, prevent reduction in, 18–19
taking, 36–37
pension choices:
engagement with, 117
pension decisions:
disengagement with, 117
pension design:
employers' discretion, 139
pension financial planning, 119–21
pension funds:
global finance crisis impact, 8
lifetime allowances caps, 104
losses in stock market crashes, 8
pension information:
in contracts of employment, 103, 112
Pension Law Review Committee, 9–10
pension membership:
charges for advice or services specifically requested by members, 31
as default position, 13
pension policies:
constantly changing, 108
occupational pension schemes as second pillar of, 6
retirement savings by individuals as third pillar of, 6
state pension as first pillar of, 6, 22
three pillars approach to, Europe, 6
pension pots:
multiple, 100, 128–29, 139
protected against future reductions, 106–107
small, 121, 128–29, 187, 189
Pension Protection Board, 10
Pension Protection Fund (PPF), 18
pension providers, ***see*** **product providers**
pension schemes:
access at particular time of life, 105
contractual enrolment, 104
pension transferability, EU, 121
pension transfers, 121
pensioners, deferred, 31
pensions:
emotional ownership, 116–17
see also entries beginning with pension
Pensions Act 1995, 1, 10
Pensions Act 2007, 1, 14, 180
Pensions Act 2008, 1, 14, 167, 171, 180
Pensions Act 2011, 14
Pensions Act 2014, 14, 22, 28, 30
Pensions Advisory Service, The (TPAS), 9
Pensions Commission:
auto-enrolment, international experiences referenced, 14
pensions provision review reports, 10–14
private pension saving, 12–13
recommendations, 13–14
road to Auto-Enrolment, 10–14
pensions mis-selling, 9
Pensions Ombudsman, 163, 168
Pensions Regulator, The (TPR):
Automatic-Enrolment legislation compliance enforcement, 28
as cost, 58

employer information to workers, guidance, 27–28
enforcement notices, 111
enforcement of AE, 165, 168, 171–72
information and templates, employers' reliance on, 127
master trusts authorisation and supervision, 36
personal pensions, 3
trustees' obligations enforcement by, 33
people, *see* **individuals**
perfectionism:
non-paternalistic legal intervention, 55
performance of contracts:
good faith in, 167
performance risks, 19
***Personal Accounts: A New Way to Save* (Pensions White Paper),** 14
personal autonomy, 40, 41, 63
personal choice, 181
personal financial decisions, 61
personal information:
consent to disclosure, Auto-Enrolment, 103
personal integrity, 52, 53–54
personal interests:
contracts of employment, 160
Personal Investment Authority (PIA):
miss-sold personal pension cases, 9
personal pensions, 3
agents, 158
Auto-Enrolment, 26
benefit transfers from final salary pension schemes to, 9
contract-based schemes, 34
contracts of employment, 154
employers, 154
Financial Conduct Authority, 3
mis-selling, 38
NEST as alternative to, 38
Pensions Regulator, The (TPR), 3
pre-existing, 19
product providers of financial advisors as employers' agents, 154
see also group personal pension schemes; grouped personal pensions
personal responsibility:
retirement savings, 19
persuasion, workforces, 19–20
PIA, *see* **Personal Investment Authority**
planning:
awareness, 21
financial, *see* financial planning
policies:
behavioural economics influence on, 70–72
behavioural economists influence, 64
considerations, Auto-Enrolment, 4–5
influencing behaviour, checklist, 72
intention, 184–88
Auto-Enrolment, *see* Auto-Enrolment
legal paternalism, 73–74
paternalism, 47
policy makers, 75, 76
poor decision-making, 55
population, ageing, 179–80
positional theories, 55
poverty:
income, US, 15
state pension designed to reduce, 11
power:
abuse of, employment relationships prevention, 164
asymmetries, 43, 118–19, 142, 160, 167
discretionary, employers, 164
economic, 151
social, 151
PPF (Pension Protection Fund), 18
pre-existing personal pensions, 19
pre-existing schemes, 18–19, 26
predictability function of law, 42
predictability of contracts, 53
preferences, 46
presentation:
behavioural economics, 67–68
preserved pensions for leavers, 8
prices, property, 69
pricing financial services products, 71
Principal Civil Service Pension Scheme (PCSPS), 3
principals:
agents' fiduciary obligations to, 157–58
private choices, 41
private companies, US, 82
private law:
agency duties, 176
areas, paternalism inferred into, 43
contractual obligations, 140
delict, 140, 176
detriment resulting from introduction of Auto-Enrolment, remedies, 139
fiduciary agency obligations, 140
information asymmetries, protection by paternalism inferred into, 43
power asymmetries, protection by paternalism inferred into, 43

protection of abuse by paternalism inferred into, 43
remedies, 139–40, 176–78
private pensions:
Australia, 15
saving:
compatible with state benefits, 21–22
Pensions Commission, 12–13
state pension and, interaction between, 109
voluntary, 5–10
see also occupational pension schemes; personal pensions
private persons:
suing intermediaries, FCA, 176
private sector:
interaction between state and, 16
pension provision, Spain and Italy, 6
proactiveness, 117, 164
probability:
degrees of, 42
difficulties in assessing, behavioural economics, 69–70
procrastination, 182, 183
behavioural economics, 66–67, 71
defaults, Auto-Enrolment, 81
joining, 105–106
key influence on decision makers, 46
opting-out, Auto-Enrolment, 80
product providers:
advisors as fiduciaries, 145–46
Auto-Enrolment information provision delegation to, 187
blamed by payroll providers, 113
changes of, 116, 118
COBS, obligations under, 176
duties owed to employees by, 173
advice provision, 173
financial regulation, reliance on, 175–76
information, fair, clear, and not misleading, 175
Law Commission on, 173
misunderstandings and mis-statements, 173–74
risks indications, 175
third party liability, 174–75
empirical research findings, 112–13, 122–30
employees:
dealing with on providers' terms, 113
information provision to, 131
overlapping roles and responsibilities and, 126
employers:
advice from, 125
choice prerogative, 118
communication with, helping shaping, 127
contract exclusions, 168
contracts between and, 125
delegating responsibility, 131
discretion on choice, 139
lack of trust in, 130
overlapping roles and responsibilities and, 126
sympathy for, 110–11
fiduciary duties to employee members, 173
fiduciary obligations, 152–53, 154
generic information provided, 123
guidance and advice, 38
information provision, 122–30, 167–68, 169, 175
movement of funds between, 139
notices from, Auto-Enrolment opting out, 103
opt-out forms, 126
over-reliance on, 125
payroll providers blamed by, 113
role of, 112–13
sending information about opting-out, Auto-Enrolment, 80
products:
financial services, 71
sale methods, FCA concerns with, 72
professional advice:
pension transfers, 121
professional help:
for employers with AE compliance, 109–10
profits:
not making at principals' expense, 152
prohibitive hard paternalism, 49–50, 63
projection biases, 70
proof:
burden of, 58
measurement, legal paternalism, 58–62
property of others:
management of, fiduciary obligations, 149
property prices, 69
prospect theory, 69, 122
protection:
financial planning, 20
providers, *see* **payroll providers; product providers**
prudent investment options:
administrators' fiduciary duties of selection of, 401k plan, US, 153

public interest, 42
public policy:
constraint, unreasonable burden on employers, 170
public sector:
choice-based system, Australia, 27
pensions, 2, 3
Public Service Pensions Act 2013, 3
purposive sampling, 95

qualifying arrangements:
Auto-Enrolment, 2
qualifying earnings:
workers, 23–24
quality:
of information, individuals, 89
minimum standards, 29
trustees, advice provided to, 34
question and answer sessions:
optional, HR personnel, 129
questions:
employees', unanswered, 170, 174

rational investors, 12, 46
rational person concept, 45–46
rational workers, 85–86
rationality, 42, 65
bounded, 73–74, 75
contracts, 53
difficult to identify, 46
full, 73–74
lacking, individuals, 85–86
RDR (Retail Distribution Review), 21, 107, 119
reason:
going with instincts rather than, 71
reciprocal duty of good faith:
contracts of employment, 162
recruitment agencies, 112
reductions, future, *see* **future reductions**
reflection periods, contracts, 54
regret:
consumers, 69
disappointment and, difference between, 53
regulation:
behavioural economists' influence on, 49
financial, 175–76
regulatory intervention:
of Auto-Enrolment, 1
behavioural economics, *see* behavioural economics
relationships:
clients and solicitors, 149
fiduciary, *see* fiduciary relationships
fiduciary duties owed by employers to employees, 141, 144–45, 148
fiduciary law, marked by asymmetries of power, 142
inherent obligations, 145
solicitors and clients, 149
reliance:
employees' expectations of, contracts of employment, 167
remedies, 139–40, 176–78, 191–92
reputational damage:
financial services industry, 9
residential property leases, 52
resources, wasting, 50
responsibilities:
employers, 113, 114, 126
individuals' retention, 41
unforeseen and unintended consequences, 191
voluntary assumptions of, 150
Retail Distribution Review (RDR), 21, 107, 119
retail sector choice-based system, Australia, 27
retention of choice, Auto-Enrolment, 61
retired population:
income poverty amongst, US, 15
retirement:
age:
compulsory, abolition, 2, 12
increase, 11–12
increased, state pension, 22
state pension and, interaction between, 109
financial planning for, 106–107
savings:
by individuals as third pillar of pension policy, 6
personal responsibility, 19
support, trustees consideration, 34
reversibility, 59–60
revisiting decisions, 105
rich, save more, US, 89
rights, egalitarian, 55
risks:
advisors' and pension providers' duties to employees, 175
investment, 19, 33
performance, 19

safeguards:
insufficient, Auto-Enrolment, 60
safety mechanisms:
opt-outs, Auto-Enrolment, 181
salaries, 22
salary related pension schemes:
closure, 8
decline in, 33
divisive issue in workforces, 8
unionised workplaces increasing, 7
salary sacrifice, 109, 111, 118
sale of products:
methods, FCA concerns with, 72
sampling, purposive, 95
'Save More Tomorrow' scheme, US, 87–88, 116, 117, 189
savings:
accessing, advice at point of, 37
decline, 8
default rate, 180
disincentive, 22
financial planning, 20
inertia working in favour of, Auto-Enrolment, 80
lump sums, taking as, New Zealand, 36
passive, 81
patterns shifts, defaults, Auto-Enrolment, 81
retirement, *see* retirement
taking as lump sums, Australia, 36
tangible benefits required, 22
voluntary barriers, 11
***Scally* case,** 160, 163–65, 168, 169
scheme administration:
trustees consideration, 34
scheme providers, *see* **product providers**
scheme selection, Auto-Enrolment, 183
schemes without advice, 139
scientific objectivity, 75
Scotland:
agents, 154, 158
good faith, 166
seasonal summer workers:
auto-enrolled, 128
inaction, 99–100
Securities and Exchange Commission (SEC), *see* **United States**
security:
of funds, 108
jobs, uncertainty, 109
***Security in Retirement: Towards a New Pensions System* (Pensions White Paper),** 14
self-control, 71
lack of, individuals, 73
self-created communities, 68–69
self-enrolment, 18
401(k) plans, US, 47
poor record, 48
switching from to Auto-Enrolment, 79
workplace pensions, 183
self-harm, 40, 43
self-interest:
fiduciaries restriction on, 152
self-selection of investments, Australia, 27
semi-structured interviews, 96
senior managers:
fiduciary obligations, 147
serfdom:
personal autonomy restrictions leading to, 41
services:
specifically requested by pension members, 31
short term workers, 100
simplicity, 32
Sims, V, 148
single tier state pension system, 22
Sitkoff, RH, 159
skill:
care and, agents' obligations, 158–59
duty of, 144
small pension pots, 121, 128–29, 187, 189
Smith, Lady, 166
Smith, LD, 143, 151
smoking, 42
social costs, 1, 191–92
social influences, 68–69
social power, 151
society, collective will of, 41
soft paternalism, 43, 48–50, 59, 63, 68, 72
Auto-Enrolment, 74, 180, 181
behavioural economics alternatives to, 77–79
legal paternalism distinguished, 48–50
solicitors, 149
solvency, minimum scheme, 10
Spain, 6
***Spring Guardian* case,** 170
staging, 1
stakeholder groups, 44
stakeholder pensions, 12
standard terms, contracts, 51
standards of care, employers, 164
state benefits, 21–22
state influences, 75

state intervention:
France, 114
legal paternalism, 46
risks for, 42
state pensions:
Canada, 11
compulsory retirement age abolition, 2
defined benefit, 7
designed to reduce poverty, 11
equalisation for men and women, 2
as first pillar of pension policy, 6, 22
flat rate system, 2
guaranteed compulsory, Italy and Spain, 6
means testing, 21–22
New Zealand, *see* New Zealand
NIC funding of, 6, 14
private pensions and, interaction between, 109
retirement ages, 22, 109
second and third pillars complementing, 6
single tier system, 22
strict paternalism, 43
uncertainty about, 108–109
worker contributions, 6
states:
intervention to mitigate irrational bias, 46
knowing individual citizens' interests best, legal paternalism, 41–42
see also entries beginning with state
status:
fiduciaries' duties not derived from, 149
fiduciary duties owed by employers to employees, 141, 144–48
status quo:
behavioural traits favouring, 43–44
biases, 66, 74, 75, 81, 83, 100
Steyn, Lord, 164
stock market crashes, 8
Strauss, L, 95
strict paternalism, 42, 43
student loans, 106, 114
subjective tests, 42
subordinate parties, 142
suitability, FCA rules, 175, 176
summer workers, seasonal, *see* **seasonal summer workers**
Sunstein, CR, 47, 64, 68, 74, 78, 84–85
superannuation:
Australia, *see* Australia
Sweden:
notional defined contributions, 6–7
tangible benefits, 22
tax incentives, 106
tax reliefs, 108
tax savings:
KiwiSaver, New Zealand, 86
taxation, 56
technical failures:
to comply, Auto-Enrolment, 168
Thaler, RH, 47, 78
third party liability:
advisors' and pension providers' duties to employees, 174–75
three pillars:
Superannuation Scheme, Australia, 7
time barriers to decisions, 105–106
tort, 165, 168–70, 176, 192
see also delict
TPAS (Pensions Advisory Service), 9
TPR, *see* **Pensions Regulator**
traditional economic principles, 65
transaction costs:
Auto-Enrolment, 32–33
contracts, 51, 61
transcripts, detailed, 96
transfers done automatically, 118
tripartite relationship complexity, 192
trust:
benefits, 59
contracts of employment operation on, 160
empirical research findings, 130–31 97
employees' expectations of, 167
employees' in employers, 130–31
lack of, 8–10
trust and confidence:
employment law, 163
mutual, *see* contracts of employment; mutual trust and confidence
trust-based schemes, 33–34
Auto-Enrolment, 153
costs, employers' commitments to, 153
default investment strategies, 34
governance, 34
trustees' fiduciary duties to members, 153
see also master trusts
trustees:
advice provided to, quality consideration, 34
beneficiaries and, relationships between, 144
default strategy design consideration, 34
fiduciaries and, 141–42, 144
fiduciary duties to members, trust-based schemes, 153

financial advice for members consideration, 34
governance, 33–34
investment performance consideration, 34
MySuper, Australia, 154
obligations enforcement by Pensions Regulator, 33
occupational pension schemes, *see* occupational pension schemes
retirement support consideration, 34
scheme administration consideration, 34
trusts, *see* **master trusts; occupational pension schemes; trust-based schemes**

unacceptably intrusive forms of paternalism, 49
unawareness:
of opt-outs, Auto-Enrolment, 129, 187
uncertainty:
advice not durable, 107
barriers, 107–109
changes causing, 107
about contributions, 108
costs, contracts, 61
over currency, 122
elements of, financial services products, 71
inaction and, links between, 108
over inflation, 122
job security, 109
state pension, 108–109
unconscionability:
contracts set aside on grounds of, 50
understanding:
action and, connection between, 101
asymmetries in, empirical research findings, 118–19
education and, 121–22
employees' lack of, 127
engagement and, 97, 115–30
foreign workers complication to, 130
illiteracy complication to, 130
lack of frustrating individual consent, 44
language barriers complication to, 130
time required, 105
unforeseen consequences:
advice, 190
of Auto-Enrolment, 137–38
barriers, 188
defaults, reliance on, 188–90
detriment, 191
misunderstandings, 188
responsibility, 191
social costs and remedies, 191–92
uninformed consent:
individuals, 44
unintended consequences, 139–40, 176–78
advice, 190
barriers, 188
defaults, reliance on, 188–90
detriment, 191
duties arising from contracts of employment, *see* contracts of employment
duties owed by employer as agent, 153–56
duties owed to employees by advisors, *see* advisors
duties owed to employees by product providers, *see* product providers
fiduciary duties owed to employees, *see* fiduciary duties owed by employers to employees
misunderstandings, 188
policy makers, 75
responsibility, 191
social costs and remedies, 191–92
unionised workplaces:
increasing salary related pension schemes, 7
United States:
401(k) plans, 47, 87, 153
annuities, 37
auto-enrolment, 23, 183
increased choice, 86–87
inertia, 87–88
introduction by private companies, 82
opting-out, 83, 85
success
UK distinction, 75
voluntary, 14
behavioural science, literature on, 64
broker-dealers, uniform fiduciary standard of conduct, 154
defined contributions, 15, 84
egalitarian impulses, 86
financial advice for rich, 89
income poverty amongst retired population, 15
investment advisors, uniform fiduciary standard of conduct, 154
libertarian paternalism, 86
mandatory pensions based on part of total career earnings, 15
paternalism debate, 40
pensions voluntary, 23
rich save more, 89

'Save More Tomorrow' scheme, 87–88, 116, 117
Securities and Exchange Commission:
advisors' and brokers' duties study, 153
unknown costs, 113
unrealistic optimism, 69
upfront payments:
financial advice, 107
US, *see* **United States**
utilitarian argument of competence, 41

value:
Auto-Enrolment, 29
measurement, legal paternalism, 58–62
for money, not to be relied on, 29
post implementation legislative changes, 29
Visa **case,** 164
volenti non fit injuria, 43
voluntariness, 43, 44
voluntary assumptions of responsibility, 150
voluntary pension saving system barriers, 11
voluntary private pensions, 5–10
voluntary scheme, New Zealand, 15
vulnerability, 142, 148

wages, minimum, 60–61
wasting resources, 50
welfare state:
subconscious reliance on, 120
will of individuals, *see* **individuals**
willpower, bounded, individuals, 75
women:
Auto-Enrolment, 24
small pension pots, 189
women and men:
state pension equalisation for, 2
workers:
definition used in other employment legislation, 22
eligible defined as 'jobholders', 22–23
employers' information provision to, 27–28
excluded, 180, 184, 187
foreign, *see* foreign workers
illiterate, 186
inattentive passive, 85, 86
information provision to, Auto-Enrolment, 27–28
lowest paid, 180, 184
myopic, 85–86
naïve myopic, 85–86
occupational pension schemes contributions, 6
qualifying earnings, 23–24
rational, 85–86
state pension contributions, 6
see also agency; employees
workforces:
education, parliamentary intent, 19–21
persuasion, 19–20
salary related pension schemes as divisive issue in, 8
workplace pensions:
self-enrolment, 183
see also occupational pension schemes; personal pension schemes

Yam Seng Ltd **case,** 166

Printed by Libri Plureos GmbH in Hamburg,
Germany

9 781509 92937